Russian Literature, 1988–1994
The End of an Era

The collapse of the Soviet Union brought about radical changes in the Russian literary world. With the state's relinquishment of control over literary production, writers acquired freedom of expression and publication. State publishing houses, now self-supporting enterprises, stopped printing money-losing books and turned to foreign detective novels and erotic literature, effecting a considerable shift in popular taste. The writer, no longer a producer of ideology, has been recast as a struggling competitor in a free-market environment.

Focusing on the current Russian literary scene, *Russian Literature, 1988–1994* examines these recent changes. Beginning with a general overview of the political, intellectual, and social atmosphere in the country and its effect on artistic creativity, Shneidman surveys the period's literature. He considers the work of succeeding generations of prose fiction writers: the 'old guard,' the writers of the intermediate generation, and the younger authors of perestroika, whose works first appeared in print after Gorbachev's ascent to power. The writing of this last group is divided into three categories: novels written in the style of conventional Russian realism; works that combine realistic prose with modernist narrative techniques; and the body of work that constitutes Russian post-modernism. Exploring artistic and social issues in an integrated manner, the volume will be of interest not only to students of Russian literature but also to those concerned with the culture and social life of the former Soviet Union.

N.N. SHNEIDMAN is Professor Emeritus in the Department of Slavic Languages and Literatures, University of Toronto. He is the author of *Soviet Literature in the 1970s: Artistic Diversity and Ideological Conformity* and *Soviet Literature in the 1980s: Decade of Transition.*

D1291925

Russian Literature, 1988-1994

1988-1994

The End of an Era

N.N. SHNEIDMAN

UNIVERSITY OF TORONTO PRESS
Toronto Buffalo London

© University of Toronto Press Incorporated 1995
Toronto Buffalo London
Printed in Canada

ISBN 0-8020-0507-1 (cloth)
ISBN 0-8020-7466-9 (paper)

Printed on acid-free paper

Canadian Cataloguing in Publication Data

Shneidman, N.N.
 Russian literature, 1988–1994 : the end of an era

 Includes bibliographical references and index.
 ISBN 0-8020-0507-1 (bound) ISBN 0-8020-7466-9 (pbk.)

 1. Russian fiction – 20th century – History and
 criticism. I. Title.

 PG3098.4.S55 1995   891.73'4409   C95-930851-2

University of Toronto Press acknowledges the financial assistance to its
publishing program of the Canada Council and the Ontario Arts Council.

This book has been published with the help of a grant from the Canadian
Federation for the Humanities using funds provided by the Social Sciences
and Humanities Research Council of Canada.

To Jessica and Michael

Contents

Preface

Literature in the former Soviet Union has always been responsive to political change. It has reflected the life of Soviet people and, at the same time, the social and ideological atmosphere in the country. To a certain degree the same is true today. Having gained power in 1985, Mikhail Gorbachev initiated a course of reform, and in the process of transformation destabilized Soviet social and government institutions. The failure of the August 1991 anti-Gorbachev coup foreshadowed the end of communist rule and the disintegration of the Soviet Union. The year 1992 marks the beginning of the post-Soviet era in Russia, and there is no end to this process of transition in sight.

Literature has been affected by these changes in many different ways. Censorship has been abolished, the old Writers' Union is no longer in existence, and many new names have appeared on the Russian literary scene. Keeping up with recent developments in Russian literature has become a challenging endeavour. Publishing and distribution structures in Russia are in disarray, and the old lines of communication with the outside world have been destroyed. The new structures that have come to replace the old ones are still in a state of flux and often lack resources, experience, and permanence. It may take years before this chaotic situation stabilizes and cultural institutions can assume their proper place in a democratic society.

The purpose of this study is to investigate the effect of the recent changes in Eastern Europe, and, in particular, of the dissolution of the Soviet Union, on Russian literature. Covering the six years from 1988 to 1994, the book is intended as a general introductory survey and as a sequel to my *Soviet Literature in the 1980s: Decade of Transition* (Toronto 1989), which investigates the period between 1978 and 1988.

The limited scope of this study prevents my giving detailed consideration to all contemporary Russian writers. My selection of authors and works for discussion is arbitrary. It may not please everyone, but it is representative of contemporary Russian literature and is determined by the artistic and social relevance of these works. The main objectives of this book are to provide a general picture of the current Russian literary scene and to sum up the Soviet era in Russian literature.

For reasons of economy I limit myself to the discussion of Russian prose fiction written by authors residing in Russia. Works by the Belorussian Vasil' Bykov and the Kirghiz Chingiz Aitmatov are included because these authors are fully bilingual and their works often appeared in Russian journals before they were published in their native republics. For reasons of convenience, experienced authors have been grouped together according to age. In many instances their current literary output is affected by the degree of their commitment to the former Soviet regime. New authors, never officially published in the USSR prior to 1987, are grouped together according to their artistic inclinations, regardless of age.

Chapter 1 provides a general overview of the political, ideological, intellectual, and social atmosphere in the country, and its effect on artistic creativity. It discusses, among other things, issues of politics and ideology, the changes in the Writers' Union, the publishing business, and the relationship between the intellectual élite and those in power. Chapter 2 gives a general overview of the literary evolution in the years between 1988 and 1994. Chapter 3 examines the prose of the so-called old guard, or writers who are over sixty, and chapter 4 the prose of the former *sorokaletnie* (literally, forty-year-olds), or those who today are somewhere between the ages of forty and sixty. Chapter 5 is devoted to new writers of perestroika. This chapter is divided into three parts: the first part discusses works written in the traditions of conventional Russian realism, the second discusses the works of writers who combine realistic prose with modernist narrative techniques, and the third is devoted to Russian post-modernism. Most works under consideration were written between 1988 and 1994.

This study is based mainly on original sources, many still unavailable in North America. Some were written prior to 1988 but never officially published before, nor ever circulated as *samizdat* or *tamizdat* literature.* All translations from Russian, unless quoted from English sources, are my own. Any transliteration system from one language into another is arbitrary; I have adopted here the widely used system of the Library of

Congress, with minor exceptions for surnames such as, for example, Yeltsin (instead of the appropriate El'tsin). At first mention, titles are given in Russian, with an English translation and year of publication in parentheses; in subsequent references, they are given only in Russian.

The term 'perestroika' is used in this study to designate the time period beginning with Gorbachev's ascent to power in 1985. It does not refer to, or connote, the success or failure of Gorbachev's policies. The terms 'Russia' and 'Soviet Union' are used interchangeably here, but, beginning with the discussion of events in 1992, 'Russia' rather than 'Soviet Union' is used consistently. Attention should be paid to the numerous changes in the names of Russian cities. For example, in 1991 Leningrad was changed to St Petersburg, and Sverdlovsk to Ekaterinburg. In this text, city names usually reflect the chronology of the discussion.

In order to make this study more useful, I have made it expository in nature, investigating artistic and social issues in an integrated manner. I hope that it will be of interest to students of Russian literature, and to all those who follow the development of culture and society in the former Soviet Union. I trust that it will stimulate a better understanding of the intricate process of transition from totalitarianism to democracy.

I would like to acknowledge my debt and express my gratitude to all those who helped me in the course of my work on this book. I am indebted to Professor K.A. Lantz, who read the manuscript and offered constructive criticism. A special note of thanks is due to writers, critics, and scholars in the former Soviet Union (too numerous to name here) with whom I have had an opportunity to meet on my recent visits to Russia. My discussions with them helped me to gain a better understanding of the social and cultural processes taking place in Russia today.

I gratefully acknowledge the generous support I have received for my research from the Social Sciences and Humanities Research Council of Canada, and the help extended by the Department of Slavic Languages and Literatures and the Centre for Russian and East European Studies at the University of Toronto.

Samizdat refers to literature unofficially published and clandestinely circulated in the Soviet Union. *Tamizdat* most commonly refers to works by Soviet authors not approved for official publication in the USSR but published abroad.

I acknowledge with pleasure the assistance of many institutions and the help and advice of my colleagues and friends, but I accept sole responsibility for any inaccuracies and errors that may exist in this book.

N.N.S.
December 1994
Toronto, Canada

Russian Literature, 1988–1994
The End of an Era

1

Politics, Literature, and Society

The ascent of Gorbachev to power in the spring of 1985 marked the beginning of the disintegration of the Soviet state and the demise of the driving force behind it – the Communist Party of the Soviet Union (CPSU). Once in power, Gorbachev proclaimed the policy of so-called perestroika, which entailed democratization and economic renewal and advanced the concept of glasnost, which provided for relative freedom of expression as well as an openness and pluralism in public life.

Little changed in the Soviet Union in the first two years of perestroika. But the introduction of glasnost, which affected in varying degrees the performance of the daily and the periodical press, opened the first cracks in the Soviet system. The years 1987–9 marked the beginning of democratization of Soviet institutions, which was followed by the intro- duction of a multi-party system of government. However, these positive changes were not reinforced by economic reforms. The national com- mand economy began to disintegrate, without anything viable to replace it. The virtual collapse of central planning, without the introduc- tion of a functioning market economy to take its place, plunged the Soviet Union into an economic crisis. National income and living stan- dards dropped drastically, and Gorbachev watched helplessly and inde- cisively as economic chaos became a way of life. The situation was made worse by the rise of national fervour and the resurgence of extreme nationalism and xenophobia, resulting in wide-ranging ethnic strife and separatist sentiments in the various republics of the USSR.

The August 1991 coup d'état had a sobering effect on most Soviet peo- ple, and apparently on Gorbachev himself. For the next four months, he was no longer the leader of the ruling party, which was banned by his saviour, the president of Russia, Boris Yeltsin, nor was he the head of an effective Soviet government, Yeltsin's Russian republic having taken over most of its important functions and finances.

The dissolution of the Soviet Union, and the rejection of communist rule, which was followed by the creation of a Commonwealth of Independent States, composed of member-nations of the former USSR, put to rest the notion of perestroika. In fact, perestroika was just another Soviet myth. It was doomed from the outset because Gorbachev never had a practicable notion of viable economic reform, nor a clear conception of the future for Russia. He steadfastly refused to accept the recommendations for change put forward by his economic advisers, because his objectives did not envisage the repudiation of socialism, or any other serious modification in the Soviet system of government. Initially he wanted to improve the existing system rather than dismantle it. As late as February 1991, in a speech to Belorussian intellectuals, Gorbachev stated bluntly that he was not ashamed to say that he was a communist and adhered to the socialist idea. He claimed that he had made this final choice long ago, and that he would remain true to it until his death.[1]

Gorbachev introduced glasnost with the purpose of strengthening his hold on power. He used glasnost as a means to discredit the old members of the Politburo, still identified with the Brezhnev regime, and replace them with his own supporters. In the beginning of perestroika Gorbachev was immensely popular in the Soviet Union. His policy of glasnost received the overwhelming approbation of all Soviet people. But his indecisiveness and incompetent handling of the economy soon lost him the support of the masses. Even many members of the liberal intelligentsia turned away from him in frustration and disappointment. Today, many former communists, as well as ordinary Russians, view him as a man who has betrayed not only the Communist Party but the Soviet Union and the Russian people as well. Only those with perspective can appreciate the great historical paradox of Gorbachev's political and economic mistakes' having made possible the beginning of a new historical era.

It thus appears that glasnost was the only successful aspect of perestroika. It slowly lifted the spectre of fear. It made possible the beginning of a gradual change in the social consciousness of the people and the transformation of Soviet public institutions. By uncovering the abuses and injustices perpetrated by the Bolsheviks, and by questioning the legality of Soviet and communist institutions, glasnost helped undermine the ideological foundations of the Soviet state. Shackled by the past, however, Gorbachev failed to understand the impact that freedom of expression could have on the masses. He still believed that, as in the past, the people would obey, or pretend to obey, and follow the dictums of the party. Glasnost provided the Soviet people with a measure of freedom and hope for a better life, but it has done little to satisfy their new heightened expectations. It helped dispel the old socialist dream, creating a new one about the allegedly beautiful and easy life in the West, which was, however, beyond the reach of ordinary Soviet people.

More by chance than by design, Gorbachev changed the destiny of the Soviet people, and in doing so helped change the face of the world. The collapse of the Berlin wall in November 1989, which was probably a surprise to Gorbachev himself, added momentum to the breakdown of the communist commonwealth, and the Soviet empire as well. It signified the failure of the socialist myth, and the end of the cold war. Gorbachev's popularity was soaring in the West. In October 1990 he was awarded the Nobel Peace Prize. But, back home, even many of his closest associates began to abandon ship when they realized that Gorbachev would not be able to bring the promised reforms to successful fruition.

Gorbachev's departure in 1991 marks the end of the Soviet state and the beginning of real perestroika in Russia – the transition to a market economy. Today no Russian talks of the old perestroika, or of glasnost. Freedom of expression has become a fact of life rather than a privilege. There is a danger, however, that, without a democratic legal system and well-defined provisions for the protection of human rights, absolute freedom of expression, in the context of economic hardship and political instability, can degenerate into proliferation of hate, falsehood, and the abuse of political and national minorities. In fact, this is the situation on the threshold of 1995. It is a reality in which extreme views have become a prominent fact of life rather than an exception. Today, calls for democracy, tolerance, and a new spirituality are heard simultaneously with xenophobic and fascist clichés, and appeals for a return to communism, dictatorship, and the rule of power.

The October 1993 anti-government revolt, crushed with the help of tanks, and the success of Vladimir Zhirinovsky's Liberal-Democratic Party in the first post-Soviet free parliamentary elections that followed were a good indication that the situation in Russia remained volatile and unpredictable. It appeared that Yeltsin's unilateral decision to disband the anti-reform Supreme Soviet had solved little. Angry masses, devastated by poverty and a drastic drop in living standards, caused by inflation, unemployment, and crime, elected to the new parliament a majority of communists and Liberal-Democrats. The latter are neither liberal nor democratic but, rather, uphold nationalistic, expansionist, and neo-fascist views, and oppose economic reforms. The meetings of the new parliament early in 1994 and the composition of the new government were a clear indication that the road to reform would not be a smooth one. The only positive sign in the current Russian political arena was the adoption of a new constitution, approved in December 1993 in a national referendum. True, the constitution provided the president with extraordinary powers, but it also enshrined basic democratic freedoms for the people. It did away finally with the amended version of the old Brezhnev constitution, and thus formally ended the legality of the Soviet communist regime.

The road from communism to democracy is difficult and thorny. Only free people can become part of a free-market system based on democratic social and political values. The peoples of the former Soviet Union have little experience with democracy and not much tolerance for the views of others. Except for the few who have already managed to adapt to the new conditions in Russia, most are still psychologically chained to the past. They lack the skills required for a competitive capitalist environment and continue to depend on hand-outs from the government. It may take years, if not generations, before their outlook changes and they learn to appreciate the true value of personal freedom. For all practical purposes, the Soviet era is over, but its residue lingers on, making a real break with the past a formidable challenge.

POLITICS AND IDEOLOGY

Literature and politics were intrinsically intertwined in the former Soviet Union. The state supported culture, and the arts and literature, in turn, promoted the political and ideological objectives of the party. Glasnost and perestroika, however, unsettled the established modus operandi of the government and brought about the gradual disintegration of Soviet social and cultural institutions. The Writers' Union, the literary bureaucracy, and the writers' community, in general, were no exception.

The first signs of ideological discord in what appeared to be a uniform writers' body came to the fore in the late 1960s. The adherents of nineteenth-century Russian *pochvennichestvo* (native-soil movement) and Slavophilism were waging battle with those who supported moderation, liberalism, internationalism, and Western values in culture and life. In the 1970s and early 1980s, those writing Russian 'village prose,' such as Fedor Abramov, Vasilii Belov, and Valentin Rasputin, were fighting against urbanization and the intrusion of technological progress and Western civilization into the Russian countryside. They decried the destruction of the old Russian village and the disappearance of the moral and spiritual values associated with Russian 'roots.' They propounded a certain philosophical conception of life which was based on the identification of nature with the motherland and the nation, and was connected with the view that native soil is the source of the national and moral wealth that was to save Russia from spiritual stagnation.

In the late 1980s ideological dissention assumed political form, and the supporters of neo-Slavophilism turned into conservative nationalists, struggling for power and the control of the Writers' Union. The battle between liberals and conservatives assumed the form of extreme belligerence, leading to an open rift within the writers' community. Ideological disputation, previously conducted under the cover of literary discussion, turned into personal attacks and political invective, and arguments were no longer generated by literary or philosophical issues but, rather, by political disagreement.

The dissolution of the Soviet Union and the total abolition of party control and censorship have brought into the open a wide range of intellectual and political opinions, and propelled the discord between the so-called liberal moderates and extreme conservatives onto a new political level. Most liberals support freedom of expression, democratic reform, and the transition to a market economy, while the conservatives, who have assumed the designation 'patriots,' advocate the overthrow of the current Yeltsin government and the establishment of the rule of power. One of the leaders of this camp, the writer, and editor of *Den'* (Day), Aleksandr Prokhanov, stated bluntly that 'if fascism is the price one has to pay for the establishment of a great Russian state ... then let there even be fascism ... our future is a civil war.'[2]

The conservative nationalist movement has lately assumed a strong religious Russian-Orthodox colouring which transcends even its previous adherence to the notion of pan-Slavism. In his statement 'Kak nam obustroit' Rossiiu' (How to Arrange Things in Russia; 1990), Aleksandr Solzhenitsyn called for the creation of a Slavic union, leaving all other Soviet republics to determine their own destiny.[3] V. Belov, however, views pan-Slavism today within the context of religious denominations and divides Slavs into Orthodox Slavs and Catholics. He proclaimed, at the International Congress of Slavic Cultures that took place on 25–30

May 1992 in Moscow and Voronezh, that 'the Slavs belong to the most important nations that defend Orthodoxy, and that is why they are hated in many European and American countries.' He attacked the Ukrainian association Rukh, alleging that it has been blinded by anti-Russian propaganda, and he berated the Russian government for not supporting the Serbs in the civil war in the former Yugoslavia: 'How did we help the Serbs? By recognizing Croatia we rather hurt them. And everybody knows, of course, what Croatia represents – they are Catholics who fight against the Orthodox.'[4]

The writers of the nationalist-patriotic camp advocate the most extreme, chauvinistic, nationalistic, even fascist views, and they have allied themselves with the most reactionary elements of the former nomenklatura, the armed forces, and the KGB. In March 1990, a group of Russian conservative writers published the so-called letter of seventy-four, addressed to the Central Party Committee and the Supreme Soviets of the USSR and RSFSR. The letter, signed by a number of well-known writers, including P. Proskurin, L. Leonov, V. Rasputin, A. Prokhanov, V. Krupin, M. Ganina, and S. Kuniaev, called for an end to the alleged Russophobia that had, according to the letter's signatories, been intensified by the assertion that a new 'Russian fascism' was in the making. Paradoxically, according to the letter, the main culprits in all Russia's misfortunes were the Zionists. The authors of the letter claimed that 'the fact that the fabrication of the myth about "Russian fascism" takes place in the shadows of the swift rehabilitation, and dashing idealization of Zionist ideology is notable in itself.'[5] It is apparent that, in the view of the 'patriots,' all that is necessary is to find a real or imagined culprit and pass on the blame. They did not see that placing blame solves nothing, least of all Russia's current problems. The letter of seventy-four met with a rebuttal from writers belonging to the liberal committee Aprel' (April). An open letter, signed by E. Evtushenko, A. Pristavkin, V. Sokolov, Iu. Chernichenko, and M. Shatrov, asserts that 'chauvinism is an attempt to transform extraction into a privilege. It is the first sign of a carefully hidden lack of talent, or of a talent beginning to decay. It is an aggressive complex of inferiority which turns imperial self-conceit into imperial paranoia.'[6] The letter also expressed dismay that Leonid Leonov, one of the oldest living Russian writers, at the time already over ninety, had obviously been pressured into signing this ignominious document.

The determination of the nationalist extremists in the Writers' Union to turn back the wheel of history and stop the reform movement in the USSR became obvious only after the failed coup of August 1991. On 23

July 1991, 'Slovo k narodu' (A Word to the People) appeared on the first page of *Sovetskaia Rossiia* (Soviet Russia). It was signed by twelve people, including the writers Iu. Bondarev, Rasputin, and Prokhanov; the Afghan war veterans Generals V. Varennikov and B. Gromov; and several other prominent party officials. The open letter exhorted the peoples of the Soviet Union to save the country from its destroyers and occupiers. It called for the 'creation of a national-patriotic movement ... with the purpose of saving the fatherland ... and strengthening Soviet power.'[7] It became clear after the failed coup that some leading members of the Writers' Union had been among those supporting the plot and were actually involved in preparing the ideological and theoretical basis for the overthrow of Gorbachev and the seizure of power.

The failed August 1991 coup is now history, but the antagonistic forces in Russian intellectual life continue the struggle to win the hearts and minds of the people. Unleashed by glasnost, the pluralism of opinions has turned into a pluralism of mutual accusations, verbal abuse, and even violence, as was evident long before the coup. On 18 January 1990, some thugs from the nationalistic anti-Semitic association Pamiat' (Memory) used violence to disrupt an open-microphone meeting, organized by the Aprel' committee, in the Central Writers' Club in Moscow.[8] Despite the fact that several participants at the meeting were roughed up and injured, the police at first ignored the incident. In the end, however, justice won out, and the organizers of the assault were put on trial.

Today the ideological battle, which has assumed a political form, continues with increasing intensity. The liberals persist in supporting economic and political reforms and the evolution of Russia into a Western-type democracy. The leadership of the patriotic nationalist camp, on the other hand, aims its activities in two distinct directions – one political, the other ideological. Its main political objective is the removal of Yeltsin and his government from power. It views the current administration as transitional and temporary and regards it as an occupational force. This opposition represents an alliance between some members of the former Soviet nomenklatura, leading figures of the former Communist Party, the leaders of the chauvinistic Russian nationalist camp, and some army generals and former KGB officers. This coalition has had full control of the Supreme Soviet, disbanded in October 1993, and it is well represented today in the new Russian parliament, being thus able to interfere with and frustrate the process of democratic reform. According to Prokhanov the opposition is well organized and ready to take over from the allegedly demoralized democrats who are in the process of disintegration.[9] The aim of the opposition is to create a strong Russian state, the future of which will be guaranteed by 'large social programs, consequently by centralized state ownership of the main branches of the economy.'[10]

The ideological platform of the conservative opposition has its roots in the late fifteenth-century Russian vision of Moscow as the 'Third Rome,' as the sole remaining stronghold of true faith in the world. The theorists of Russian nationalism assert that the messianic appointment of Russia to serve as a saviour of, and an example for, the whole world is a 'special reward for all its deprivation and suffering.' They claim that the Russian people have a great soul and are imbued with a special spirituality which makes it possible for them to suffer and to save others at the same time.[11] This philosophy of national exclusiveness is extremely anti-Western and anti-Catholic. It propounds the view that, since Western society lacks the required spiritual foundation and is permeated by egoism, atheism, and Catholicism, it cannot provide the necessary guidance for mankind. 'Such a spiritual base can be found only in the old Russian and Byzantine cultural heritage.'[12]

The notion of Russian spiritual superiority is today combined with Russian imperial ambitions and is placed in a geopolitical context by its blending with the concept of Eurasianism. Eurasianism, a philosophy developed in the nineteenth and early twentieth centuries and promoted by some members of the Russian émigré intelligentsia, proceeds from the assumption that the future of Russia will be determined by its geopolitical position at the crossroads of Europe and Asia. Furthermore, the alliance between Russia and the Moslems, who have the same political enemies, is highly advantageous to both. Today the Russian patriotic nationalist movement is divided on the issue of Eurasianism. One group 'insists on the purely Slavic and ethnic confessional specific of Russia and its historical mission. While the other "Eurasians" regard fundamentalist Islam as an ally, because they agree with its anti-materialism ... and hostility towards universal usury, as well as its stand against liberal economic systems.' They suggest that 'today the main, and only geopolitical enemy of both, the Russians and the Moslems, are the United States of America and the liberal, cosmopolitan, anti-spiritual, anti-religious system which is inseparably linked to the image of the USA ... The American Masonic anti-spiritual civilization corresponds to the Christian notion of Antichrist.'[13] It is further intimated that the essence of capitalism is not determined by economic modes of production or trade patterns. Since 'capitalism is an outgrowth of Protestantism, its American-type liberal economic system contradicts the religious, spiritual, and emotional cast of mind of all Moslem nations as well as of most European states.'[14] It is clear that the revived Eurasian ideal, perverted and propounded by Prokhanov's weekly *Den'*, is a cover for the imperial ambitions of Russian extreme nationalist politicians who cannot reconcile themselves with the fact that the Soviet Union is no longer in existence, and that the union republics of the former USSR have by now declared their sovereignty.

Today what appear to be most dangerous are the ideals of those who, under the cover of modernization and economic development, preach revanchism and try to combine elements of fascist ideology with the interest of the new Russian financial and industrial élite.[15] These new perpetrators of fascist ideology attempt to gain power by infiltrating the economic infrastructure of the nation.

It is clear that, compromised by its collaboration with the former regime, Orthodox Christianity cannot, in the short term, fill the ideological and spiritual vacuum created by the demise of official Soviet Marxist-Leninist dogma. Hence, Russian national ideals are gaining popularity even among recently liberal writers and politicians. The term *russkost'* (Russianness), widely used today in intellectual circles, can be viewed as a new version of the former notion of *sovetskost'* ('Sovietism'). It shields those in the ideological void from a sense of inferiority, and it gives them something with which to identify. Political nationalism, however, is fraught with dangerous consequences, particularly in a multinational state having the dimensions of the Russian Federation.

The conservative elements in the writers' community play a prominent role in promoting extreme nationalist ideas. Well-known writers such as Rasputin, Krupin, V. Lichutin, V. Gusev, and Kuniaev were, until recently, members of the editorial board of *Den'* which was the main ideological mouthpiece of the so-called patriotic Russian nationalist opposition. The writer Timur Pulatov, an Uzbek of Turkic extraction and Muslim background, has recently joined the camp of those who promote Eurasianism. In one of his recent speeches, 'he called for Russian Orthodox unity with Islam in their common struggle against Catholicism and Zionism, against the "devils".'[16] It is unfortunate that many good Russian writers, such as Rasputin, have abandoned their calling and turned from creative literature to politics and ideology, wasting their talents on writing social sketches and political pamphlets that will surely soon be forgotten.

Today the political battles between the supporters of democracy and the conservative camp are as fierce as ever before. The outlawed Communist Party has been legalized again, and some leading members of the former CPSU suggest that the notion of 'socialism with a human face' be replaced by the concept of 'communism with God.' The proposed fusion of communism with religion may sound ludicrous, but it reflects the current crisis of intellectual thought and the perplexed state of affairs in Russia today.

THE WRITERS' UNION

The Writers' Union has for years been an important professional organization which reflected well the ongoing struggle between different groups of intellectuals and politicians representing diverse views on the fate of Russia and the destiny of mankind. Lately it has mirrored convincingly the process of disintegration of Soviet social and professional institutions, which until recently formed the basis of Soviet and Russian cultural development.

The Eighth Congress of Soviet Writers, held in June 1986, was the last relatively peaceful gathering of this group.[17] Liberal changes in the leadership of the union were achieved at that time through compromise rather than open warfare. Nevertheless, the control of the daily operations of the union, and of the Litfund, which was in charge of most union property and financial resources, continued to be in the hands of the old, party-run literary bureaucracy. The acceleration of political turmoil in the country in the last years of Gorbachev's rule affected also the state of affairs in the union. Ideological disagreement turned into an open battle for the control of union property, while different factions within the union were vying for power and control.

The disintegration of the Writers' Union gained momentum in March 1989 with the proclamation of a manifesto and resolution by the newly formed Committee of Writers in Support of Perestroika, 'Aprel'.' The committee included a number of prominent writers and poets such as A. Adamovich, B. Okudzhava, A. Rybakov, V. Kondrat'ev, S. Kaledin, and V. Dudintsev. At the inaugural meeting of this committee, which took place on 10 March 1989, in Moscow, its first elected chairman, Anatolii Pristavkin, denounced the leaders of the Writers' Union for their conservatism and refusal to democratize the union bureaucracy in keeping with the new spirit of glasnost and perestroika. He also called for a full disclosure of the union's role in the purges and suppression of Soviet writers. The resolution adopted at that meeting stated bluntly that the

Writers' Union was ill equipped to bring about perestroika in literature. It called on the union's leadership to reinstate Solzhenitsyn's membership in the Writers' Union and permit the publication of his works in the USSR.[18]

A few months later, on 10 May 1989, at Maastricht, the Netherlands, the 53d International Congress of the PEN Association adopted a resolution concerning the creation of a Russian-Soviet chapter of PEN. PEN had previously excluded the USSR because of Soviet persecution of writers and other intellectuals; the Soviet government, on the other hand, had viewed PEN as an anti-Soviet institution. Anatolii Rybakov assured the congress that all worthy Russian writers would be able to join the PEN chapter. However, Andrei Bitov warned that '"there can't be any guarantee" that the Soviet PEN chapter would not be suppressed or taken over by authorities.'[19] The fact that a chapter of PEN was founded in Moscow, bypassing the official administrative structures of the Writers' Union, could be regarded as a further expression of internal rebellion against the old literary bureaucracy in Moscow.

In Leningrad, where liberal writers were in control of the local branch of the Writers' Union, a conservative nationalist group of some twenty-five writers formed the association Sodruzhestvo (Commonwealth). A delegation from Sodruzhestvo arrived at the Sixth Plenary Session of the Board of the RSFSR Writers' Union that took place in November 1989, and demanded that it be recognized as an independent body within the Writers' Union. It requested also that the journal *Leningrad* (Leningrad) be designated as the group's official organ. The board approved these requests with little opposition.[20] It decided also to remove A. Anan'ev from the position of chief editor of *Oktiabr'* (October) and replace him with V.V. Lichutin. It accused Anan'ev of defaming the memory of A. Pushkin by publishing *Progulki s Pushkinym* (Strolling with Pushkin; 1976) by A. Siniavskii, and of spreading Russophobia by publishing V. Grossman's novella 'Vse techet' (Forever Flowing; 1989). Anan'ev rejected the board's decision and refused to relinquish his post.

Whether under the pressure of Aprel', or under the influence of the general atmosphere in the country, the board of the USSR Writers' Union soon revoked the 1969 resolution of its RSFSR branch, which had approved the expulsion of Solzhenitsyn from the union. The board also requested that writers who were deputies of the USSR Supreme Soviet petition the Soviet parliament to repeal its resolution of 12 February 1974, according to which Solzhenitsyn had been deprived of Soviet citizenship and expelled from the country. It was more than a year later that

Soviet citizenship was restored to twenty-three previously expelled and victimized Soviet writers, including Solzhenitsyn, V. Aksenov, G. Vladimov, and V. Voinovich.[21]

The increasing political polarization within the writers' community alienated a number of writers who preferred not to get involved in political activity and refrained from participating in the acrimonious ideological debates. In June 1990, a group of these writers, which included V. Astaf'ev, V. Tokareva, V. Shugaev, A. Kim, and Iu. Rytkheu, announced the creation of an association of independent writers. They stated that, since 'various politicized writers' associations introduce into the writers' community tension, animosity, and hostility ... and are often motivated by personal ambitions and hidden desires for material gain, which harm the cause of perestroika,'[22] a new association of independent writers was being formed with the purpose of promoting the cause of literature and assisting in the development of a harmonious life. It was also announced, late in 1989, that a federation of women writers, attached to the USSR Writers' Union, had been formed. By Western standards the objectives of this federation were tame: the resolution of its founding conference did not address the issue of sex discrimination, nor did it call for equality within the writers community.[23]

The disintegration of the Moscow writers' organization was, in fact sanctioned at its general meeting held late in 1990. More than three quarters of its members, including the most prominent Moscow liberal writers, refused to attend. The newly elected chairman, V. Gusev, who had claimed in his pre-election speech that he had no special administrative skills or ambitions but was known for his 'innate honesty,' later turned out to be a supporter of the most reactionary forces within the writers' community.[24]

Soon after, in December 1990, Russian writers gathered at the Seventh Congress of the RSFSR Writers' Union. Iu. Bondarev, the new chairman of the board, decried the current state of Russian literature and 'the total confusion of ideas, styles, heroes, and ethical doctrines.'[25] Most speakers at the congress attacked the liberals and accused them of all manner of deadly sins. Some sober voices, however, like that of Viktor Astaf'ev, tried to turn the discussion to literary issues, but they were ignored by the majority. The congress approved new union statutes, and elected delegates to the ninth congress of Soviet writers. But the ninth congress, which was to take place early in 1991, was postponed several times; when it finally took place, the Soviet Union was no longer in existence.

Just prior to the coup, in July 1991, a group of progressive writers promulgated a manifesto about the creation of an independent writers' union. The manifesto was signed by Ch. Aitmatov, A. Bitov, V. Voinovich, F. Iskander, and D. Likhachev.[26] It was not clear whether they intended to act as a faction within the existing Writers' Union or wanted complete separation. It was apparent, however, that they did intend to share the social services and financial resources provided by the Litfund.

The August 1991 coup changed drastically the political situation in the country. It affected also the domain of culture, literature and the arts, crystallizing the formal ideological and political break-up of the Writers' Union. A meeting of the union's secretariat, on 23 August 1991, at which its liberal members, for years shunned by the union bureaucracy, participated, clarified the situation. It appeared that the bureaucracy of the union, including board members such as Sergei Mikhalkov, Feliks Kuznetsov, and Prokhanov, had not opposed the anti-Gorbachev plot. At the meeting a resolution was passed whereby all those who had supported the coup were to be removed from the board. The resolution stated further that the so-called 'Slovo k narodu,' published just prior to the coup, and signed by, among others, Bondarev, Rasputin, and Prokhanov, was to be considered a document 'which secured the ideological background of the anti-state conspiracy. It demanded that Iu. Bondarev, V. Rasputin, and A. Prokhanov resign from their posts as secretaries of the boards of the USSR and the RSFSR writers' unions.'[27] The Writers' Union elected new leaders, most of whom belonged to the liberal camp.

The conservative elements in the USSR Writers' Union did not submit easily. They were in an overwhelming majority on the board of the RSFSR Writers' Union, and they adopted a resolution according to which the RSFSR union became an independent body and no longer a member of the USSR Writers' Union. A few weeks later, the Extraordinary Congress of the RSFSR Writers' Union was called to approve the adopted resolution. The fact that this congress had no legal status, since there was no formal election of delegates did not matter much; those present had previously been elected to the ninth all-union congress of Soviet writers. The extraordinary congress proclaimed the RSFSR Writers' Union as the legal heir of the USSR Writers' Union, claiming jurisdiction over the whole territory of Russia. Most liberal writers refused to belong to this newly defined RSFSR union; they announced the formation of an alternative union of Russian writers and made public its statutes.[28] On 21 October 1991, in Moscow, the founding congress of this new union took place. It was claimed that close to 1,300 writers had applied for membership in this organization, among them most writers who supported the platform of Aprel' and opposed the coup.

Despite the fact that the old USSR Writers' Union was formally still in control of the Litfund and the union's property, for all practical purposes it continued to exist only on paper. The writers of the Baltic republics – Lithuania, Latvia, and Estonia – had left the USSR Writers' Union more than a year earlier, as had the writers' organization of Georgia. The RSFSR Writers' Union had withdrawn from the 'big' union after the August coup. As well, many splinter groups had been formed in the local branches of the union, and several writers' organizations were operating in Moscow, Leningrad, Smolensk, Irkutsk, and other cities and regions. By December 1991, there were two national writers' unions; three writers' organizations in St Petersburg; and three in Moscow, including the club of independent writers comprising some older writers such as S. Zalygin, Mikhalkov, M. Aliger, and V. Rozov, who wanted to avoid becoming embroiled in political infighting.[29]

The formal dissolution of the USSR in December 1991, and the formation of the Commonwealth of Independent States, created a new situation. On 10–11 January 1992, the founding conference of a new body which called itself the Commonwealth of Writers' Unions, and regarded itself as superseding the USSR Writers' Union, took place in Moscow. The Uzbek writer Timur Pulatov was elected first secretary of the executive committee. Among the commonwealth's founding members were writers' unions of independent and autonomous republics, the cities of Moscow and St Petersburg, as well as other writers' organizations. The Ukrainian delegation, which participated in the work of the conference, refused to sign the program documents. Delegates from Latvia attended but only in the role of observers. The RSFSR Writers' Union at first conducted a vigorous campaign against this new organization but later expressed some interest in participating under certain conditions. However, that did not stop some RSFSR union members, under the leadership of Bondarev and Prokhanov, from organizing a meeting of protest against the newly formed Commonwealth of Writers' Unions. They attacked the political stance of, heaped personal abuse on, and even used violence against those who occupied the offices of the former Writers' Union.

Discord was rife within the ranks of the liberal writers' community as well. Community members turned into political democrats without a unifying political platform, administrative experience, or a clear notion of their true objectives. It did not take long for infighting to begin among the democrats. Timur Pulatov, first secretary of the executive committee of the Commonwealth of Writers' Unions, was soon removed from his position, and, by the middle of April 1992, for all practical purposes, two committees were allegedly charged with the responsibility of organizing the Ninth Congress of Writers of the Former Soviet Union.[30] Expelled from the now fractured liberal camp, Pulatov joined the conservative RSFSR Writers' Union, and helped organize the Ninth Congress, to be held on 2–4 June 1992, in Moscow. The congress was attended by delegations from Russia proper, its autonomous national regions, and Moscow and St Petersburg. There were also delegations from the five former Soviet Central Asian republics. Liberal writers and members of the recently organized Commonwealth of Writers' Unions and the Union of Russian Writers did not participate. Thus, the majority of leading writers and poets from Russia, Ukraine, Belorussia, Armenia, and other former Soviet republics did not attend the congress, and some of those who did left soon after it began because 'the dictate of the mob silenced all attempts to discuss literature.'[31]

According to a declaration adopted by the gathering, the congress marked the founding of the International Association of Writers' Unions, which regarded itself as displacing the former USSR Writers' Union and taking control of all its property, as well as of the Litfund. At the congress, the delegation from Russia announced the formation of an association of Russian writers within the structure of the RSFSR Writers' Union to which all 'those who write in Russian and adhere to the traditional values of Russian culture'[32] might belong. The proposal was signed by most members of the conservative wing, including V. Rasputin, P. Proskurin, E. Safonov, M. Lobanov, V. Gusev, S. Kuniaev, and V. Krupin. One might wonder who was to determine what constituted the 'traditional values of Russian culture.' Whatever those values were, it was obvious that those who signed the proposal did not consider that liberal writers such as A. Siniavskii and V. Voinovich 'adhered' to them.

In 1993, the organizational fervour had died down somewhat, but the appearance of unity among the different camps is misleading. The so-called liberals were poorly organized, and squabbled with one another on many issues of substance. Some leading conservatives were accused of abusing their positions and paying little attention to the needs of average writers. Personal strife lurked behind the façade of organizational unity in both camps. In November 1992, S. Iu. Rybas, one of the secretaries of the conservative RSFSR Writers' Union, came out with a scathing attack against Iu. Bondarev, who, he alleged, took advantage of his post as chairman of the board for personal enrichment and to the benefit of his friends.[33] In fact, by the middle of 1993, most writers' associations had turned into public corporations, involved in a variety of commercial activities, such as publishing and trade. These new formations were controlled by former literary bureaucrats and were concerned more with profit than with creative activity. In June 1994, at the Ninth Congress of the Writers' Union of the Russian Federation in Moscow, Bondarev resigned his position as chairman. Most speakers at the congress attacked Yeltsin's administration, the current system of government, as well as the liberal intelligentsia. However, some decried the fact that few young writers were present at the congress and called for greater harmony in the writers' community. Similar calls were later heard from the ranks of liberal writers. Disappointed with the current state of affairs, Iu. Arakcheev and some others began to seek new paths for a rapprochement with the conservatives.

In the meantime, the fight for the right to inherit the property of the former USSR Writers' Union was in full swing. In June 1992, it was taken over by the Committee for State Property and the Moscow civic department in charge of protecting historical monuments. The property was then divided between the two warring writers' organizations, a solution that was rejected by the International Association, which appealed to the courts. Early in 1993, a lower court overturned the decision of the Committee for State Property, and the issue of property ownership was once again moot. On 26 January 1994, the Supreme Court of the Russian Federation considered the request to transfer all property of the Litfund to the International Association of Writers' Unions. During the session of the court, the well-known liberal writer Ales' Adamovich suffered a fatal heart attack and the court postponed proceedings before it had reached a formal decision. The discord continues, with no end in sight.

Why all this fuss about organizations and meetings of creative writers, things that have little to do with literature proper? Is not creativity a personal matter, rather than a collective endeavour? In fact, many of those most actively involved in the political battles have almost completely stopped writing fiction or poetry. For them, being a writer is a struggle for power and money. Most members of the former USSR Writers' Union are, at best, average writers, with the barest modicum of talent, and have no chance of surviving in the new competitive conditions of a free-market economy. Thus, they have to join forces in order to protect their access to journals and publishing houses and ensure access to whatever benefits accrue to members of a formal group. In fact, today, serious literary discussion among writers is a thing of the past. Life is difficult and the situation in the country is serious. The incomes and pensions of most writers have declined dramatically, and the question of physical survival is imminent. It is, however, clear to any outsider that once the wealth accumulated by the superseded union is divided and spent, new sources of income will have to be found, and a creative artist will once more have to depend on talent, ingenuity, and perseverance.

GORBACHEV, YELTSIN, AND THE INTELLIGENTSIA

In 1989 the prestige of, and public support for, Gorbachev and the policies of the Communist Party began to dwindle rapidly. None the less, the party continued its efforts to control and influence the intelligentsia and intellectual élite. Under the cover of democratic reform, Gorbachev initiated the reorganization of the old Supreme Soviet into a two-tiered parliament, comprising the Congress of People's Deputies and a Supreme Soviet, elected by the Congress. Some deputies were to be chosen in general free elections, but a substantial number were to be appointed by various political and social institutions, thus ensuring that the party could control the new congress and that Gorbachev could be elected to the position of president. The intelligentsia was assigned an important role in the congress. The USSR Writers' Union was allotted twelve seats in the new parliament, and V. Astaf'ev, V. Bykov, S. Zalygin, L. Leonov, and V. Rasputin were among the union appointees to Congress. The CPSU Central Committee included among its nominees the writers Ch. Aitmatov, V. Belov, I. Vasil'ev, D. Granin, V. Karpov, and B. Oleinik. In addition, E. Evtushenko, F. Iskander, D. Likhachev, Iu. Kariakin, A. Adamovich, and Iu. Chernichenko were elected by the public at large. A year later Gorbachev formed a small presidential advisory committee, on which the creative intelligentsia was represented by Ch. Aitmatov and V. Rasputin. By selecting two writers, representing diametrically opposite views on issues of ideology, nationality, and politics, Gorbachev wanted to affirm his middle-of-the-road position – a dangerous tactic in times of social upheaval.

The Congress of People's Deputies turned into a new forum for writers to vent their frustrations and advocate their narrow, clannish views. The liberal writers were calling for complete democratization, economic reform, and the repeal of Article 6 of the USSR constitution, which made communist rule in Russia legal. The conservatives claimed that they were not against democracy, yet objected to the changes that new democratic policies would bring to bear. According to Rasputin, 'extreme freedom creates the greatest and harshest slavery ... and the pluralism of morality is even more dangerous than bombs of any kind.'[34] In this multinational forum, Rasputin attacked, the alleged anti-Russian outbursts in Union republics and castigated national minorities for blaming Russia for all their troubles; at the same time, he asked, rhetorically, whether it would not be better for Russia to leave the Soviet Union altogether. The tone of Belov's speeches at the congress was even more belligerent. He came out against the moral decay that allegedly spread under the cover of glasnost and perestroika. He attacked the newspaper *Komsomol'skaia pravda* (Young Communist Truth) for its sex-education program for the young, and called for the introduction of a new censorship law that would prevent such activity.[35]

Unable to control the political actions of different members of the intelligentsia in the congress, the party tried to influence them in other ways. Between 1989 and 1991, Gorbachev invited leading scientists, intellectuals, and writers to several meetings in the Kremlin with the purpose of seeking support for his policies. In the beginning, he did it in the role of general secretary of the CPSU Central Committee; later, he issued such invitations as head of state. In many instances, when Gorbachev sought support for his policies, he was forced to defend himself against those who attacked the aimlessness of perestroika and the inability of the government to provide positive leadership. In his speech of 6 January 1989 he defended socialism and pluralism, but came out against those 'who under the cover of glasnost make attempts to discredit the Communist Party.'[36] He censured the creative intelligentsia for the squabbles within their ranks and called for more civilized behaviour. However, writers representing different clans were not deterred from assailing one another. Thus, the editor of *Molodaia gvardiia* (The Young Guard), A.I. Ivanov, attacked the journal *Iunost'* (Youth) for publishing the novel *Zhizn' i neobyknovennye prikliucheniia soldata Ivana Chonkina* (The Life and Extraordinary Adventures of the Private Ivan Chonkin; 1975), by V. Voinovich, because it allegedly slandered the good name of the Soviet soldier and denigrated the Soviet army, which had saved mankind from fascism.[37]

In July 1990, the Twenty-Eighth Congress of the CPSU gathered in Moscow. The Soviet economy was already on the verge of chaos, and Soviet culture and literature were being threatened under the onslaught of commercialism and the free market. Furthermore, the Communist Party was no longer a unified body, under the control of a central bureaucracy, but rather had splintered into different ideological, political, and national factions. The congress resolutions called for creative freedom in the arts; for the competition of different cultural trends, styles, and schools; for the adoption of a state law in defence of ethics and morality; and for the creation of a commission on culture, education, and science, attached to the CPSU Central Committee.[38] The programmatic statement of the congress made no direct reference to political and ideological interference in the arts. However, it did contain an assertion to the effect that the party opposed the free-market approach to, and the commercialization of, artistic production, thus supporting the subsidization of culture and the arts. It was not made clear who would provide the necessary funds, especially since N.N. Gubenko, the USSR minister of culture, shortly afterward declared that 'no funds for culture [had] been allocated in the 1991 Union budget' and that whatever money was available was in the hands of separate republics, which meant that a unified cultural policy was no longer possible.[39] The congress elected to the CPSU Central Committee the writers V. Karpov, V. Belov, P. Proskurin, and A. Gel'man, some of whom supported opposing political factions. In fact, Karpov soon relinquished his position as first secretary of the USSR Writers' Union, and Gel'man resigned from the Central Committee in protest over state and party policy. However, at this point, such gestures were of little consequence. The party had already lost much of its former power and was in a state of disintegration. Soon after the congress, the Party Central Committee discussed 'Measures to Overcome the Increasing Tendencies of Commercialization in Culture.'[40] It called on the government to fight commercialism in culture, stating that commercialization undermined the ethical foundations of the nation and promoted aggressiveness, eroticism, and bad taste in the arts. It proposed also that a law 'On the Protection of Ethics and Morality in the USSR' be adopted.

Several months after the party congress, Gorbachev invited the cream of the Soviet cultural élite to the Kremlin. His goal was obvious: he wanted to use the prestige of the intelligentsia to repair his own sagging political fortunes and help curb the disintegration of society. The meeting did not produce the expected results, nor did the participants show any respect for their host. Instead, by attacking others and accusing opponents of political betrayal, each tried to protect his own political turf. As leader of a party that had lost much of its former power, and as head of a state that was in total disarray, Gorbachev was unable, at this point, to influence or provide leadership to an intelligentsia which had witnessed the destruction of its cultural institutions and lost faith in perestroika. Gorbachev admitted at the meeting that, without the help of the intelligentsia, there could be no perestroika. But M. Shatrov countered that the intelligentsia could rock the boat, but whether they could keep it on course when the waves become too strong was questionable.[41] A. Kamshalov, a bureaucrat in charge of Soviet movie enterprises, decried the fact 'that commercialization of art, which destroys the soul, destroys also the ethical health of the nation.'[42] Bondarev attacked the very essence of Gorbachev's policies. He claimed that all current difficulties were the result 'of the destruction of the triad which connected statehood, *narodnost'* [national spirit], and faith, interpreting here faith in a broad sense.' He asserted further that 'glasnost was a lie which was more similar to the truth than the truth to itself. Glasnost destroyed our past and our foundation ... our history, our roots, our spirituality, our culture, and our economy.'[43] Rasputin continued in the same vein. He stated that 'culture had turned into anti-culture ... aggressive words, plots, and heroes appeared in literature ... the initiative was taken away from us, not by the intelligentsia, but rather by semi-intellectuals.'[44] In his concluding remarks, Gorbachev expressed despair that even warnings of possible plots from the right, as well as from the left, went largely unnoticed, and he called for unity and compromise as the only means to ensure renewal and survival. It was the speech of an impotent captain at the helm of a ship that had lost its direction in the stormy waters of history. After the meeting, a group of leading intellectuals published an open letter to Gorbachev in the press, requesting that changes be made to the state budget for 1991, which allocated no funds for the development of culture.[45]

The disintegration of the Soviet Union and the formation of new state structures precipitated the decline in prestige of the creative intelligentsia and removed most of its representatives from positions of power. None the less, President Yeltsin did pay heed to the political stance of the intellectual élite and tried to keep in touch with it. An important meeting between Yeltsin and members of the liberal creative intelligentsia took place on 15 September 1993, just a few days prior to Yeltsin's fateful decision to disband the obstructionist Supreme Soviet. It is interesting to note that most of the meeting's participants, including Iu. Chernichenko, M. Chudakova, A. Nuikin, and Iu. Kariakin, urged Yeltsin to get rid of the pro-Communist parliament and call new elections.[46] At the same time, an open letter signed by the writers B. Okudzhava, D. Granin, G. Baklanov, V. Astaf'ev, Iu. Nagibin, S. Kaledin, and many others, appeared in the press. It came out against the propaganda of fascism, racism, and chauvinism, and it urged the government to outlaw all communist and nationalistic parties and organizations. It also called for a ban of the publication of *Den'*, *Pravda* (Truth), *Sovetskaia Rossiia*, and *Literaturnaia Rossiia* (Literary Russia).

THE LITERARY PRESS

Before the advent of perestroika, the Soviet literary press was regarded as a vehicle of education and ideology, and all newspapers and journals were published by state-approved institutions. Creative literature was subject to editorial control and official censorship, which was managed by the bureaucracy of GLAVLIT – the Chief Administration for the Protection of State Secrets in the Press. The introduction of glasnost and perestroika in 1985 engendered the first cracks in this well-established system, but it took almost five years for this repressive edifice to begin its final collapse.

A decisive blow to the existing system of state control over literature was inflicted in 1990 by the USSR Supreme Soviet's, adoption of a new 'Law on the Press and Other Means of Mass Information.' This law abolished official censorship and proclaimed the freedom of the press. According to the new regulations, newspapers, journals, and other vehicles of mass information could be established by state institutions; social agencies; creative unions; religious, cooperative, and other associations; as well as by collectives of workers and other Soviet citizens.[47]

The new law started a mutiny in the media and the literary press. Many publications rebelled against their sponsoring parent organizations and sought total independence. *Literaturnaia gazeta* (Literary Gazette), for years the organ of the board of the USSR Writers' Union, dropped this designation on 2 May 1990. In September 1990, the workers,' collective of *Literaturnaia gazeta* registered the newspaper with the RSFSR Ministry for the Press and Mass Information, thus becoming the paper's founding body. Beginning with its 18 September 1990 issue, *Literaturnaia gazeta* began to appear as an independent paper and a 'free writers' tribune.' Similar steps were undertaken by a number of literary periodicals. Thus, *Znamia* (Banner) declared its independence from the USSR Writers' Union, while *Oktiabr'* severed its ties with its patron, the RSFSR writers' organization. The Writers' Union did not give in easily. It fought the decision of *Literaturnaia gazeta* tooth and nail, and it took *Znamia* and its editors to court. The conflict was both financial and ideological. The popular *Literaturnaia gazeta*, under the editorship of F. Burlatskii, had a liberal publication policy, while the board of the USSR Writers' Union was, at that time, still controlled by conservative writers. In addition, the paper and its printing plant were major sources of income for the Writers' Union.

Having lost its official mouthpiece, the board of the USSR Writers' Union decided to establish as its organ a new paper, *Den'*, under the editorship of the well-known conservative and Russian nationalist A. Prokhanov. The objective of such a move was obvious. It intended to draw away readers from *Literaturnaia gazeta* and lay claim to its printing plant. *Den'* advocated conservative nationalistic and chauvinistic policies, and it opposed Gorbachev and his reforms. Prokhanov abused freedom of expression by publishing in *Den'* articles that openly called for sedition. Yet he made the ludicrous claim that 'unfortunately the freedom of the press was concentrated in the hands ... of democrats, representatives of the liberal intelligentsia. Thus an imbalance was created, and not everyone could benefit from this freedom.'[48] After the unsuccessful August 1991 coup, *Den'* was closed by the new liberal board of the USSR Writers' Union. It was accused of being in the forefront of the anti-Gorbachev plot. But, a few days later, *Den'* was taken over by the conservative leadership of the RSFSR Writers' Union, and publication recommenced. Prokahnov declared that he did not need any financial support because he could receive it from other patriotic sources. It was well known in Moscow's literary circles that, even before the coup, *Den'* was patronized by generals and military commanders, and that it ran its operations in Soviet Army premises.[49] With a circulation of close to 150,000, *Den'* has become the mouthpiece of the ultra-conservative National Salvation Front. It called itself the 'newspaper of the spiritual opposition,' devoting little space to literature but continuing its anti-Yeltsin, anti-reform, nationalistic propaganda. The paper's calls to mutiny, and its thinly veiled appeals to the military to disobey presidential orders in time of political crisis, prompted the government early in 1993 to launch prosecution with the purpose of banning the publication of *Den'* altogether. The courts declined the request submitted by the Ministry of Information and the Press, and *Den'* continued publication until October 1993. After the anti-government mutiny was crushed, *Den'* was banned, but it was soon replaced by the new weekly *Zavtra* (Tomorrow), which continues, under the editorship of Prokhanov, to promote the extreme views of its defunct predecessor.

In 1993, except for the weekly *Literaturnaia Rossiia* and the conservative journals *Moskva* (Moscow) and *Nash sovremennik* (Our Contemporary), which are still organs of the Writers' Union of the Russian Federation, most other journals, such as *Znamia*, *Oktiabr'*, *Zvezda* (Star), *Iunost'*, *Neva* (Neva), and *Druzhba narodov* (Friendship of Peoples) are independent publications, registered with the Ministry of the Press by workers' collectives and run by independent editorial boards. The city of Moscow has two literary weeklies. *Moskovskii literator* (Moscow Writer), founded in 1958, was taken over by conservative writers, members of the Writers' Union of the Russian Federation. The newly established *Literaturnye novosti* (Literary News), on the other hand, is a liberal paper published by the progressive Union of Moscow Writers and the Association Aprel'.

Prior to glasnost, the Soviet literary periodical press was a tool of ideology, but it also reflected, better than the general media, the social and political atmosphere in the country. With the help of a variety of artistic contrivances and the use of Aesopian language, Soviet literature was able to provide, within certain limitations, a truthful and realistic picture of Soviet daily life. The gradual removal of censorship widened the perspectives and changed the face of the periodical press.

In 1986–8, literary journals published works previously forbidden in the USSR by Soviet writers such as Aleksandr Bek, Anatolii Rybakov, Boris Pasternak, Vasilii Grossman, Evgenii Zamiatin, Andrei Platonov, and Andrei Bitov, as well as novels by Vladimir Nabokov, Franz Kafka, and George Orwell, among others. In 1989–92, previously banned novels by Soviet dissidents such as Vladimir Voinovich, Andrei Siniavskii, Vladimir Maksimov, and Vasilii Aksenov were published. In the Soviet Union, 1990 was rightfully regarded as the year of Aleksandr Solzhenitsyn. *Novyi mir* (New World), *Nash sovremennik*, *Neva*, *Zvezda*, and *Druzhba narodov* simultaneously published his works. The journals also published significant novels written prior to glasnost by authors previously unknown in the USSR and at present residing in the West, such as Fridrikh Gorenshtein[50] and Iurii Miloslavskii.[51] The novels by the late Iu. Karabchievskii,[52] written prior to glasnost, also appeared in print. By the middle of 1992, the supply of formerly forbidden prose started to dry up, and works of well-established Soviet writers of the older generation, such as Astaf'ev, Vasil' Bykov, Sergei Zalygin, and Belov, as well as contributions by young and aspiring authors began to appear more frequently in the main journals. The quality of the prose in the periodicals varied, but it attracted the interest of the reading public, after many years of censorship still hungry for information and cultural enlightenment.

The popularity of the periodical press could, in part, be attributed to the fact that the balance between the space allotted to literary and to sociopolitical subjects changed considerably, with the latter assuming an important, if not a dominant, role. Debates on economic and political issues have become part of the regular contents of literary journals, and articles by leading politicians and economists, such as N. Shmelev, G. Popov, and A. Strelianyi, began to appear regularly. As a result, the success of the literary press was guaranteed, and prior to 1990 circulation grew steadily. In 1985, *Novyi mir* printed 430,000 copies; in 1989, 1.5 million copies; and, in 1990, 2.6 million copies. *Literaturnaia gazeta* almost doubled its circulation in one year – from 3.5 million in 1988 to 6.2 million in 1989. Most other journals increased circulation between 1986 and 1990 by at least 25 per cent. This success created a larger demand for an already limited supply of paper and strained to the extreme the capabilities of Soviet printing plants. A situation arose whereby some periodicals that did not have their own printing facilities could not publish their journals on time. *Novyi mir*, for example, was able to produce only eight monthly issues in 1990.

The good fortunes of the literary journals was not shared by scholarly and academic publications. When the literary press became financially self-supporting, the government cancelled all such subsidies and endangered the very survival of many important academic journals. In 1990, the USSR Writers' Union found it necessary to step in and provide financial support from its own resources to *Literaturnoe obozrenie* (Literary Review), *Voprosy literatury* (Problems of Literature), *Sovremennaia dramaturgiia* (Contemporary Drama), and *Teatr* (Theatre) in order to save them from extinction. It also decided to stop publishing *Sovetskaia literatura* (Soviet Literature) in French and Spanish, limiting it to Russian, English, and German editions.

The year 1991 marked the end of the boom of the periodical literary press, but the early signs of its imminent decline were already evident in 1990. The sources of previously forbidden and unpublished literature had been exhausted, and the public had become disenamoured with words that produced little practical benefit. Readers had also tired of the continuous squabbles between different clans of intellectuals, and the new economic situation emptied the pockets of the intelligentsia and middle class, in the past the main supporters of the literary press. In addition, rising paper prices and printing expenses connected with the transition to a market economy unsettled the publishing business, and complicated the life of editors. In 1991, the literary euphoria of 1988–90 became a thing of the past. The circulation of journals plummeted drastically; for example, the circulation of *Znamia* dropped from one million in 1990, to 48,750 in October 1994; the circulation of *Oktiabr'* dropped from 335,000 in 1990 to 38,200 in November 1994; and the circulation of *Novyi mir* dropped from 2.6 million in 1990 to 250,000 in 1992, and to 29,000 in November 1994 – a far cry, even, from the 335,000 copies produced in 1981 under Brezhnev. The same was true of literary weeklies. The circulation of *Literaturnaia gazeta* dropped from its high of 6.2 million in 1989 to 1.2 million in December 1991, to 510,000 in 1992, and to 310,000 in December 1994.

Today, the literary periodical press in Russia reflects a broad spectrum of political, ideological, and aesthetic opinion. Despite numerous changes in editorial management, the old and established journals keep close to the policies and ideals they adopted during the early days of perestroika. Thus, *Nash sovremennik* and *Molodaia gvardiia* propound rabid nationalistic and xenophobic views. They glorify the achievements of the former Soviet state and assail everything new and experimental in life and in the arts. *Moskva* is close in spirit to these journals; it projects a conservative, neo-Russophile point of view and devotes most of its space to the discussion of national-Christian and patriotic issues. *Znamia*, *Oktiabr'*, and *Iunost'* promote liberal democratic views and open their pages to a variety of artistic trends. *Novyi mir* maintains a middle-of-the-road position, yet some accuse it of being close to the conservative wing. Some have even derisively suggested that it has become a variant of *Nash sovremennik* for the intelligentsia.[53] It is accepted currently in Russia that, in a broad sense, *Novyi mir* reflects the views of Solzhenitsyn, while *Znamia* continues along the path envisaged by A. Sakharov.[54]

The decline in the popularity and public appeal of *Novyi mir* could be attributed, in part to the change in its editorial policy. Under the editorship of Zalygin, the journal avoids controversiality and tension. It has opted to steer a moderate national-religious-philosophical course, much in tune with the line of thinking of Russia's nineteenth- and early twentieth-century philosophers, such as Vl. Solov'ev and V. Rozanov, which does not necessarily appeal to the mainstream of contemporary Russia's middle class. None the less, the journal does publish polemical critical material and opens its pages to young writers and their experimental prose.

Along with the central monthlies, published in Moscow and St Petersburg, established Russian provincial journals such as *Volga* (Volga; Saratov), *Ural* (Ural; Ekaterinburg), *Sibirskie ogni* (The Flames of Siberia; Novosibirsk), *Sever* (The North; Petrozavodsk), *Pod"em* (Ascent; Voronezh), *Kuban'* (Kuban'; Krasnodar), and *Dal'nii vostok* (The Far East; Khabarovsk) continue publication. It is interesting to note that, despite difficult economic conditions and the decline in the popularity of established periodicals, new literary journals and almanacs come into existence almost daily. In 1991 alone some four hundred such new publications were officially registered with the government.[55] Some of them are founded by social, educational, political, or lay organizations; others are launched by commercial and business outlets; and still others are the result of individual initiatives by writers and poets. Unfortunately, the existence of many new journals is short-lived, and they disappear soon after they appear. Among the better-known new periodicals is the monthly *Soglasie* (Concord), which commenced publication in December 1990. A serious publication, dedicated mainly to prose fiction and poetry, it is produced by the Moscow editorial and publishing network Miloserdie (Charity). The long list of new publications established in the last several years includes *Moskovskii vestnik* (Moscow Herald), *Solo* (Solo), *Zolotoi vek* (The Golden Age), *Lepta* (Mite), *Vestnik novoi literatury* (The Herald of New Literature), *Diadia Vania* (Uncle Vania), *Konets veka* (The End of the Century), and *Strannik* (The Wanderer). Some established journals, such as *Iunost'* and *Literaturnoe obozrenie*, have been riven by internal bickering, and the newly established *Novaia iunost'* (New Youth) and *Novoe literaturnoe obozrenie* (New Literary Review) reflect this internal break-down. Among the provincial new periodicals, *Ekstsentr-Labirint* (Eccentricity-Labyrinth), established in 1991 as a joint venture by writers from Leningrad and Sverdlovsk, is worth a mention. The journal provides a forum for the experimental prose and poetry of young writers, and it is published alternately in St Petersburg and Ekaterinburg. It has already become known as an original and aspiring publication with its own values, world-view, and language.

Some of the new journals espouse the views of their sponsoring organizations, but most refuse to join established political camps and limit their interest to literary and social issues. Some, such as *Vestnik novoi literatury* and *Solo*, publish mainly former underground and post-modernist literature. Others, such as *Moskovskii vestnik* and *Diadia Vania*, continue in the old realistic tradition. *Strannik* devotes most of its space to the denunciation of Bolshevism and the Soviet system. *Konets veka* publishes the works of well-established Soviet and Russian émigré writers, as well as experimental prose and poetry. But the very fact that most new journals stress artistic innovation, experimentation, and the repudiation of old Soviet values makes them suspect to conservative critics who would like to stop the process of change and bring about the return of censorship.

It is worthwhile to note that, with the demise of the Soviet state two of its harshest critics, the Russian journals *Grani* (Boundaries) and *Kontinent* (Continent), published, respectively, in Frankfurt/Main and Paris, have moved their editorial offices to Moscow and are now published in Russia. Similarly, the periodical *Strelets* (Sagittarius) has moved its publishing operations from the West to Moscow.

Thus, it appears that, despite the decline in the popularity of the established periodical press, literary journals continue to play an important role in Russia's social, political, and cultural life. They are an important tribune for airing new ideological and philosophic ideals, as well as the political, national, and economic views of the Russian intellectual élite. They also provide a publication outlet for established as well as young and aspiring Russian authors. It is deplorable, however, that the literary press pays little attention today to the discussion of serious theoretical literary issues or to the review of currently published prose and poetry.

BOOK PUBLISHING AND CULTURE

The current transition to a market economy complicates the situation of most Russian writers. Before perestroika, generous state subsidies made possible the survival of many periodicals and the publication of huge editions of ideologically correct, but artistically deficient, works. The subsidies also made possible the printing of scholarly and academic books aimed at the specialized reader. Since 1990, publishers have been able to decide for themselves what to ignore and what to publish. Censorship has been removed, and they are now in the business of making money rather than fulfilling official plans. The decision of the government to lease state enterprises to collectives of workers, giving them the right to manage their own affairs, as well as the rise of a number of new independent small publishing enterprises have greatly influenced publication policy. Today, instead of publishing academic books and classical prose for marginal gain, printing houses have turned to the publication of foreign detective novels, manuals, and erotic literature, which bring in huge profits. They also publish low-quality works at the authors' expense.

Thus, most publishing houses, including the former Soviet giants such as Sovetskii pisatel', Khudozhestvennaia literatura, and Sovremennik, have curtailed the publication of classical literature and scholarly books, seeking instead more profitable printing and publishing contracts in other fields. The head of the editorial department of Khudozhestvennaia literatura, G. Ivanov, despairs that 'before, censorship used to choke us; today, we are choked by the ruble.'[56] Most affected by this situation is contemporary Russian literature. The number of published works by young contemporary writers drops from year to year. Thus, in 1990, Khudozhestvennaia literatura published seventy books by contemporary authors; in 1991, it published twenty-five; and, in 1992 it published only five. The numbers speak for themselves.

The predicament of Sovetskii pisatel' is not much different. According to the chairman of its board, Anatolii Zhukov, '70 per cent of the books approved for publication in 1991 will never appear in print. There are valid contracts with authors, and advances, in the amount of 25 per cent of the royalties due, have already been paid, but their books will hardly be published ... the reasons are simple: there is no paper.'[57] The budget of Sovetskii pisatel' for 1991 projected a deficit of close to four million rubles, which the publishing house hoped to recover by working closely with cooperative enterprises and publishing mainly commercially viable literature, such as reference books, manuals, foreign detective novels, and erotic and pornographic literature.

The situation is somewhat alleviated by the ingenuity of the young, who manage to form joint publishing ventures with representatives from the West or establish their own small publishing operations, requiring minimal cash outlay. These new publishing ventures, springing up daily and disappearing as fast, make possible the appearance of hundreds of booklets, pamphlets, and almanacs. They are also responsible for the publication of the new *samizdat* brochures and newspapers. In Leningrad alone, close to two hundred such publications appeared in print in 1989.[58] But most of these small publishing outfits are little concerned with Russian culture; their mandate is to satisfy public taste, serve a political purpose, and make a profit. Among the new publishing houses that endeavour to produce some high-quality books and replace, at least in part, the former Soviet publication giants, Terra, Tekst, and Ex Libris in Moscow, and Severo-zapad in St Petersburg, are the most prominent.

The situation in the Russian publishing business is indeed difficult. Russia produces no more paper than does a country the size of Finland – hence, the continuous shortages and high prices. Printing plants are old, poorly equipped, and lacking in new technologies. By 1993, 'over six thousand new publishing houses [had] been registered with state authorities, yet not a single new printing plant [had] been constructed.'[59] The situation is further exacerbated by growing inflation and the drop in the living standards of the population. It is also affected by the fluctuating tastes and changing interests of the current reading public. It is obvious that the first to suffer in these tough circumstances are expensive scholarly books and the Russian classical literary heritage. V. Vatsuro despairs that the publication of new scholarly books on literature has ceased almost completely. At best, defective reprints of books written long ago occasionally appear in print.[60] G. Baklanov decries the fact that no writer of his generation was able to publish a single book in 1992.[61] About 90 per cent of all printed matter in Russia today consists of pirated translations from foreign sources.[62] It appears thus that, while having satisfied their long craving for creative freedom, Russian scholars and many writers have lost the opportunity to publish and to sustain the literature and culture in whose name many of them have endured suffering and repression.

The question as to whether financial independence is a necessary prerequisite for complete artistic freedom is academic. It is well known that real art and culture cannot survive anywhere without public support, and that even in the West few writers and poets can support themselves from the incomes derived from selling their books. But, in the West, the situation is alleviated by the existence of charitable foundations, endowments, and state subsidies, independently distributed and managed, which assist individual artists and support cultural institutions. In Russia, the lay support system is still in its infancy, and many continue to look to the state for assistance. But, in times of transition, economic difficulties, and rising budget deficits, the government has little cash to spare. Furthermore, money taken from the state is suspect because it may mean that the artist surrenders his independence to a government which claims to be democratic but is still controlled by former communist bureaucrats.

The emphasis on the development of culture in the former Soviet Union was greater by far than in most countries in the West. The state supported the arts because artists, in turn, propagated the values and ideals advocated by the party and government. The number of people employed in literature and other fields of artistic and cultural endeavour was in the millions. It is evident that no democratic state, accountable to the taxpayer, can maintain such a structure. Hence, today, many writers, poets, playwrights, and translators seek work in areas little related to their main professions. Russian writers and artists, educated and nurtured by the Soviet system, have difficulty accepting this new situation, which signifies the loss of earning potential and prestige as well as a decline in the general level of cultural development. The only thing both liberals and conservatives can agree upon is the demand for public support of culture. According to Evgenii Evtushenko, commercial censorship is just as dangerous as political control: 'It can lead to the flowering of the so-called entertaining literature which, in the final analysis, corrupts the taste of the reader ... There should certainly be books which are destined from the outset to lose money.'[63] And the well-known writer Boris Mozhaev warns that the 'decline of culture is the first sign of degeneration and the death of a state. And literature is the backbone of our culture.'[64]

An acrimonious debate on the pages of *Literaturnaia gazeta* between Lev Losev, an émigré poet and currently professor at Dartmouth College, and the well-known Russian scholar and critic Vladimir Lakshin is instructive. Losev asserts that all a writer needs is freedom to create, and that there is a price to be paid for the opportunity to become part of the contemporary market economy. Lakshin retorts with a rhetorical question: 'What is the price that Russian culture has to pay? Or what if the price is so high that it would be better to return the ticket to this kingdom of bliss?'[65] In fact, the Russian government does support the creative arts. In 1994, close to two hundred writers, from both the liberal and the conservative writers' unions, including V. Belov, D. Galkovskii, and G. Vladimov, received state stipends. The government also subsidizes the daily and periodical press, but it can spare little for the publication of academic books and works of literature. According to M. Poltoranin, the minister responsible for the press, all newspapers, including the extreme nationalistic *Den'* and *Sovetskaia Rossiia*, received support from the state in 1992.[66] And *Znamia* has been able to wipe out its deficit only with the help of a state subsidy.[67]

The liberals and conservatives agree on the basic principle of public assistance to culture, but they argue vehemently on the very essence of the culture they are ready to support. The liberals promote a culture based on general human values, as well as on Russian traditions and heritage. It is a culture which advocates democracy, tolerance, and human rights. The conservatives see culture as a reflection of Russian national-orthodox values, and as an expression of Russian state interests. One of them asserts that 'the recent fashionable variety of the "pluralistic" way of making fools of the people is shrewd and dangerous, because it hides itself under the cover of the priority assigned to general human values ... The former abuse with the help of ideological means has been today replaced by more subtle methods – namely, abuse with the help of pornography, the cult of cruelty, and permissiveness which are masked by the enlightened symbols of freedom, equality, and brotherhood ... But under the surface there is always the same objective – to level and uproot everything that is national and distinctive.'[68] By questioning the very principle of self-management in the publishing business, *Pravda* has come out openly in support of conservative values in Russian literature. According to *Pravda*, this new business approach allegedly 'does not lead to the discovery of new interesting names, but rather to the flooding of the market with works which are produced with the only objective of being hastily sold ... Today's book-selling business ... subverts the development of literature; it chokes much of what is on the way to the reader.'[69]

It is true that the current chaotic conditions of transition to what intends to be a market economy are not conducive to an orderly publication process which would serve well the objective of preserving Russian cultural heritage in its entirety and, at the same time, satisfy the interests of the reading public. Today, inflation, rising paper prices, and declining demand pose a grave danger to the publishing of literary books, as well as to the periodical press. In 1994, even established journals, such as *Druzhba narodov* and *Znamia*, faced the perils of possible extinction. In the meantime, Russian trade, and the Russian economy in general, including the book-selling business, resemble a bazaar rather than an orderly market-place – hence, the numerous abuses of accepted business practice perpetrated for material gain, as well as for ideological and political reasons. But that does not justify the all-round condemnation of everything that is new, or the calls for a return to the past voiced by some conservative thinkers.[70]

The Russian government tries its best to shield culture from the dangers of a market economy, but its means are limited. In December 1991, it adopted a special document concerning the protection of Russian cultural heritage, in which it stated clearly that cultural institutions are not subject to privatization.[71] In April 1992, the Russian government adopted another resolution 'about the support of culture and the arts in the period of economic reforms.' It is questionable whether Soviet-style resolutions are an adequate means of saving Russian culture – the more so since many remember Yeltsin's supercilious attitude towards the Sverdlovsk writers.[72] The appointment of the well-known literary critic and former rector of the Literary Institute in Moscow Evgenii Sidorov to the position of Minister of Culture may be of some help, but the Ministry of Culture today is an institution with little power, no prestige, and no money.

It is evident that the development of culture and literary production in Russia is today closely related to social and political transformation, and economic well-being. Literature is currently no longer a vehicle of ideology and is gradually becoming an ordinary form of art. With the decline of its ideological significance, literature is no longer a priority for the Russian government, and writers, critics, as well as publishers have to compete for scarce financial resources with other branches of the national economy. The future of Russian culture will depend, to a large extent, on the speed with which individuals and cultural institutions will be able to adapt to these new conditions. Sheer ingenuity, as well as public and government support, is essential for the successful transformation of Russian literature from a tool of indoctrination into a vehicle of democratic cultural enlightenment, tolerance, and education.

2

The Russian Literary Scene

The writer in the former Soviet Union was not only a creative artist, but simultaneously also a historian, philosopher, sociologist, politician, and student of human relations. Since the media and daily press were in no position to satisfy the thirst of the people for information and knowledge, it was the role of imaginative prose to lift thematic taboos, provide a critique of social institutions, and question the ethical values of society in general. All that amounted to indirect scrutiny of the workings of Soviet institutions, and of the leadership of the Communist Party. It was natural, therefore, that the government followed literary production closely, because it was sensitive to the issues discussed in imaginative fiction.

The literary treatment of social and political phenomena by Soviet writers reflected the political situation in the country at any given time. In many instances the intentions of writers differed from official party policy, and their conclusions were contrary to those postulated by Marxist ideology. As a result, it was often the case that literature contained less that was apparent than was insinuated, and the message was often hidden deep under the surface. The state reacted forcefully to any insubordination. At one time, culpable authors were expelled from the Writers' Union, arrested, or banished from the country. At other times, they could get away with a minor reprimand. In the Brezhnev era, writers were at once useful and dangerous to the regime. The state made use of the educational potential of creative prose, having ascertained in advance that Soviet literature was free of what it regarded as pernicious ideas.

Until the middle of the 1980s, the government treated writers selectively, using the carrot-and-stick approach. It weighed carefully the balance of benefit and harm before taking decisive action against individual authors. The last major onslaught on the writers' community took place prior to the Olympic Games in Moscow, in the summer of 1980. The clandestine publication of the almanac *Metropol'* (1979) was one of the last attempts by Soviet writers to challenge the literary bureaucracy and defy established criteria. It irked those in power. In an effort to rid the capital of undesirable elements of questionable political reputation before the Olympic Games, writers such as Vasilii Aksenov and Vladimir Voinovich were forced into exile. Two other contributors to *Metropol'*, Viktor Erofeev and Evgenii Popov, were expelled from the Writers' Union but were permitted to remain in the USSR.

With the advent of the Gorbachev regime, and the introduction of glasnost, the situation changed drastically. By 1990, censorship had been abolished, and the literary bureaucracy had lost much of its power. The disintegration of the USSR in 1991 destabilized former Soviet cultural institutions and undermined their financial base. The publication of works by Soviet dissident and Western authors, formerly forbidden in the USSR, has become the order of the day.

Prior to glasnost, the relationship between Russian émigré literature and Soviet prose was a sensitive issue. The question as to whether there was one Russian-language literature, to which all those who write in Russian belonged, regardless of their place of residence, or two separate Russian literatures – one written by Russian Soviet authors residing in the USSR and the other produced by Russian émigré writers – was debated in both the USSR and the West. Guided by ideological considerations, most Soviet scholars and critics refused to recognize émigré literature as part of Russian culture. However, most Western scholars supported the notion of a single Russian-language literature. Much of this debate was stimulated by political acrimony rather than by cultural and artistic considerations. Today, this issue is academic. The boundaries between Russian writers residing in different parts of the world have come down, and anyone can publish whatever and wherever he or she wishes.

None the less, while it is difficult to deny that emigration and residence in a foreign environment may effect the creative output of any artist, only a detailed study contrasting the works produced by certain authors prior to their emigration with those written by them after can provide the necessary evidence to make a conclusive evaluation. Even then the results may be different in each separate case. It is worthwhile to note that many prominent nineteenth-century Russian writers, including Ivan Turgenev, Fedor Dostoevsky, and Nikolai Gogol, lived abroad for extended periods of time and wrote many of their works there. Yet the situation in those days was different. Writers were seldom subjected to ideological pressure, nor were they exiled from their native land. Furthermore, they were then little affected by the local print or electronic media, and their manuscripts, written in a foreign country, were always shipped back to Russia for publication. Today the situation is different. With the exception, perhaps, of Solzhenitsyn, who has lived in the United States for many years in total seclusion, very few can avoid the impact of Western civilization, including its social values and commercialized environment. It is apparent that circumstances of life affect everyone. The degree of influence to which authors are exposed, however, is different in each individual case. Former dissident and exiled writers are free today to return to Russia. But, except for Solzhenitsyn and Iu. Mamleev, and E. Limonov, who has come back to join the conservative nationalist political camp, most others visit Russia regularly, but retain residence in the West. Aksenov lives in Washington, DC; Andrei Siniavskii in Paris; and Voinovich in Germany.

Solzhenitsyn arrived in Vladivostok on 27 May 1994 and travelled with his entourage across Russia in two luxurious train cars, sponsored and paid for by the BBC. On his way he appeared at numerous meetings and press conferences, but it seemed that the seventy-five-year-old bard had little new to say. He claimed that he was not interested in becoming involved in political activity, yet he did not fail to criticize Gorbachev, the liberal reformers, the communists, as well as the right-wing leader Vladimir Zhirinovsky. He refrained from attacking Yeltsin directly, but he was contemptuous of the present system of government, asserting that 'the country is currently in a state of pseudo-democracy which is a cunning hybrid of the nomenklatura bureaucracy and rapacious commercialism.'[1] Solzhenitsyn decried the fact that most young Russians did not read his books and paid little attention to his exhortations. Solzhenitsyn's return to Russia generated a mixed reaction which was mainly determined by his political stance. Most agreed, however, that his return was badly mistimed and long overdue, and expressed doubt as to whether his return could seriously affect the political and cultural state of affairs in Russia today.

The early 1990s were witness to many other changes on the Russian literary scene. Where literature was once a state affair, now it has become a private business. Where writers and scholars once set the tone of social and intellectual discourse in the country, today journalists and television commentators excite the imagination of the masses. Where once, under the cover of imaginative fiction, writers conducted ideological battles, today, under the cover of ideological warfare, they are fighting for money, property, and political power. Where once there was much talk in literature about communist ethics and morality, today the Soviet ethic has been repudiated by most, even though nothing tangible has replaced it. Where once the writer's decision about what to write was determined by ideological restrictions and editorial policy, today that decision is influenced by the realities of the market-place. Literary criteria that were once established by official state policy today are determined by public taste. Russian literature was used in many instances as a vehicle of silent opposition. Since literature was under constant pressure to conform, the need to articulate in a whisper, or under the surface, prompted the creation of special forms of artistic expression, perfected over the years. Today there is no need to hide anything, no need any longer to rely on elaborate literary subterfuge in order to deliver the intended message. Once, there was no freedom of expression, but there was political and economic stability. Today, public institutions are in disarray, the economic situation is chaotic, and the new social ideals are vague. Few authors have definite ideas about the future, and most of them try to come to terms with their own past. They endeavour to assess in their works the general phenomenon of Soviet life. Where once literature was, in a sense, a mission, and the writer was a missionary, seldom concerned with issues of physical survival, today the writer is a struggling competitor in a free-market environment, and the creation of literature is no longer an occupation of influence. Step by step, literature is shedding its non-literary trappings and becoming mainly a form of art.

Prior to glasnost, most Soviet authors were identified with certain thematic streams. Writers such as Fedor Abramov, Vasilii Belov, and Vasilii Shukshin were associated with so-called village prose in Soviet literature. Vasil' Bykov and Iurii Bondarev were the leading exponents of war prose. Iurii Trifonov and Iurii Nagibin explored the city *byt*, or daily life of the urban middle class, and investigated the intricate family relationships of the city intelligentsia. Similarly, the labour theme, historical novel, and the so-called *delovaia proza*, the prose which explored Soviet trade and service industries, have had their proponents. Today, this thematic classification is no longer valid. Many authors have broadened their thematic range and changed the emphasis in their novels. Belov and Rasputin need no longer the cover of 'village prose' to expound con-servative views. Their message is now on the surface.

The war theme evolved for different reasons. It was affected by the end of the cold war, by the unification of Germany, by the dwindling number of survivors and veterans of the Second World War, as well as by the changing interests of the readers. That is not to say that the war theme has been totally discarded. Viktor Astaf'ev, for example, is cur-rently in the process of producing a major realistic tragic narrative, *Prokliaty i ubity* (The Cursed and the Slain, Book one; 1992),[2] based on his personal experience in the Second World War. None the less, the former prestige of the Soviet Army has been greatly reduced, and most current literature about war deals with the Afghanistan débâcle, which is por-trayed convincingly in the prose of, among others, the young war vet-eran Oleg Ermakov. The hideous conditions of army service and the difficult lot of Russian conscripts are described in the prose of Aleksandr Terekhov, Iurii Poliakov, and Sergei Kaledin.

Literature about the Russian and Soviet historical past has always reflected more accurately the times in which it was written than the period that it describes. The same is true, to a certain degree, today. Where once authors manipulated historical facts in order to produce manuscripts acceptable to the party, today many writers make good use of the new research possibilities in former Soviet archives and concen-trate their efforts on bringing out into the open the falsification of history perpetrated by Soviet writers and historians. Others, however, continue to manipulate facts to suit their own narrow clannish interests. In the early days of perestroika, the denunciation of Stalin and his reign of ter-ror was the rule rather than the exception. Today, Russian nationalists and neo-communist writers, such as Belov and Petr Proskurin, vindicate Stalin and absolve him of any guilt, blaming instead non-Russians and foreigners for all Russia's troubles.

The political changes of the early 1990s shattered the former unifor-mity of mainstream Russian literature. Today the writers' community is utterly fragmented along ideological, social, and aesthetic lines, and dif-ferent groups and associations of writers are held together by political and commercial interests. In addition, a writer's age and place in the former Soviet literary hierarchy are important factors which determine his or her current position on the literary scene. Writers of the older gen-eration may change their interpretation of some social phenomena, but their world outlook and literary style remain essentially the same. Writ-ers of that generation, such as Anatolii Rybakov, Boris Mozhaev, Anatolii

Anan'ev, and Bondarev, continue to turn out conventional realistic novels in which they propound views similar to those they expressed early in perestroika. Some older writers such as Chingiz Aitmatov have a hard time coming to terms with the new situation. They are confused and dejected, and produce little of substance.

Most writers who matured in the days of Brezhnev and are at present in their fifties are in the process of transformation and adaptation. The former *sorokaletnie* (forty-year-old), or 'Moscow school' authors, continue to work within their former artistic perimeters, at the same time extending their artistic and philosophical range. Vladimir Makanin continues to place an introspective but ambivalent intellectual at the centre of his novellas. He locates him in a new environment, and raises the level of his metaphysical contemplation to a new plane. Anatolii Kim continues, in his novel *Otets-les* (Father-Forest; 1989),[3] the exploration of the relationship of man and nature, but attempts also to provide, in artistic form, a philosophical substantiation of Russian social history of the last century. He tries also to assess the psychological and ethical state of the young generation of Soviet people.

Prior to perestroika most editors refused to publish Liudmila Petrushevskaia's grim stories, which lack both a positive message and any visible sign of optimism. The current difficult economic situation in Russia makes her plots even more telling. Individual hardship and anguish are augmented in her stories by the picture of family disintegration and moral decay. She illustrates convincingly the processes that destroy the ethical fabric of society. Petrushevskaia identifies with the suffering of her heroes, but she does not spare them. Her stories make a statement to the effect that both individual fortitude and a healthy social environment are required for life to become bearable.

Among the middle-aged writers whose creative talents have been dulled by recent political events, Valentin Rasputin (b. 1937), one of the most gifted and promising Russian authors of the 1970s, stands out most prominently. Rasputin's novella 'Pozhar' (The Fire; 1985) is an early reaction to glasnost. It uncovers the ethical disintegration of peasant society in the remote regions of Siberia and denounces Soviet official policy in the Russian countryside. Since the appearance of 'Pozhar,' however, Rasputin has failed to produce a single work of art. He has become, instead, a politician, public tribune, defender of Lake Baikal,[4] and an ardent proponent of Russian nationalistic orthodox ideals. In his articles and speeches, he denigrates democratic reform and those identified with it. He idealizes the Russian past, and the role of the church in

Russian history. He claims that 'Russianness ... is a spiritual quality,' inherent to the Russian people.[5] He pronounces his invectives in a strident voice which rejects compromise.

Today some Russian literary critics are taking a second look at Rasputin's prose of the 1970s and searching for the roots of his current transformation in his earlier stories and novellas. Pavel Basinskii has suggested that Rasputin has always expressed deep pessimism in his prose: 'He has always exhibited a lack of faith in life, and a strange and morbid interest in everything connected with death.'[6] Basinskii claimed that Rasputin treats his heroes with unnecessary harshness. He makes them suffer because, allegedly, only suffering can save them. He acts not as a detached observer but as a judge. None the less, there is no denying that Rasputin is an accomplished craftsman, and his place in Russian literature is secure. One can only regret that, by assuming the thankless role of saviour of Russia pitted against its internal and foreign enemies, Rasputin wastes his creative talent.

The new writers of perestroika defy classification. Those who have just recently emerged from the literary underground are already in their fifties. Others, with no previous experience of writing 'for the drawer,' are still in their twenties and early thirties. Most of them write short fiction – stories, novellas, and sketches – although some do try their hand at novels. In the late 1980s, works by some of these authors were dubbed 'drugaia proza,' or 'the other prose.' By the early 1990s the thematic and stylistic distinctions in the prose of these new authors had become apparent, and today they can be grouped, albeit arbitrarily, into several separate categories. Writers belonging to one group produce thematically innovative but conventionally realistic prose. Others reject the old manner of writing, discarding the accepted forms of narration and often sacrificing substance for style, and turn literature into word play. They experiment with language and meaning and reduce the social and ethical significance of a work of art. Most of these writers belong to the stream of what is known today as Russian post-modernism. The division between these two extremes, however, is not as clear as it might seem initially. Many writers, such as Mark Kharitonov, Anatolii Korolev, Aleksandr Lavrin, and Aleksandr Vernikov, are somewhere in between. They combine realistic and modernist narrative modes, and despite their emphasis on the stylistic aspects of narration, their prose may provide a social or philosophical message of considerable significance.

The new authors of the realistic stream produce thematically controversial and provocative plots, containing, in most cases, some social message. Their characters are usually unconventional, and the settings new to Soviet and Russian literature. Kaledin, for example, sets his novellas at a cemetery, at an army construction battalion, and in a church, respectively. The action in Leonid Gabyshev's novel *Odlian, ili vozdukh svobody* (Odlian, or the Air of Freedom; 1989)[7] takes place in a correctional institution for juvenile delinquents. Most of Ermakov's works are set in Afghanistan. The heroine of one of Aleksandr Rosliakov's novellas is a prostitute, and the main protagonists in Terekhov's stories are young people disenchanted with life. In his stories about the army, he debunks the romantic notion of brotherhood-in-arms, and in his narrative about student life, he portrays the higher school as a repository of depravity and moral rot. Other young writers of the realistic stream, such as Dmitrii Bakin, Ivan Alekseev, Iurii Buida, Ivan Oganov, and Aleksei Varlamov, are good stylists who explore in their stories different aspects of life in contemporary Russia.

The current version of Russian post-modernism is a peculiar post-Soviet phenomenon.[8] The application of this term reflects, in a way, the old Soviet addiction to high-sounding phrases of questionable meaning. Soviet official language has always had a predilection for the use of elaborate slogans and clichés, and, in that sense, the designation 'post-modernism,' widely used in the West for years, has come to replace in Russia the by-now defunct notion of socialist realism. In general terms, post-modernism is regarded as a reaction to modernism, and as a statement to the effect that humanity has found modernist ideas inadequate. In Russia today, post-modernism refutes the aesthetics of socialist realism, as well as old Soviet values. In contemporary Russian fiction, post-modernist art is usually identified by a heightened self-consciousness, authorial self-reflexiveness, and a reliance on secondary literary and cultural sources. Among the writers who identify with current Russian post-modernism are authors as diverse as V. Erofeev, E. Popov, Vladimir Sorokin, and Valeriia Narbikova. Each creates in his or her own peculiar manner, yet all are united by their rejection of the Soviet past. Post-modernist literature is not for everyone. It is for the sophisticated reader and the adherent of 'art for art's sake.' It is popular among those who have come out of the literary underground, and a small group of young literati. It has, however, few followers among the mass readership, who have, for years, been nurtured by solid and prosaic realistic fare. The print runs of post-modernist publications are small, and some could hardly survive without outside financial support.

The theoretical premises of Russian post-modernism are elaborated in works of young Russian critics and scholars, such as V. Kuritsyn, M. Lipovetskii, and M. Epshtein. These critics draw parallels between Russian post-modernism and its predecessors in the West, and try to substantiate the essence of the Russian variant of this vague phenomenon. Kuritsyn, for example, asserted that 'the post-modernist sap enmeshes our communal body, ... the vertical, hierarchical, rough, and classified image of the world is being replaced today by the horizontal, pluralistic, flexible, and the destructive. Everything flows ... Such are the times.'[9]

Many literary scholars and writers of the older generation oppose post-modernism vehemently. Solzhenistyn is one of those who do not mince words in their assault on post-modernism. He asserts that 'for a post-modernist the world does not posses values that have reality. He even has an expression for this: "the world as text," as something secondary, as the text of an author's work, wherein the primary object of interest is the author himself in his relationship to the work, his own introspection. Culture in this view, ought to be directed inward at itself ... it alone is valuable and real.'[10] According to Solzhenitsyn, 'the artist must not forget that creative freedom can be dangerous, for the fewer artistic limitations he imposes on his own work, the less chance he has for artistic success ... Many young writers have now given in to the more accessible path of pessimistic relativism ... They say ... absolute truths do not exist anyhow, and trying to find them is pointless.'[11] Solzhenitsyn's opposition to post-modernism is prompted by ideological as well as artistic considerations. He cannot accept the chaotic vision of life promoted by some post-modernists, nor can he concur with their choice of words, images, or ideas. According to him, post-modernism is dangerous to Russian culture, because it is an expression of novelty without spirituality and it advances an objective without substance.

Solzhenitsyn is not the only one to take exception to the proliferation of post-modernism in Russian culture. Caryl Emerson has suggested that, 'if our Western commercialized postmodernism, with its superficial attitude toward art ... is enjoying a temporary and transitory bestseller status in Russia, because of its novelty and its formerly forbidden status, this state of affairs will not last – or so thoughtful Russian intellectuals now insist ... The West can afford to place aesthetic emphasis "not on depth or intensity, but on slipping over the surface" ... But Russians ... will return, sooner or later, to a form of realism. Postmodernism can teach Russians ... only one important thing: how to philosophize intelligently about art as process.'[12]

WRITERS FROM THE PROVINCES

One of the positive developments in Russian literature of the late 1980s and early 1990s is the appearance of a number of new provincial authors. Close to half of all members of the former Writers' Union of the Russian Federation lived in Moscow and Leningrad. Only a small number of established writers resided in the provinces. Belov lived in Vologda, and Rasputin in Irkutsk. They became, however, well known all over Russia only after their works began to appear in the main journals or were published by major Moscow publishing houses. Currently the situation is somewhat different. Provincial journals, such as *Ural*, *Volga*, *Sibirskie ogni*, and *Pod"em*, have gained relative independence because they are no longer supported by the Writers' Union in Moscow and are free to follow the publication policy of their choice. In addition, the abolition of censorship and transition to a market economy have made possible the appearance of many new provincial almanacs, journals, and independent publishing outlets which cater to the needs of the local population. These new conditions have helped many new provincial authors to gain recognition in the national literary scene and become well known all over the country. The long list of newly successful provincial writers includes Aleksandr Ivanchenko, Andrei Matveev, and Vernikov (Ekaterinburg region); Ermakov (Smolensk region); Gabyshev (Volgograd); Aleksei Slapovskii (Saratov); Anatolii Gavrilov (Vladimir); and Nina Gorlanova (Perm'). Ivanchenko's novels *Avtoportret s dogom* (Self-Portrait with a Great Dane; 1990) and *Monogramma* (Monogram; 1992) and Ermakov's novel *Znak zveria* (Sign of the Beast; 1992) are considered by some Russian critics to be among the best prose narratives recently produced in Russia. *Monogramma* was short-listed in the competition for the Booker Russian Novel Prize for 1992, and *Znak zveria* was one of the leading contenders for the 1993 Booker Award.

It is interesting to note that some young Ekaterinburg writers maintain that Moscow and St Petersburg have now relinquished to Ekaterinburg their leading positions in Russian letters. They even produce a special series of publications under the general heading 'Tret'ia stolitsa,' or 'The Third Capital,'[13] suggesting that Ekaterinburg has currently become the 'Third Rome' of Russian literature and the centre of Russian creative activity. Ekaterinburg writers and critics such as Ivanchenko, Vernikov, A. Matveev, V. Iskhakov, Kuritsyn, and Lipovetskii are indeed very active in the local and central literary press. Their prose and ideas are innovative and unconventional, yet in literature quantity seldom translates into quality, and the issue of cultural leadership is of little consequence to the ordinary writer. In fact, Ivanchenko, the leading prose writer of the Ekaterinburg region, has recently become a bureaucrat in the liberal Writers' Union of the Russian Federation and spends most of his time in Moscow.

THE LANGUAGE OF PROSE

The language promoted by any dictatorship is usually simple, concrete, succinct, and free from abstractions. It avoids different shades of meaning, or unnecessary metaphors, because they stimulate thinking. Phrases are functional, and the general vocabulary is limited. In Soviet literature prior to perestroika, structure, composition, and language stressed the message inherent in a work of art, and the tone of a narrative was most often kept neutral. Editors made sure that the choice of words did not upset established stylistic criteria and did not obscure the message. Today most writers of the older generation continue to produce narratives similar in style to their earlier works. Glasnost has affected the subject-matter of Bondarev's, Astaf'ev's, or Mozhaev's prose, but their language remains essentially the same. They continue to rely heavily on straightforward third-person narration, interspersed with some flashbacks, dialogue, and internal monologue. The language of Fazil' Iskander has also changed little. It is witty and full of irony, and it conveys a sense of earnestness under the cover of what might appear to be trivial occurrences. In the works of many new writers language has acquired new meaning. The harsh or 'tough' prose, or, as it is dubbed, 'zhestkaia proza,' by realistic authors such as Kaledin and Gabyshev verges on naturalism and the physiological sketch. It is close in tone and diction to the so-called zhestokaia proza, or 'cruel' prose, and to 'chernukha,' the profane slang used to portray the seamy sides of Russian life. Harsh prose is close in spirit to the so-called oblichitel'naia proza, or denunciatory prose, the objective of which is to uncover the transgressions and abuse of power by the former Soviet regime. The language of this prose has many parallels with that of literature which often expresses despair. In some of Petrushevskaia's stories, peculiar language features accentuate personal anguish, social despair, and the feeling that people have lost their way in this God-forsaken world. In other instances, the language of Petrushevskaia resembles skaz, or oral narration full of colloquialisms, slang, and vulgar expressions.

For many contemporary modern writers, language is the message.

They combine different narrative techniques with a number of thematic variations. Viacheslav P'etsukh, Korolev, Viktor Pelevin, and Lavrin, among others, freely mix reality with fantasy and myth. In the prose of Kharitonov and Popov, a secondary text provides the basis for plot development, and realistic prose is often intertwined with narration in the form of verse. Erofeev's prose presents a mixture of different styles in which the 'low' and the 'high' intermingle freely. His prose demystifies, mocks, and brings down to an ordinary human level the false ideals of a corrupt world. Some of his stories are monologues in epistolary form; others emphasize the vulgar and profane in speech, as well as in human behaviour.

Sorokin's stories combine realistic narration with stylistic incongruities. His is the language of the absurd. Many passages are compilations of incoherent sounds which appear to have no meaning whatsoever. On the surface he subverts language and destroys meaning, but within the general context of his stories the combination of realistic prose with nonsensical language may intimate some hidden and symbolic purpose. The language of Narbikova appears somewhat artificial. Full of slang, new idioms, and clichés, it reflects the inconstancy of the environment portrayed, providing, at the same time, some stylistic unity to her narratives. Mikhail Kuraev's language is ornate and metaphorical, while Nina Sadur's voice is geared to the exploration of the subconscious and surrealistic.

Erofeev, Narbikova, and Sorokin describe explicit sex scenes and freely mix elevated speech with obscene language. This trend is new to Russian literature, and it is resisted by many. Even in today's atmosphere of total freedom of expression, established journals refuse to accept manuscripts containing what is regarded to be unacceptable language. But editorial policy can no longer affect the realities of the market, and writers such as Erofeev and Sorokin find other publication outlets. In general terms, the boundaries between erotic literature and pornography are today often blurred.

WOMEN WRITERS

The number of women writers in the former Soviet Union was very small indeed. In 1986, female membership in the Writers' Union was, close to 15 per cent of the total. Among delegates to the Eighth Congress of Soviet Writers in 1986 there were only forty-four women, 7.7 per cent of the total. Only 5 per cent of elected members of the board of the Writers' Union were women, and no women were elected to the union's highest governing body, the so-called bureau of the secretariat. Similarly few women were in the élite of Soviet prose writers. Soviet official women writers, with the exception, perhaps, of Maiia Ganina, were not interested in furthering the aims of emancipation, or in advancing the cause of feminism as it is understood in the West. And, besides, Soviet self-styled feminists were persecuted, driven underground or into exile.[14] Leading Soviet women writers and critics, such as Petrushevskaia, Tat'iana Tolstaia, and Natal'ia Ivanova, have long regarded the term 'woman writer' as derogatory and condescending because it implies that prose written by women has thematic and artistic peculiarities and limitations.[15] The term 'women's prose' was used and misused, but never properly explained, in the former Soviet Union. Even today, it is not clear whether 'women's prose' is defined by gender, subject-matter, or a feminist approach to individual human problems as well as to social phenomena.

In the late 1980s, the composition of the women writers' community started to change rapidly. Mariia Prilezhaeva and Irina Velembovskaia died. Other woman writers of the older generation, such as I. Grekova (b. 1907) and Natal'ia Baranskaia (b. 1908), have curtailed their literary activity to a minimum. Established middle-aged women writers such as Petrushevskaia, Viktoriia Tokareva, Tolstaia, and Tat'iana Nabatnikova continued to write but, with the exception of Petrushevskaia, produced less than expected. This situation has been alleviated by new publication possibilities, and the appearance of a number of promising new female authors. Some of them are very young; others have already managed to graduate from the Gorky Literary Institute. Many reside in the provinces. Writers such as Marina Palei, Irina Polianskaia, Valeriia Narbikova, Nina Sadur, Mariam Iusefovskaia, Nina Gorlanova, Svetlana Vasilenko, and Liudmila Ulitskaia have already gained recognition, and their prose appears regularly in the main periodical press. The prose of Palei and Polianskaia is in the tradition of realism. Sadur explores the darker sides of the human psyche. Narbikova's prose is in the realm of post-modernist absurd. Several collections of what is called today 'zhenskaia proza,' or women's prose, including Ne pomniashchaia zla (She Does Not Remember Evil; 1990), Novye amazonki (The New Amazons; 1991), and Abstinentki (Women Who Abstain; 1991), have been recently published in Moscow. The prose in these collections varies in style, subject-matter, and quality, but it provides exposure to women writers unknown until recently. Most new women authors concentrate on the investigation of the female character, employing women narrators to provide a female perception of events described and discussing issues of concern to women, such as motherhood, abortion, loneliness, and infidelity. That is true of Polianskaia, Palei, as well as Petrushevskaia.[16]

LITERARY CRITICISM AND SCHOLARSHIP

In the former Soviet Union, no manuscript was ever officially published, without editorial scrutiny and the approval of the censor. None the less, the critical reception a novel manuscript received could often determine the fate of the book and the destiny of its author. Prose fiction was regarded by the state as a social and ideological document and as such was accorded proper critical attention. Official criticism emphasized political relevance and conformity with the requirements of socialist realism over artistic merit. Today prose fiction is no longer treated as a political and ideological phenomenon. Even a work of prose that is ideologically significant and contains a social message in most cases is regarded as a work of art and is treated as such. The role of literary criticism has changed accordingly – but only up to a point. The ideological rift in the writers' community affects the critical opinions of those who belong to different political camps. As a rule, most prose fiction produced by the so-called liberals, and in particular by post-modernist authors, is assailed by conservative critics. Equally, liberal critics usually attack the conservative nationalist message contained in the prose of their opponents.

In the 1970s and early 1980s critical opinion was dominated by the so-called *shestidesiatniki* (literally, 'those of the 1960s'), or moderately liberal intellectuals, who believed in the social function and ethical essence of literature. They matured in the days of the Khrushchev thaws and were active in the official press in the years of Brezhnev stagnation. They were sympathetic to the literary dissidents but refused to join them. Today, well-known literary critics of that generation, such as Lev Anninskii, Igor' Zolotusskii, Igor' Vinogradov, Benedikt Sarnov, and Andrei Turkov, are still active. Most of them promote liberal ideals and support democracy but are cautious in accepting extreme radical positions in life, and in the arts. They are not ready to accept the chaotic state of affairs in Russia and the declining role of literature in this new social order. They are uncomfortable with the intrusion of unacceptable phraseology and obscene diction into Russian literary language, and they express doubt whether culture and the arts can survive in a free world without outside support. They value highly the creative freedom in democratic society but resent the corrupting effect of commercialization in the arts. The current views of some critics of this generation reflect the difficult process of adaptation. Whereas they appreciate the new freedoms of expression, publication, and foreign travel, they sorely miss their former security and prestige.

The younger generation of critics have no such impediments. Some become entangled in political infighting, but most concentrate on the aesthetic analysis of new works of prose and on the general elaboration of the situation in Russian literature today. Among the critics of the younger generation most often appearing in the daily and periodical press, are Aleksandr Ageev, Mikhail Zolotonosov, Mark Lipovetskii, Dmitrii Lekukh, Viacheslav Kuritsyn, Andrei Nemzer, Oleg Dark, and Sergei Kostyrko.

Prior to glasnost, no more than 10 per cent of all new books published in the USSR were ever mentioned in literary criticism. The books reviewed could be divided roughly into two extreme categories: in one group were dull, artistically insignificant, but politically important novels by literary bureaucrats such as Georgii Markov, Mikhail Alekseev, and Aleksandr Chakovskii; in the other group was the innovative and refreshing prose of liberal authors such as Iurii Trifonov, Iurii Nagibin, Vasilii Aksenov, and Andrei Bitov. Today a work of prose is selected for critical consideration in the conservative press on the basis of political merit, although, in most other literary publications, this choice is influenced by artistic significance. In general, however, most contemporary works of prose fail to attract the attention of reviewers – the more so since even literary weeklies, such as *Literaturnaia gazeta* and *Literaturnaia Rossiia*, devote little space to literary criticism and focus instead on the discussion of social and political issues. Similarly most established monthly periodicals have curtailed their review sections and limit themselves to the occasional publication of survey review articles. Many established critics, such as N. Ivanova, S. Chuprinin, and V. Oskotskii, are now employed full-time by the main journals, which has changed the focus of their literary activity considerably. The situation is somewhat alleviated by the publication of *Literaturnoe obozrenie* and the sporadic appearance of critical articles and book reviews in daily newspapers, such as *Izvestiia* (News), *Segodnia* (Today), and *Nezavisimaia gazeta* (Independent Newspaper); however, the new journals and almanacs, mushrooming all over the country, devote little room to literary criticism.

In the West, literary criticism is closely intertwined with literary scholarship. In the former USSR, literary theory and criticism have always been interlaced with ideology, and the study of artistic form has been secondary to the examination of ideological and social relevance. Today, the situation in Russia is different. Literary scholars have acquired the long-cherished freedom to engage in intellectual and scientific inquiry. Unfortunately, literary scholarship – particularly, literary theory – is virtually moribund. Scholars whose reputation has been irreparably marred by their association and cooperation with the former regime, and by their ardent promotion of the school of socialist realism, are in no position to make advances in scholarship or to develop progressive new theories. Some young Russian scholars and critics draw upon the experience of Western literary scholarship. Unfortunately, Western theoretical literary thought is fragmented, and far from uniform, and Russian students have a hard time finding their way in the thicket of Western literary theory. It will take time before Russian literary theoreticians will be able to rid themselves of the effects of their Soviet education and develop new theoretical premises, which wil be rooted in and inspired by the Russian tradition and the accomplishments of Russian thinkers and scholars of the early 1920s. In the meantime many Russian literary scholars are involved in the arduous task of trying to fill in the gaps in Russian literary history caused by censorship and the intrusion of communist ideology.

THE BOOKER PRIZE

One of the most important literary events of 1992 was the competition for the First Booker Russian Novel Prize. Of the fifty-one works submitted for consideration, six were short-listed by the panel of judges chaired by the Russian literary critic Alla Latynina. The panel also included the British scholar John Bayley, Ellendea Proffer from Ardis (United States), as well as A. Siniavskii and A. Bitov. The six titles singled out for detailed consideration included *Linii sud'by, ili sunduchok Milashevicha* (Lines of Fate, or Milashevich's Little Trunk; 1992) by M. Kharitonov, V. Makanin's 'Laz' (Manhole; 1992), L. Petrushevskaia's 'Vremia noch'' (The Time: Night; 1992), A. Ivanchenko's *Monogramma*, V. Sorokin's unpublished manuscript 'Serdtsa chetyrekh' (Four Stout Hearts), and *Mesto* (Place; 1991) by the émigré writer F. Gorenshtein. Three judges – Bayley, Siniavskii, and Latynina – voted for Kharitonov.

The £10,000 prize was intended for the best Russian novel of 1992, yet two of the short-listed works were published in 1991, and one was accepted for consideration in manuscript form. Furthermore, only three titles were full-length novels; the others were in the realm of short fiction. It appeared, then, that Russian writers had ceased producing good novels. V. Semiletov suggested in *Literaturnaia gazeta* that the nominations for the prize had been engineered, and determined by political considerations, with writers from the capital receiving favourable treatment. He supported his allegations by noting that the panel of judges refused consideration of the novel *Znak zveria* (Sign of the Beast) by the Smolensk writer O. Ermakov, submitted by the journal *Znamia* in page-proof form, yet made an exception for the unpublished experimental prose work of Sorokin.[17]

Thirty-nine nominations were proposed for the 1993 Booker Prize. Works published between April 1992 and March 1993 were accepted for consideration. The chairman of the jury, which included Geoffrey Hosking, Bulat Okudzhava, and the Russian émigré critic Aleksandr Genis, was the respected scholar Viacheslav Ivanov. In October 1993, six titles were short-listed, Astaf'ev's *Prokliaty i ubity*, Ermakov's *Znak zveria*, Semen Lipkin's *Zapiski zhil'tsa* (Notes of a Lodger; 1992), Makanin's 'Stol, pokrytyi suknom i s grafinom poseredine' (Cloth-Covered Table with Carafe in the Middle; 1993), Liudmila Ulitskaia's 'Sonechka' (Sonechka; 1992), and Narbikova's *Okolo ekolo ...* (Around and About; 1990, 1992).

The list of titles selected for detailed consideration raises some questions. It is evident that the decision to short-list works by representatives of different generations and different artistic inclinations had been determined by political, rather than artistic, considerations. There are only two full-length novels in the list, those by Ermakov and Lipkin. Astaf'ev's novel is incomplete, since only Book One has been published so far. Makanin's and Ulitskaia's works are novellas rather than novels, and Narbikova's *Okolo ekolo ...* is a collection rather than a single work of prose fiction. In fact, the novella 'Okolo ekolo ...' included in this collection was originally published in 1990 in *Iunost'*. Just prior to the final-selection stage, the jury acknowledged their mistake by removing *Okolo ekolo ...* from the list of contenders.

It was announced on 14 December 1993 that Makanin had won the Second Booker Russian Novel Prize. There is no question that Makanin is one of the best contemporary Russian prose writers, yet his 'Stol, pokrytyi suknom i s grafinom poseredine' is not a novel but a forty-four-page *povest'* (novella). Nor is it one of his better works. It is evident that by awarding the prize to Makanin the judges violated the basic rules of competition: the Booker Prize is intended for the best novel of a given year rather than for the quality of a writer's general creative output.

In addition to the major prize, a 'Little Booker Prize,' worth £2,500 is awarded annually. In 1992 the journals *Solo* and *Vestnik novoi literatury* (The Herald of New Literature) were awarded the special prize for their contribution to the development of contemporary Russian-language literature. In 1993, Viktor Pelevin received the 'Little Prize' for his *Sinii fonar'* (Blue Lamp; 1992), the best collection of short prose.

It is worth mentioning that most works under consideration were submitted by liberal journals and publishing houses. The only novel nominated by the conservative *Nash sovremennik* was B. Mozhaev's *Izgoi* (The Outcast; 1993). In fact, many conservative writers and critics, including E. Limonov and V. Bondarenko, oppose the presentation of the Booker Prize altogether. They claim that it is an expression of foreign interference in Russian affairs and offends Russian dignity. Furthermore, they object to the acceptance of money allegedly derived from the exploitation of slave labour by British imperialists. It is evident that the Booker Prize has become another pawn in the ongoing struggle between representatives of different political camps in the Russian cultural arena.

Early in May 1994 a list of thirty-nine works nominated for the 1994 Booker Russian Novel Prize, has been made public. Works published between 1 January and 31 December 1993 are eligible for consideration. The jury, chaired by the Russian writer and critic Lev Anninskii, included the writer V. Voinovich, the editor and translator Natasha Perova, as well as the Western academics Martin Dewhirst (Great Britain) and Marina Ledkovsky (United States).

The list of authors whose works have been nominated contains the names of well-known writers such as V. Bykov, B. Okudzhava, Iu. Davydov, A. Bitov, M. Kuraev, A. Kurchatkin, and L. Petrushevskaia. It also included young and aspiring authors such as Petr Aleshkovskii, Aleksandr Borodynia, Iurii Buida, Viktor Pelevin, Mikhail Shishkin, Igor' Doliniak, and the Saratov writer Aleksei Slapovskii, whose name appeared on the list three times for works published in different journals. On 27 September 1994, six titles were short-listed: Aleshkovskii's 'Zhizneopisanie Khorka' (Polecat's Biography), Buida's 'Don Domino' (The Domino-player), Doliniak's 'Mir tretii' (Another World), Mikhail Levitin's 'Sploshnoe neprilichie' (Total Indecency), Bulat Okudzhava's *Uprazdnennyi teatr* (The Closed-Down Theatre), and Slapovskii's *Pervoe vtoroe prishestvie* (The First Second Coming).

It was announced on 19 December 1994 that Bulat Okudzhava had won the Third Booker Russian Novel Prize. The 'Little Prize' for the journal outside Moscow and St Petersburg that, in the opinion of the judges, had done most to support Russian fiction was awarded to *Volga*, published in Saratov. The task of the jury was not an easy one. Unfortunately the nominated works of most well-established writers appeared slight in comparison with their earlier works. The nominated works of most of the young writers, on the other hand, make up for in being innovative and refreshing what they lack in sophistication and depth.

SOCIALIST REALISM

The censor was the final judge of what might, or might not, appear in print in the Soviet Union. But literary theory was the vehicle that helped to deliver to the reader the politically correct ideological message. In the West, literary theory concerns itself with the study of the basic principles of literature, its categories and criteria. It investigates the poetics of artistic creativity in terms of genre, style, and the modes of narrative fiction. In the Soviet Union, on the other hand, instead of explaining literature, literary theoreticians have attempted for years to regulate literary production.

Since 1934, when it was adopted by the First Congress of Soviet Writers, socialist realism was the official 'method' of Soviet literature. It required 'from the artist a truthful, historically concrete representation of reality in its revolutionary development,' whereby 'truth and historical completeness of artistic representation must be combined with the task of ideological transformation and education of the working man in the spirit of socialism.'[18] In practice, socialist realism limited the stylistic range of artistic prose and made a positive hero and a didactic message imperative in any work of art. In many instances, the party interfered in the creative process to ensure that literature was not out of step with the political objectives of the state. After the death of Stalin, the application of the stringent requirements of socialist realism was somewhat relaxed, with the result that the disparity between theory and literary practice was often immense.

Glasnost unsettled the established balance between the artist's freedom of expression and the official guidelines for artistic creation. In October 1988, the Politburo of the CPSU Central Committee recognized as erroneous and repealed the resolution of the All-Union Communist Party (Bolshevik) Central Committee of 14 August 1946 – 'On the Magazines "Zvezda" and "Leningrad"' in which it accused those journals of publishing 'ideologically harmful' works and singled out for special condemnation the writer Mikhail Zoshchenko and the poet Anna Akhmatova. By the middle of 1988 it was no longer a secret in the Soviet Union that socialist realism was 'neither an aesthetic nor ethical term, but rather a political and ideological notion.'[19] Nevertheless, in 1988, socialist realism was still the subject of academic discussion, and a number of Soviet scholars and critics continued to interpret it as an aesthetic notion.[20] In 1988, the Writers' Union still regarded socialist realism as an indispensable component of Soviet literary theory.

The first substantial, albeit contradictory, changes in this long-standing tradition became visible in 1989. There was no mention of socialist realism in the projected new statutes of the Writers' Union, published early in 1989.[21] Instead, the statutes asserted that the union 'is guided in its work by the principles of socialist democracy, glasnost, personal initiative and responsibility of each member ... It also considers the freedom of creative activity as an indispensable condition for the development of literature.' And yet, the same document states that 'partiinost' [partyness, party principles and spirit] and narodnost' [national spirit] of artistic creativity are the basic principles of Soviet literature,' and that 'guided by the pluralism of opinions ... the union supports works which are realistic in style and uphold the socialist ideal.'[22]

Nine months later, a new version of the statutes of the USSR Writers' Union appeared in print.[23] The new version still 'adheres to the principles of socialism and democracy, glasnost and creative freedom,' but it also asserts that 'creative freedom is incompatible with any kind of censorship, except for instances where it protects military and state secrets, and prevents the kind of propaganda which runs counter to all-union and republican laws.' Most important is the inclusion in the statutes of the statement that 'the controversial nature of the author's social and aesthetic views cannot serve as an obstacle to his or her inherent and guaranteed rights of self-expression.'

In May 1991, a new, drastically changed, version of the statutes was published.[24] This time, the statutes concern themselves more with organizational and business issues than with ideology. The statutes assert the equality of all union members; the writers' freedom of self-expression; and the freedom to form, within the framework of the union, different factions, associations, or groups united on a national, ideological, or territorial basis. They also state that the Writers' Union 'is independent of any political party or movement, and does not pursue any political aims.' This new document, which resembles in many ways the rules of professional associations in the West and was published several months prior to the anti-Gorbachev coup, is a reflection of the social, political, and ideological upheavals within the writers' community and in Soviet society in general, as well as a reaction to the revocation by the USSR Supreme Soviet of Article 6 of the Soviet constitution, according to which 'the leading and guiding force of Soviet society and the nucleus of its political system ... is the Communist Party of the Soviet Union.' The repeal of Article 6 abolishes, in fact, the rule of the Communist Party and opens the door for a multiparty system of government in which different parties may represent a variety of different political agendas.

The new version of the projected union statutes strikes the final blow to the myth of socialist realism, an artificial creation of the Soviet totalitarian system, which has managed to survive for more than fifty years not because of its viability as a literary theory, but rather because the government mercilessly enforced its acceptance. And yet, it is necessary to note that socialist realism is not totally dead. Many years of indoctrination have left a mark on the psyche of Soviet writers. Today, some of them continue to advocate in their works old Soviet values and policies, making ample use of the compromised precepts of socialist realism. Others apply the old methods and devices with the purpose of obtaining results contrary to the initial objectives of socialist realism. In the process of demythologizing Soviet literature, the former positive hero is often turned today into a negative hero, or anti-hero. The communist utopia portrayed in former works of socialist realism has evolved into an anti-utopia. The optimistic conclusion, an important device in socialist realist novels, is frequently replaced today by an ending full of pessimistic doom and gloom. The positive social background that compensates for individual tragedy in a work of socialist realism is today most often replaced by a picture of stagnation, corruption, and social decomposition. The conventional structure of a socialist realist work, and its language, accessible to the masses, are in many instance replaced by innovation and experimentation with structure and form, and a language often incomprehensible to the average reader. In many contemporary works we witness what can be termed 'socialist realism in reverse.' This transition from one extreme to another is a phenomenon not limited to literature alone but characteristic of life in the former Soviet Union in general.

In general terms, the contemporary Russian literary scene is dynamic and vibrant, but it is also volatile and lacking stability. Its main characteristic is artistic and thematic variety. The fragmented structure of many new novellas reflects the fractured state of affairs in current Russian society. Artistically, this prose is uneven. Many novels imbued with serious ideas are artistically deficient. In other instances, artistic sophistication covers up the lack of meaning. The most promising new authors are concerned with ontological issues. They search for faith, new values, and the meaning of life, yet often fail to address coherently the complex issues of ethics, human nature, and spirituality.

By the end of 1993, Russian literature had reached a certain critical juncture. Most *samizdat* and *tamizdat* literature had been already published in Russia, and former underground authors who have been writing for years 'for the drawer' have come out into the open. Thus, most manuscripts published today in the periodical press were written in the last several years, and reflect accordingly the new conditions of the day. It appears, however, as Aleksandr Vial'tsev suggests, that 'the level of contemporary Russian literature is indeed not very high.'[25] Creative freedom has turned into a burden, 'driving literature into a stupor.'[26] Pavel Basinskii corroborates this view by asserting that the new literature by writers such as V. Sorokin, V. Narbikova, E. Laputin, and D. Galkovskii is *fundamentally* deprived of the possibility of growth,' not because of its moral shallowness, but rather because of its 'aesthetic irresponsibility, which is, perhaps, its most characteristic trait.'[27]

Indeed, most new authors from the realistic stream have come to literature with their own consuming themes and have been unable to diversify. They have a narrow view of life. Post-modernist and avant-garde literature, on the other hand, has lost much of its early freshness and attraction for most Russian readers. This has made room for the appearance of a number of novels by writers such as Vladimir Sharov who cater to the lower tastes of the mass readership and create in the realm of kitsch.[28] Important manuscripts by other writers, such as Dmitrii Galkovskii, are only marginally connected with creative fiction. Galkovskii's narrative *Beskonechnyi tupik* (The Endless Impasse; 1992)[29] is so long that no journal or publisher would accept its complete text for publication. It is a book in the form of comments on a non-existent text, which are followed by comments on comments ... on comments ... The book, which combines autobiography with cultural and intellectual history, is regarded by many as an intellectual provocation because it offers many contradictory insights and caters to a variety of whims. In a cold, detached manner, Galkovskii disparages A. Chekhov and L. Tolstoy, but shows favour to V. Rozanov.

Russian prose is currently in a state of transition. Some see its future in modernist innovation and stylistic experimentation, but most agree that a literature without depth has no future in Russia. I. Rodnianskaia suggests that 'literature can only be great or nothing at all. If it is great, then it draws its excitement and its inspiration from more than artistic technique, from a source beyond and greater than literature.'[30] That is not to say that there is no room in Russian literature for artistic variety and the exploration of non-realistic narrative modes, but the future of Russian prose is apparently in a new realistic art infused with significant ideas. The influx of many new authors bodes well for the future of Russian literature. They are still inexperienced, their craft needing polishing, but they are young and have time to mature. None the less, few of these new writers have yet been able to produce memorable manuscripts of lasting artistic, social, or intellectual significance. The current unsatisfactory state of Russian literature could be alleviated by the sudden appearance of several new great talents who may raise the level of creative prose to new heights and set the tone for other contemporary writers to follow.

3

The Old Guard

The years between 1989 and 1994 have witnessed the demise of many important literary figures connected with the Soviet literary past. Among those departed are V. Kaverin (1902–1989); S. Dangulov (1912–1989); V.S. Pikul' (1928–1990); the former editor of *Druzhba narodov*, S. Baruzdin (1926–1991); the former chairman of the USSR Writers' Union, G. Markov (1911–1991); A. Strugatskii (1925–1991); G. Semenov (1931–1992); Iu. Semenov (1931–1993); V. Kondrat'ev (1920–1993); A. Chakovskii (1913–1994); I. Stadniuk (1920–1994); and Iu. Nagibin (1920–1994). Other established writers of the older generation, who are today over sixty, have been affected in different ways by the rapid political changes occurring in the Soviet Union in the late 1980s and early 1990s. Change for them does not come easily. Years of adaptation and acquiescence have perverted their talents. Some have tried to cash in on the new freedoms by resorting to subjects unacceptable to the editors and censors of the former regime. Others have dealt with old problems, changing the emphasis and interpretation of the issues discussed. Still others have attempted to modify the impact of their early published works by preparing revised versions in which they introduce changes and additions. But most writers of the older generation who formerly published their prose in official Soviet journals are disturbed by the proliferation of experimental and innovative works by young authors in which eroticism, adultery, and *poshlost'*, or banality, are the main subjects, and in which substance is sacrificed for external stylistic effect. Viktor Astaf'ev bluntly states that 'there is no use expecting creative discoveries from those who have not endured any major shock in their lives, or have little life experience. People ask, but what about Lermontov or Pushkin? Indeed, but they are geniuses, hence a special case ...

Unfortunately, our new prose is stylistically untidy. The authors think that they write in a contemporary vein, when in fact their prose is primitive.'[1] Anatolii Rybakov's comments on Viktor Erofeev's *Russkaia krasavitsa* (Russian Beauty; 1990) are similar; he asserts: 'I read the novel ... but what could one say? A lot of *poshlost'*, and little talent.'[2]

In recent times, few writers of the older generation have written anything of great artistic significance. The prose of many is autobiographical and reflects the changing social and political conditions in the country. Indirectly it bears witness to many personal dramas in the writers' community. Some writers of the older generation make an attempt at a new beginning and try to repudiate their recent past, but most cling to their old themes, ideas, and values.

VIKTOR ASTAF'EV

Viktor Astaf'ev (b. 1924) is one of those who make good use of the new possibilities of glasnost. He remains, however, true to himself. Substance is always his main concern. In response to the early relaxation of perestroika, he came out with a hastily produced and artistically deficient novel, *Pechal'nyi detektiv* (The Sad Detective Story; 1986), in which he decries the prevalence of evil and injustice, which have become a daily occurrence in Soviet life, and expresses anguish for the future of Russia. Astaf'ev continues also to add new chapters to his *Poslednii poklon* (Last Respects), a loosely connected, episodic narrative, begun over thirty years ago, portraying friends, family, and his native Siberia, and with particular emphasis on the character of his loving, selfless, and compassionate grandmother.[3] 'Ne khvataet serdtsa' (Not Enough Heart; 1988),[4] and 'Liudochka' (Liudochka; 1989)[5] provide further evidence of Astaf'ev's disenchantment with and despair over the state of affairs in contemporary Russia.

In 1976, Astaf'ev published his long lyrical and philosophical allegory *Tsar'-ryba* (Queen Fish) in which he contrasts the rapacious nature of human beings with the serenity and infiniteness of nature. 'Ne khvataet serdtsa,' a new chapter of *Tsar'-ryba*, for obvious reasons could not have been published in 1976. The story begins with the author-narrator's encounter with a bureaucrat from the city of Noril'sk, in Siberia's far north, who travels with him in the same compartment, down the Enisei River. The narrator is on his way to seek help for his dying brother, while the nameless bureaucrat travels to join a group of officials on a tour of Paris. The narrator resents the condescending tone and the air of superiority in the voice of his travelling companion and is full of scorn for the man's incessant bragging about his good life in Noril'sk, a city whose horrible history is unknown to him.

This introduction places the story in proper perspective. It is followed by a flashback to the 1930s when the city of Noril'sk was constructed in the tundra with the help of slave labour. Most convicts are victims of Stalin's rule of terror, condemned to die in the inhumane conditions of the far north. Some try to escape, but perish in the taiga or are caught and returned to work in the mines and quarries. One such convict, previously a colonel in the Soviet Army, tries to escape. Despite all tribulations, he retains his faith in the goodness of people and renews his belief in God. In his naïvety he is sure that Stalin is unaware of the injustice and cruelty to which Soviet people are exposed, and he seeks a meeting with the leader in order to tell him the truth.

The harsh reality described is rooted in Astaf'ev's autobiography. It leads the author to the blunt conclusion that the human product of the Soviet era is a heartless, cruel, and often evil individual.[6] This is true of most run-away convicts, who even resort to cannibalism as a means of survival in the taiga, as well as of the nameless bureaucrat, whose current pleasures of daily life in Noril'sk have been made possible by the blood of innocent victims.

The spirit of gloom is also pervasive in the realistic third-person narrative 'Liudochka.' Liudochka, a country girl, comes to the city to learn a trade and build a life for herself. She has little ability and not much education, but a warm heart, full of compassion and tenderness. Unprepared for the callous and brutal reality of city life, she is abused, raped, and driven to suicide, her sensitive soul uable to withstand humiliation. 'Liudochka' is a tragic story about an unfulfilled and wasted life, rendered by a sensitive but detached observer. Astaf'ev does not judge or moralize, but instead allows harsh reality to speak for itself. In a sense, the story harkens back to 'village prose,' and to Astaf'ev's earlier stories, set in the remote Russian countryside. Villages are desolate and abandoned, and their inhabitants have been uprooted. Those who move to the city, hoping for a better life, soon become bitterly disappointed, or corrupted and destroyed by the effects of this 'progressive' urban civilization.

Astaf'ev's most recent novel, *Prokliaty i ubity* (The Cursed and the Slain; 1992), a tragic narrative about the Second World War, is thematically different but similar in spirit. The first book of the novel, which is appropriately entitled 'Chertova iama' (The Devil's Pit), is based on the author's personal experience, and is set in 1942–3 in the Siberian city of Novosibirsk. The novel is about soldiers in time of war, but most of the action takes place in the hinterland, far from the front line, in military barracks which resemble a Siberian prison camp, and there are few scenes in which the Nazi enemy appears. The soldiers, who are readied to join the Soviet army at the front, are treated like convicts – victimized, abused, exploited, and starved. The depiction of the execution of two brothers, accused of desertion for visiting their old mother in a nearby village shocks the reader. In the novel, Astaf'ev questions the true reasons for war, the depravity of the young, and the lack of ethics in the military establishment. He challenges the idealized image of the Russian peasant advanced in Soviet village prose, and the notion that evil and corruption have been brought in to the Russian countryside from outside. The seeds of evil, according to Astaf'ev, are in everyone, are part of human nature. And the 'devil's' pit is a metaphor for the Soviet system, which perverts and dehumanizes those in power and subverts and subjugates the weak.

Astaf'ev is a compassionate observer, and an invisible participant in the action. The narrative is realistic, and portrayal verges on the naturalistic. It presents a compilation of seemingly minor incidents, full of dramatic tension, slowly evolving into major human tragedies. The author reproduces accurately, and without embellishment, the soldiers' slang and the lexical features of Siberian peasant language. It is impossible to pass final judgment on the artistic merits of the novel, since so far only one book has appeared in print. It is apparent, however, that since it belongs to the so-called *oblichitel'naia proza* (denunciatory prose), or the literature that unmasks and repudiates the Soviet system and communist rule, it had no chance of being officially published prior to glasnost in the USSR.

Astaf'ev's recent stories are thematically innovative, but otherwise similar to his earlier works. His characters are usually simple people, facing a difficult life, and those who are weak in body are usually imbued with inner strength and spirituality. His imagery is harsh and realistic, and the language is characteristic of the milieu he describes. He contrasts the inner goodness of those who are connected with their past and with the land with the base and perverted impulses of those who are removed from the soil and exposed to a new life with which they are neither familiar nor comfortable. Astaf'ev's plots evolve slowly, but dramatic tension grows continuously, leading inevitably to a tragic end. Astaf'ev's prose of the post-Brezhnev period is imbued with an air of pessimism. The inner goodness, expressed by some of his heroes, is overshadowed by a pervasive evil that determines the actions of most characters. The author's anxiety about the future of Russia, ravaged by seventy years of Soviet rule, is on the surface, and it permeates all his recent works.

CHINGIZ AITMATOV

Chingiz Aitmatov (b. 1928) is another writer of the older generation who has responded to the political changes in the USSR in a peculiar way. His case is special. He is Kirghiz by birth, but perfectly bilingual, and, to the chagrin of his Kirghiz colleagues, writes mostly in Russian. However, Russian conservative nationalists are no better pleased: in their view, works by writers such as Aitmatov introduce alien elements into Russian culture and contaminate the Russian national spirit.[7] In addition, although in his previous works he trod dangerously close to the boundary of what was permitted, Aitmatov always supported party policy and was himself a member of the Soviet élite. In 1989 he was nominated to the USSR Congress of the People's Deputies, and later became a member of President Gorbachev's Advisory Committee. In November 1990, he was appointed Soviet ambassador to Luxembourg.

Sensitive to political change, Aitmatov has always managed to react to the needs of the regime with the necessary spirit. In the stifling atmosphere of the final days of Brezhnev's rule, a new positive hero was required, and Aitmatov created, in his *I dol'she veka dlitsia den'* (The Day Lasts More than a Hundred Years; 1980) the character of Edigei, an upright and decent man, dedicated to his job, family, friends, and nature.[8] In his early response to glasnost, Aitmatov published the novel *Plakha* (The Execution Block; 1986) in which he uncovered the evil and corruption prevalent in Soviet society.

Aitmatov is, of course, a good writer, an accomplished craftsman who integrates reality with elements of myth, folklore, and fantasy. His conflicts are always charged with dramatic tension, and his style is terse and expressive. But he is also a product of the Soviet system and the son of a purged father. It has been suggested that the higher Aitmatov climbs on the social and political ladder, the cooler and more sceptical we grow when we read his novels.[9] It has become apparent recently that the issue of Aitmatov's sincerity and integrity has become amplified by his guilty conscience. This new state of mind has led him to rewrite and revise some of his earlier works. He is aware of the fact that some may view with scorn his attempt to vindicate himself in the eyes of the reading public and he asserts, in self-defence, that 'surely we are now different people ... people with a different thinking.'[10] One wonders, however, whether any one can change his way of thinking overnight, and whether Aitmatov's efforts to show that he has changed are not an expression of a new opportunism, or, as the Russians call it, *koniunkturshchina*.

'Beloe oblako Chingizkhana' (The White Cloud of Genghis Khan; 1990)[11] is a new addition to *I dol'she veka dlitsia den'*. It combines an old legend with the reality of Stalin's Russia. In the original version of the novel, Abutalip Kuttybaev is a secondary, albeit important, character. He comes with his family to work at the railway siding of Boranly-Burannyi, in the Kazakh steppe, after being fired from his job as a schoolteacher in town. Abutalip, having been a soldier, prisoner of war, and partisan in Yugoslavia, is no longer trusted with the responsibility of educating the young; at this time, being a prisoner of war in Nazi Germany is tantamount to being a traitor. For a while, Abutalip and his family are left in peace. He works, teaches his children, and, in his spare time, writes down the old legends from the people's lore, as well as reminiscences of his prison and partisan experiences during the war. It is not long before Abutalip is arrested. On 5 March 1953, the day of Stalin's death, his wife, Zaripa, receives a note informing her that her husband has died in prison from a heart attack. In 1956, after the Twentieth Party Congress, Abutalip is rehabilitated with the help of his neighbour and friend, Edigei.

The new novella, intended to be read as a constituent part of the novel, changes the perspective and revises Abutalip's life story. It includes a new legend from eastern lore, full of symbolic meaning, which alludes directly to the despotism of Stalinist rule. The external frame of the novella is composed of realistic details about the workings of the Soviet system of justice and the security forces in the days of Stalin. Aitmatov illustrates clearly the modus operandi of the security officers who justify their indispensability and promotions by creating a myth about an alleged danger to the Soviet state. Investigating officers spare no effort in fabricating evidence and coercing prisoners to admit to crimes they have never committed. Abutalip refuses to yield to pressure. He has nothing to admit. His conscience is clear, and he chooses suicide rather than surrender.

A major part of the novella is taken up with the legend of 'The Serozek Execution,' written down by Abutalip and viewed with suspicion by his interrogators. This story of Genghis Khan and the white cloud that shows him the road to success exposes his immeasurable cru-elty, pride, and thirst for unlimited power and new conquests. It is also a story about the embroiderer of military banners, Dogulang, and her tragic end. Genghis Khan forbids women to bear children until his great victory, but Dogulang conceives and gives birth in secret, and is denounced and condemned to die. The executioners demand that she disclose the name of the child's father, but she refuses. Her husband, Ederne, is in despair, tortured by love and guilt. He wants to commit sui-cide, but instead he comes forth and admits that he is the father of the child. They are both executed by hanging. Their slave, the old woman Altun, hides with the child in the steppe. There is no food for the baby, but suddenly milk appears in the old woman's breast and the white cloud over the head of Genghis Khan disappears, reappearing in front of Altun and the baby.

'The Serozek Execution' is a beautiful story which fits well with the legend about the mankurts, and with Aitmatov's earlier works, which also feature elements of folklore, legend, and mythology. Aitmatov him-self views the legend about Genghis Khan within the context of the eter-nal conflict between the individual and those in power.[12] As a corollary, the legend can also be interpreted as a comment on the relationship between the artist and those who rule. Dogulang is an artist at her trade. Her artfully embroidered and decorated banners accompany Genghis Khan's hordes in their battles and conquests, thus adding to the glory of their leader, but once Dogulang is murdered, her name disappears into oblivion. The theme of the artist's subservience to those in power is not new. Aitmatov illustrates convincingly that, by destroying the artist physically, Genghis Khan dispossesses her of her creation, making use of her art to his own advantage. The allusions to Stalinism and to the Soviet state are obvious. For years, nineteenth- and early twentieth-century classic works of art have been manipulated, misinterpreted, and mis-quoted to convey an impression contrary to that intended by the artists who created them. The legend is also a warning that no one should dare assume that he or she is infallible and that, the higher those in power rise, the more dangerous and devastating their fall. Those who interro-gate Abutalip have good reason to be in awe of the legend 'The Serozek Execution.' After all, deep in their hearts, they know that they serve a false idol that is not eternal.

The portrayal of the work and life of the Soviet security officers, including the description of Abutalip's interrogation and torture, is a new dimension in Aitmatov's work and was apparently written quite recently. Prior to perestroika, Aitmatov, the Soviet bureaucrat, would have never dared to deal with such sensitive anti-Soviet issues. In the 1970s and early 1980s, a new novella by Aitmatov would have been considered an important event in Soviet intellectual circles. However, under the current conditions of political, economic, and cultural disintegration, the novella's publication has been greeted, relatively speaking, with limited critical attention. It is a sign of the times, but also, perhaps, an indication that interests are changing with the generations.

In 1994, Aitmatov added another chapter to *I dol'she veka dlitsia den'*.[13] The main character is again Abutalip, who visits the respected scholar academician Chaadai and is amazed by the latter's philosophical musings about nature, God, and eternity. In the stifling atmosphere of Stalin's Russia, Chaadai's ideas are not only refreshing, challenging, and revealing, but also dangerous and risky.

Aitmatov has also embarked on rewriting and producing a new version of his story 'Litsom k litsu' (Face to Face), originally published in 1957. In this story, a Kirghiz peasant woman betrays her husband, a deserter from the Soviet army in time of war. She places the importance of a social cause above the value of her personal relationship with the father of her children. In the new version, the conflict between personal interest and social duty, as well as the issue of class struggle in the countryside and its effect on the peasantry, is amplified. Otherwise, except for toning down the pro-Soviet message and shortening the story somewhat, Aitmatov has changed little of the old version.[14]

In 1988, Aitmatov announced the forthcoming publication of his new novel 'Bogomater' v snegakh' (Madonna of the Snows), which was due to appear in the 1989 volume of *Novyi mir*.[15] Several excerpts from the novel have appeared in the periodical press. One excerpt was published 12 December 1988 in *Pravda*, and later in English translation in *Soviet Literature*.[16] It is a story of a young Russian artist, an officer in the Soviet army, who accompanies the art treasures of the Dresden Gallery on their way to Russia. He is obsessed with the idea of creating a picture of a contemporary 'Madonna with Child' which would symbolize the return of his generation to old humanistic ideals after having gone through the hell of the Second World War. Another excerpt from the announced novel, 'Bakhiana' (Bakhiana),[17] relates the story of a mysterious young Bulgarian woman, who, at the time of war, endeavours to join a Greek monastery on an island in the Sea of Marmara. Both excerpts are written in Aitmatov's intense but laconic prose, and keep the reader in suspense. Unfortunately, the complete version of the novel has yet to appear. Today, Aitmatov doubts whether he will ever be able to finish 'Bogomater' v snegakh.' Much in this novel is connected with the image of Stalin and Stalinism, and according to Aitmatov it is a worn-out subject, lately much abused.[18]

An excerpt from another novella, 'Ubit' – ne ubit" (To Kill, or Not to Kill), due to appear in *Znamia*, was published in January 1992.[19] It is also a story about the Second World War. A young conscript, preparing to leave his native Saratov to join the army at the front, is told by his father that, in order to win the war, one has to kill, and is admonished by his mother not to kill. She cannot understand how anyone could live in a world in which only victorious killers remained.

The same notion, the biblical 'Thou Shalt Not Kill,' is the subject of a story, 'Vstrecha' (A Meeting), published late in 1992.[20] In this autobiographical sketch, based on an experience from Aitmatov's youth, the fifteen-year-old Aitmatov, the oldest of four children of a widow whose husband was shot in 1937 by Stalin's henchmen, assumes many of his father's responsibilities. When the family's cow is stolen, during the difficult days of war, he sets out, rifle in hand, and chases the culprits, intending to kill them. During the pursuit, he encounters an old man riding a small donkey. When the man sees the excited and armed youth he realizes that something is wrong. A conversation follows, during which the old man dissuades the young Aitmatov from his evil intentions. The old man cautions him by saying: 'Do not go to kill ... remember life will punish those who do evil. Punishment will follow them day and night. And you will be rewarded ... Never think of vengeance.'[21] Mollified, the young Aitmatov returns home.

Whether motivated by political change, in Russia or by the reassessment of life experience that comes with age, Aitmatov turns, time and again, to the old injunction 'Thou Shalt Not Kill,' which is a precept closer to Tolstoy's pacifist conception of life than to Soviet ideology or the Muslim creed. He applies it in his creative work, as well as in his social and political activity. Aitmatov continues to advocate internationalism and the brotherhood of nations, and he supports the federation of former Soviet republics. But the recent changes in the former Soviet Union have hurled him into a state of shock. He is uncomfortable with the past but has a hard time coming to terms with the present. In a letter to the editor of *Literaturnaia gazeta*, he justifies his silence, admitting that he is not ready for unexpected changes. Refusing to accept the new idols of the market-place, he contemplates life and is unable to write. He criticizes the new wave of Russian prose, asserting that 'the discoveries of post-modernist literature do not make [the reader] happy ... The schizo-phrenic vision of life, characteristic of postmodernism, and its obsession with the spontaneity of the subconscious do not provide the reader with the promised super insights ... while old positive stereotypes are replaced by new, negative ones.'[22]

Aitmatov's destiny reflects well the predicament of many writers of the older generation. He has loyally served the old system, seldom ques-tioning its ruthless policies, and has been rewarded accordingly by the state. The sobering belated realization that he has served a false idol, wasting his life in the process, has a devastating effect on his talent and paralyses his creativity. The situation Aitmatov find himself in is more complicated than that of most other Russian writers of his generation. His native Kirghizia nurtures his talent but is too small a readership after the exposure he became accustomed to in the years of Soviet rule. The question whether Aitmatov is a Kirghiz or Russian writer is aca-demic, as he has made a considerable contribution to both cultures. He will certainly be remembered in Russia by all those who appreciate good literature, for his inventive plots, acute dramatic sense, and ability to blend myth and the reality of Soviet daily life.

Early in 1994, Aitmatov made known his intention to leave his ambas-sadorial position in Luxembourg and to devote, in future, most of his time to literature. He also announced that he had completed a new novel, entitled *Tavro Kassandry* (The Brand of Cassandra), which is to be published in the near future in *Znamia*.[23]

IURII BONDAREV

The writing of Iurii Bondarev (b. 1924) in the 1960s and 1970s was in the mainstream of official Soviet literature and reflected accordingly the changing political and social realities in Soviet society. His moderately progressive novel *Tishina* (Silence; 1962) was an appropriate reaction to the Twentieth Party Congress and the Khrushchev thaws in Soviet cul-ture, and his subsequent war stories and novellas, promoted the ideals and values propounded by the Brezhnev regime. Beginning in the mid-1970s, Bondarev embarked on a study of the Soviet post–Second World War creative intelligentsia. His trilogy, in which war scenes are juxta-posed with the postwar experiences of the survivors, includes the novels *Bereg* (The Shore; 1975), *Vybor* (The Choice; 1980), and *Igra* (The Game; 1985). The heroes of these novels – Nikitin, a writer; Vasil'ev, a painter; and Krymov, a film director – are all members of the Soviet cultural élite.[24] In the 1990s, Bondarev remains true to himself. At the centre of his new novel, *Iskushenie* (Temptation; 1991),[25] are scientists and highly placed Soviet bureaucrats. And although the subject of the novel is not new to Soviet fiction, its treatment reflects the changing political situation in Gorbachev's Russia.

The plot of the novel hinges on an artificial conflict between those who support the construction of a huge hydro-electric station in Siberia and those who oppose it. The project requires the joint blessing of the state and party administration, as well as of the leadership of the Institute for the Study of Ecological Problems, of the USSR Academy of Sciences. This planned undertaking has the full support of the Central Party Committee but encounters some opposition at the institute. The opinion of the director of the institute is crucial, but academician Grigor'ev's, death has left the position vacant, and his deputies, Chernyshev and Drozdov, are in contention for the job. Drozdov, the husband of Grigor'ev's daughter, who has died in unexplained circumstances, appears to be an independently minded scholar whose views on ecological issues are far from extreme. He is regarded as a centrist, capable of objectivity. Chernyshev, on the other hand, is a weakling, ready to acquiesce and satisfy any demands made by the party leadership.

The controversy around the construction of the Chilim hydro-electric station turns into a struggle between those who promote the preservation of the environment and the members of the Communist bureaucracy, whose aims allegedly entail the destruction of nature in Russia. Dr Tarutin, a lonely, divorced alcoholic, is the main representative of those who allegedly want to save Russia. He is an impulsive man of strong opinions, and a friend of Drozdov; however, his undisciplined nature and extreme opinions turn most scientists at the institute against him. Tarutin is an ardent Russian nationalist. He advocates the preservation of Russian spiritual purity, regarding those who support the intrusion of technological progress in the remote regions of Siberia as traitors who are consciously turning Russia into a cheap source of natural resources for America.

In an effort to forestall the inevitable, Tarutin goes to Chilim to investigate. He learns there that the Chilim project is already under way, even though formal approval to proceed has not yet been given by the appropriate higher authorities. But Tarutin does not live long enough to return to Moscow with this news; he is murdered by unknown culprits in Siberia. When Drozdov goes to Siberia to inquire about the fate of his friend, he learns nothing. In fact, Tarutin's murder appears to be a conspiracy by those in power, and the local police investigators spare no effort in covering up all traces of the crime. Tarutin is a leading figure in the novel, but his character is poorly developed and his role is limited to delivering the author's political and ideological message. Drozdov returns from Siberia a shattered man, shaken by the death of Tarutin; he turns down the offer to become the director of the institute. He cannot, in good conscience, back the construction of the Chilim station, and refusing to commit to the project would prevent his appointment to the position anyway. At the end of the novel, Drozdov is overwhelmed by persecution mania, and he dreams about unknown intruders who attack and threaten to kill him.

In December 1985, when he had just begun work on the novel, Bondarev expressed views strikingly similar to those voiced by Tarutin. In a speech delivered at the Sixth Congress of Russian Writers, he attacked vehemently official plans to reroute some rivers in the Arkhangel and Vologda regions of northern Russia in order to accommodate construction of a new hydro-electric system. He also assaulted technological progress, cosmopolitanism, and Western influences as the main adversaries of Russian culture.[26]

The character of Drozdov, the main protagonist of the novel, forms the structural foundation of the narrative, connecting the beginning with the end of the novel. But his personality is indistinct, and his image is often blurred. In the opening pages of the novel Bondarev describes death and a funeral – the passing of an era, making way for a new generation to come to the fore. On the concluding pages of the narrative, we see Drozdov, with his small son, Mitia, clinging to each other. The boy jealously protects his father from all outsiders, including the woman Drozdov apparently loves. The scene is symbolic: it appears that the good and peaceful life of the upper middle class in post-Stalinist Russia has corrupted the Soviet intelligentsia, and the only hope for the future is the children, who will guard the heritage of their forefathers and bring about a revival of the Russian spirit.

Bondarev obviously has good intentions but apparently not enough talent to turn Drozdov into a fully realized, sincere, and memorable character. The title of the novel, 'temptation,' alludes to the fact that, by refusing to join the establishment and accept the position of director, Drozdov withstands the temptations of power and evil and remains a decent human being. But Bondarev fails to see that Drozdov, a careerist who marries the boss's daughter as a sure step towards professional advancement, is in no position to continue the struggle initiated by Tarutin. In fact, Drozdov's refusal to accept the position of director is an admission of failure and a silent acquiescence to the deeds of those in power. Drozdov is a coward, and his centrist position on ecological issues is probably motivated by convenience rather than conviction.

Bondarev's new narrative is no great work of art. The main conflicts are poorly delineated, characterization is inadequate, and most heroes are little more than mannequins. The actions of the protagonists are poorly motivated and lack psychological substantiation. Furthermore, the novel is stylistically deficient, and its political and ideological message is intrusive. Glasnost has made it possible to attack the political establishment and the cultural élite, and Bondarev creates caricatures of highly placed party officials and leading scholars who express views different from his own. He portrays the so-called party mafia as a group of depraved and power-hungry people without morals or scruples. They enjoy the good but shallow life, and will go to any length in order to attain their personal objectives or to satisfy their whims. But glasnost has also given Bondarev an opportunity to expose his own narrow nationalistic views and his lack of tolerance for the opinions of others.

It is difficult to write a good novel in which an abstract notion is the main subject. Prose fiction requires that the characters that represent serious ideas and propel the dramatic narrative be artistically drawn. In *Iskushenie* the preservation of the environment remains an abstract notion to the very end. It is detached from the emotions, experiences, and the fates of most of the main characters, and its connection with their actions is tentative at best.

Bondarev's new novel about the Russian intelligentsia, which turns his former trilogy into a tetralogy, is reminiscent of his previous works. In many ways Drozdov resembles the main protagonists of *Bereg*, *Vybor*, and *Igra*. They are all contradictory, confused, and depressed. In the end, each of them disintegrates emotionally and physically. Tarutin, who is pictured as a selfless man of high moral values, has his predecessors in Kniazhko (*Bereg*) and Skvortsova (*Igra*): all of them are idealized and not very realistic; all die in unexplained circumstances; and all are invested with an emblematic ethical superiority over the corrupt majority that surrounds them. Women protagonists in Bondarev's novels are usually strong and independent professionals, married to the heroes. They are loved and respected by their husbands, but they seldom reciprocate in full measure by providing emotional support when necessary. In *Iskushenie*, the only woman, Valeriia, is a junior scientist at the institute. Divorced and single, she becomes Drozdov's companion and confidante, but their relationship is nebulous, and her role remains obscure. To his surprise, Drozdov discovers that, although married in the past, Valeriia is still a virgin – which may hint at lesbianism.

Iskushenie is the first of Bondarev's novels in which events during the Second World War do not form a constituent part of the narrative. Most of the novel's characters belong to the postwar generation; however, there is one war scene in the novel. Drozdov recalls his father, a war veteran, relating to his mother some of his war experiences.

Some Soviet critics compare the war against Nazi Germany to the war with Russia's internal enemies. It is suggested in *Literaturnaia Rossiia* that 'there is an associative connection, in the minds of the heroes, between the old Great Fatherland War, and the current "undeclared war".'[27] Today, the proponents of extreme Russian nationalism view the encroachment of cosmopolitan values, and the influence of Western civilization and culture on Russian life and society, as as much of a threat to the survival of the Russian nation as the physical annihilation during the Nazi onslaught. In the same way that *Iskushenie* evokes the war without depicting it at length, it is the first novel in the tetralogy in which no scenes are set in the West. According to Bondarev, there is no longer any need to go to Germany, France, or the United States to learn about Western society. Today, Western social and economic values overwhelm Russia. The novel suggests, in fact, that these influences have penetrated Russia so deeply that 'democratization ... has been transformed into Americanization.'[28]

The critical response to *Iskushenie* is also a reflection of the current situation in Russian literature. Bondarev, is one of the leaders of the Russian conservative nationalist intellectual and political élite, and this novel received rave reviews in right-wing publications such as *Literaturnaia Rossiia*[29] and *Molodaia gvardiia*.[30] A more balanced and objective review, published in the independent *Nezavisimaia gazeta*, stated, bluntly that 'Bondarev had great possibilities and a theme of abundant potential. He lacked unfortunately the indispensable linguistic and mental abilities required to master the subject.'[31]

Indeed, Valentin Rasputin, in 'Proshchanie s Materoi' (Farewell to Matyora; 1976), addressed the same issues Bondarev deals with in his novel but did so with much more subtlety and greater ease. At the centre of 'Proshchanie s Materoi' are real people with real problems. Rasputin concentrates on the investigation of the fate of those who are mostly affected by the disruptive effects of technological progress on the long-established pattern of life in the remote villages of Siberia. Bondarev, on the other hand, places an abstract idea at the fore, leaving emotions and personal experiences in the distant background. In prose fiction, philosophical or social notions are only as good as the artistic dimensions of the characters who express them. The difference between Rasputin's narrative and Bondarev's underscores the distinction between art and journalism. One is left to wonder why it was necessary to read several hundred pages of dull prose to receive a message which could have been delivered with ease in a short newspaper column.

Today, Bondarev devotes little time to literature proper, and is mostly concerned with business and politics. He has replaced his former communist cloak with a national-orthodox one, and he continues to advocate his regressive views against everyone and everything that is modern and innovative in life and in literature. In a recent article, he attacked contemporary Russian prose as well as American culture and Western literature,[32] paying homage to the literature of socialist realism, and affirming his adherence to Russianness and religious spirituality in life. He also voiced his support of psychologism, sincerity, and simplicity in literature. All of that is fine theory, but conspicuously lacking in Bondarev's recent novel.

VASIL' BYKOV

The name of Vasil' Bykov (b. 1924) has always been associated with the theme of war in Soviet literature. Most of his mature works deal with the fate of Soviet soldiers and partisans in the Great Fatherland War of 1941–5. Bykov's stories are usually terse and cover a short period of time. In them, a limited number of characters are placed in most unusual and difficult situations. Most of his heroes are of simple peasant stock, and until the appearance of 'Znak bedy' (Sign of Misfortune; 1983), Bykov had concerned himself mainly with the fate of the individual on the battlefield. In combat with a mortal enemy, his characters are challenged by internal ethical conflicts of insurmountable magnitude. Their choice between life and death is always determined by their moral fortitude. 'Znak bedy' is also set during the Second World War, but the main characters are not young soldiers or officers, confronting the Nazi enemy, but rather old peasants who are abused and humiliated by the occupiers in their own home.[33] 'Znak bedy' is Bykov's first attempt to combine a story about war with the theme of collectivization in the Russian countryside. Bykov illustrates convincingly that most Belorussians who collaborated with the Nazis were people who had been victimized by the

Soviet regime in the past. Injustice and evil, it is suggested, usually beget more evil and hardship.

'Oblava' (The Cordon; 1990)[34] is the first novella of Bykov's maturity that is not set in wartime. Instead, the action takes place in the late 1930s. Khvedor Rovba, the hero, and the only character we get to know well, is hiding in the swamps adjacent to his native village. The name of the village, Nedolishche, which means 'bad luck,' symbolizes the fate of the main character. A poor peasant before 1917, he is given some land and a new lease on life after the revolution. But hard work is his undoing. At the time of collectivization, jealous and envious neighbours dub him a kulak, and he is expelled with his family to the far north. His only son, Mikolka, a Komsomol member, disowns his parents and stays behind, eventually becoming the leader of the local district communists.

Despite his suffering and tribulations, and the loss of wife and daughter, in exile Rovba is driven by a blind and insatiable urge to return to his native village: 'Life taught him to bear quietly any servitude, but he could not overcome the deep yearning for his native places.'[35] Returning is, of course, a virtually impossible dream. No one waits for him there, and, if he is caught, he will be arrested immediately and sent back to jail or exile. He fails to realize that Stalinist collectivization has turned him into a class enemy and a rootless non-person. When he does return, he is recognized by some of his former neighbours and is hunted down by the police, soldiers, and a group of villagers led by Rovba's son Mikolka. Khvedor does not surrender; instead he commits suicide by drowning himself in the swamps. He prefers the peace of eternity to a life full of new suffering and humiliation. And is life worth living when a son consciously drives his own father to death? Despite these trials, the submissive Rovba blames no one for his suffering and even tries to excuse the actions of his ruthless son. There seems to be no answer to the question he asks himself time and again: 'Za chto?' – What for? Why so much injustice? Why do good and decent people turn into cruel animals? Why is everyone against him when he has not hurt or abused anyone?

The story is a poignant denunciation of Stalinism and its policies of class war and collectivization. These policies have unsettled the peasant's life and brought out the worst traits in his character, yet they have failed to provide the people with bread. Furthermore, the war against the class enemy has degenerated into a war between neighbours, friends, and relatives. Many nineteenth-century Russian thinkers, including F. Dostoevsky, propounded the notion that physical suffering and submission lead to moral elevation and spiritual regeneration, but the Russian critic V. Oskotskii asserts that the 'philosophy of suffering, humility, and moral forbearance has turned into immeasurable losses and calamity for human destiny.'[36] Indeed with the help of brainwashing and intimidation, Stalin abused the patience and traditional respect for authority of the Russian people, and forced them to support political adventures whose meaning few could comprehend.

The title 'Oblava' has deep symbolic meaning. Bykov's concern is not limited to the fate of his hero. The attack on Khvedor Rovba is an attack on all the Soviet countryside, on all Soviet people, and on the social fabric of society in general. The fate of the individual represents here the destiny of a whole class. Infected with the poison of Stalinism, people have lost the ability to see clearly and make a rational distinction between good and evil. According to Bykov, passive submission makes the rule of totalitarian monsters possible. However, that does not mean that the submissive Rovba is viewed negatively by Bykov; rather the author identifies with his hero. He appreciates his good human qualities and is sorry for him. But he makes also clear that social justice is not something that can be expected of people hungry for power. Social justice can be acquired only by those with determination and strength. Rovba's death symbolizes, in a sense, his victory over Stalinist evil. There is no room for honest and decent people in a world full of wickedness, where tyrants can corrupt, abuse, and repress the living; however, no tyrant has power over the dead.

Artistically, 'Oblava' is similar to Bykov's earlier novellas, but it also contains new elements. It is a conventional third-person narrative which covers several days of actual time in the life of Khvedor Rovba, but equally covers his entire life span. We learn about Rovba, his family, and their past through numerous flashbacks, internal monologues, reminiscences, and meditations. The time and place of action shift continuously, but inevitably return to the swamps near Nedolishche, where our hero is to face his 'bad luck' and his final destiny. The narrator expresses his views and emotions through Rovba, whom the reader perceives as a positive character, as Rovba perceivces himself. The slow-moving narrative lacks the dramatic intensity of Bykov's war stories. The conflicts and collisions are different; the warring parties are not equal. Instead of confronting his adversaries in open battle, Khvedor hides and runs away, an underdog with no chance of success. The conclusion of the story, however, is as dramatic and full of tragic suspense as the endings of most of Bykov's war stories. The scene of intended patricide, when the son, assisted by a gang of vengeful locals, is ready and willing to kill his own father, is a clear indication that the corrupting power of evil ideas is overwhelming and can drive even honourable individuals to heinous acts.

The thematic shift in Bykov's prose is a sign of the times. In the early days of perestroika, there were still limits to what could be discussed and aired publicly in Soviet literature. But, in 1990, when the old censorship machine was no longer active, Bykov created a picture of collectivization that is much harsher than that provided by S. Zalygin in his 'Na Irtyshe' (By the Irtysh; 1964).[37] Instead of limiting himself to the portrayal of the initial stages of collectivization, as Zalygin does, Bykov examines its effect on the psyche of the peasant and shows that Soviet rule in the countryside has done irreparable damage to his mind and soul.

In his next novella, 'Stuzha' (Cold Spell; 1993),[38] Bykov again blends the themes of war and collectivization. In this novella a young man is caught in a web of lies and deceit. Egor Azevich, a trusting peasant with little education, is induced to become a minor official in the Soviet bureaucracy and unwittingly turns into an accomplice to the crimes perpetrated by the regime. Years later, when the Germans occupy Belorussia, Egor is part of a group of local Soviet functionaries who flee the scene, hide in the forest, and try to mount some resistance to the Nazi occupiers. Soon, however, the group disintegrates. Some of its members join the local police; others perish; Egor remains utterly alone in the forest to fend for himself. In the end, he realizes that he has served a false idol and is a victim of circumstance. Since Egor is essentially an upright man, his conscience does not permit him to join the Nazis and he is forced to pay the price for the mistakes of his youth.

'Stuzha' is similar in style to Bykov's earlier stories. It is a third-person narrative, interspersed with dialogue, internal monologue, and digressions on the political situation, the excesses of the regime, and the corruption of its leadership. The number of characters in the story is limited, and the time span is short, the action taking place simultaneously in two different periods. Chapters dealing with collectivization alternate with those describing Egor's predicament in 1941.

'Stuzha' was nominated for the 1994 Booker Prize, yet in many ways it is inferior to Bykov's earlier stories. The main conflict is not clearly established, and there is little dramatic intensity in the plot. At times, the narrative becomes tedious because the struggle is internal and the real enemy is invisible.

On 19 June 1994, Bykov celebrated his seventieth birthday. He resides today in Minsk, the capital of independent Belorussia, but he continues to be very much a part of Russian culture and literature. His prose has always been set in the difficult days of the Soviet past, and it is doubtful whether he will ever be able to diversify his style or change his thematic interests.

FAZIL' ISKANDER

Fazil' Iskander (b. 1929) is a native of Abkhazia, until recently an autonomous region within the Soviet Georgian republic and at present vying for total political independence. He resides permanently in Moscow and writes exclusively in Russian. Iskander is one of the few Soviet writers who prior to glasnost, published in official Soviet journals; those of his works not approved by Soviet censors have appeared in Western publications. Iskander is one of the few liberal authors who have managed to retain their creative independence without being expelled from the Writers' Union or forced into exile. This leniency towards Iskander can be explained by the peculiarity of his prose, which has, in a sense, always been outside the mainstream of Soviet literature. Most of his work is set in Abkhazia and touches little on current sensitive issues of Soviet life. Iskander's main opus, *Sandro iz Chegema* (Sandro of Chegem; 1983), is a picaresque novel, comprising of a collection of interrelated stories. Started in 1973, it has, until recently, been continuously supplemented with new episodes. In it, Iskander satirizes the vagaries of the Soviet system and mocks its bureaucracy, but he does so in a light-hearted, gentle, and humorous manner. His prose is direct and witty – full of anecdotes, absurd characters, and fantastic tales.

Recently, Iskander started a new novel, entitled 'Chelovek i ego okrestnosti' (Man and His Surroundings). Similar in style and structure to *Sandro iz Chegema*, it too will comprise separate interrelated stories and novellas. The first chapters of this novel, published in the 1992 volume of *Znamia*,[39] are set in Abkhazia, and much of the action takes place in the restaurant Amra, located at the pier in the town of Mukhus. In *Sandro iz Chegema*, Stalin is a recurring character. In the new novel, he is replaced by Lenin. In the first story of the new work, 'Lenin na "Amre"' (Lenin at the 'Amra'), the reader is introduced to a deranged impostor, a former poet and professor of Marxism who imagines himself to be Lenin. Iskander uses him as a device for an investigation of Lenin's character and describes the character as baffled by the 'contradiction between the energy of Lenin's mind, and the continuous banality of his thoughts.'[40] Further, he is dismayed by the fact that, while Lenin exhibits extreme self-control and never panics, he is also biased and conceited, and does not understand what moves ordinary people.

Iskander's recent stories are placed in an autobiographical framework and are narrated in the first person. They combine reality and fantasy, and intertwined lyrical digressions, flashbacks, and philosophical deliberation. Some themes and characters, including Uncle Sandro, from Iskander's earlier novel, reappear here in new roles. Although the recent stories are humorous and full of anecdotes, they also convey an air of seriousness. It seems that it is no longer necessary to satirize everything, or to disguise ideas of substance, including the fact that the writer, Iskander, elected to the Supreme Soviet, falls asleep during one of its sessions. Iskander contrasts in the novel the narrow, often unethical, objectives of politicians and revolutionaries with the morality and goodness of the simple folk in his native Abkhazia. He alludes to the fact that corruption, prevalent in Soviet life, has left few untouched. Unintentionally, perhaps, and certainly indirectly, Iskander provides in his new stories a commentary on the social ills of Soviet society, and on the effect of Lenin's rigid ideals on the fate of Russia and its adjacent lands.

Affected apparently by the civil war in Georgia and a nostalgia for his Abkhazian roots, Iskander recently published a short novella 'Pshada' (Pshada; 1993).[41] This tale of a Soviet general, a native of Chegem, is full of autobiographical elements and provides a perceptive elaboration of the relationship between different nationalities in the allegedly happy family of Soviet nations. Professional advancement in the Soviet Union does not come easily for members of national minorities. In his old age, the retired general still speaks Russian with a foreign accent, but he has completely forgotten his mother tongue, Abkhazian. The general, is baffled, as is the narrator, by the contradictory phenomena of the changing times, wherein new freedoms and material abundance are juxtaposed with a lack of values, extreme poverty, and a new slavery of thought. The search for new values leads to religion, but change in old age is difficult. The title of the story is symbolic: 'Pshada' is the name of a village where peace always reigns. Nature creates there an atmosphere of tranquillity conducive to relaxation, and people escape to Pshada from their turbulent experiences of daily city life. It appears that neither the narrator nor his hero can find peace in today's confusing environment, and the general is condemned to a lonely death among strangers. 'Pshada,' a straightforward third-person narrative, is different from Iskander's other works. There is no humour, hyperbole, or fantasy in the story, and few hints of hope for a better future; instead, there is a pervading sense of dejection and resignation.

In spite of old age, Anatolii Rybakov (b. 1911) continues to produce mountains of prose. He is indefatigable. Despite its artistic shortcomings, his *Deti Arbata* (Children of the Arbat; 1987), which appeared early in perestroika, was timely and topical. It was received with great interest and approbation. In 1988, Rybakov published the first part of an intended trilogy, entitled *Tridtsat' piatyi i drugie gody* (Nineteen-Thirty-Five and Other Years),[42] which was followed by *Strakh* (Fear; 1990).[43] The recent novels are a continuation of *Deti Arbata*, and turn it into a long epic with two basic plot lines. One deals with the fate of a group of young adults, previously classmates and now residents of the Moscow district of Arbat; the other deals with the personality of Stalin and those around him. *Deti Arbata* is set in 1933–4, *Tridtsat' piatyi i drugie gody* in 1935–6, and *Strakh* brings us up to 1938. *Deti Arbata* concludes with the assassination of Kirov, which is the prelude to the great purges of the late 1930s. *Strakh* culminates with the execution of Marshals Tukhachevsky and Bliukher, and thousands of other Soviet political and military leaders. The action in the last part of his trilogy, *Prakh i pepel* (The Dregs and Ashes; 1994) is set in 1944, with some flashbacks to 1939.

One of the main protagonists of *Deti Arbata*, the student and dedicated party member Sasha Pankratov, is arrested, convicted, and exiled for alleged anti-Soviet propaganda. Sasha is also the central character in the sequel novels. First, he is exiled to Siberia, then he is released but denied permission to return to Moscow. He lives most of the time in fear, roaming from place to place. In the concluding pages of *Strakh*, Sasha works in the city of Kalinin, in central Russia, but when a special passport regimen is introduced in the city he is ordered to move within twenty-four hours.

Rybakov's saga is no great masterpiece. It is apparent that the sprawling narrative has been hastily written, and its different plot lines are poorly delineated. As well, some characters are oversimplified, while the actions of others lack psychological motivation. No wonder little attention has been paid to Rybakov's recent novels. In the early days of perestroika, the personality of Stalin and the workings of the Soviet security and penal systems were still partially cloaked in secrecy, and *Deti Arbata* was an eye-opener for many. Today, however, most party and security archives are open to public scrutiny, and readers have lost much of their former interest in manuscripts about the purges of the 1930s.

Rybakov's significance for Soviet and Russian literature is social and political rather than artistic. He is a pioneer who stretches to the extreme the limits of what was officially permissible at a given time. He opens new vistas to Soviet readers and writers alike. And that is no minor feat under the conditions of oppressive censorship.

In 1987, Boris Mozhaev (b. 1923) published the novel *Muzhiki i baby* (Countryfolk) in which he criticized Stalinist collectivization policies. Similar thematic reverberations are present in Mozhaev's new novel, *Izgoi* (The Outcast; 1993),[44] set in the 1950s in the Soviet Far East. At the centre of the novel is the determined, truth-seeking, and somewhat arrogant navy officer Borodin. He is the son of an exiled 'enemy of the people' who refused in the 1930s to join the kolkhoz in his native village. Borodin resigns his commission and becomes a poet-journalist.

The novel is written in good Russian, but its structure is confusing, and, except for Borodin, most characters are drawn sketchily and are soon forgotten. The author idealizes the hero, and one wonders whether Borodin's bold anti-Soviet actions are indeed characteristic of life in Russia in the middle 1950s. The first book of *Izgoi* is similar in style and tone to Mozhaev's earlier novels, but the emphasis is different: here, Mozhaev satirizes and ridicules the provincial bureaucracy and intelligentsia and decries the devastation of nature, the poverty of the native people, and the needless destruction of the communities of God- fearing old believers.

Vasilii Belov (b. 1932), who is still remembered for his 'village prose' classic, 'Privychnoe delo' (That's How It Is; 1966), is also active, but his attention is devoted today more to political and historical issues than to imaginative fiction. He has published recently *God velikogo pereloma. Khronika deviati mesiatsev* (A Year of Great Change. A Chronicle of Nine Months; 1989–91 and 1994),[45] which is a continuation of his *Kanuny. Khronika kontsa 20-kh godov* (Eves. A Chronicle of the Late 1920s; parts 1 and 2, 1976, part 3, 1987) and deals with the situation in the Russian countryside in the period of collectivization. The socialist-realist hack Petr Proskurin (b. 1928) deals in his novels *Sud'ba* (Fate; 1973) and *Imia tvoe* (Your Name; 1978) with a similar subject. Both Proskurin and Belov exhibit in their novels a special affection for the personality of Stalin. In his new novel *Otrechenie* (Disavowal; 1987 and 1990),[46] Proskurin uses the new possibilities of glasnost to suit his own fancies and changes the conception of Stalin by portraying him as a tool of Kaganovich, who is allegedly bent on destroying Russia. In the 1970s, class struggle and the support of party policy were at the centre of Proskurin's prose, and the so-called kulaks were portrayed as enemies of the people. Today, those victimized by the regime are vindicated, and the commissars are presented in a negative light. In response to the changing times, the message in Proskurin's prose changes accordingly. Formerly he glorified Stalin and whole-heartedly supported collectivization and the theory of class struggle; today he promulgates a new brand of national patriotism, which combines old-style communism with Russian nationalism and orthodoxy.

Until 1987, Anatolii Pristavkin (b. 1931) was known as an official Soviet writer, producing tedious stories and novels about the taiga and the heroic exploits of construction gangs in Siberia. The appearance of 'Nochevala tuchka zolotaia' (The Golden Cloudlet Passed the Night; 1987)[47] changed the reader's perception of Pristavkin's talent, but only for a while. 'Nochevala tuchka zolotaia' is set in 1944, and it deals with the fate and suffering of homeless orphans during the war. It addresses also the sensitive issue of intranational relations in the Soviet Union. The story is rooted in reality, and based on the author's personal war experience. The indigenous population of the Chechen republic in southern Russia are expelled from their native land for alleged collaboration with the Nazi occupiers, and Russian settlers from all over the Soviet Union are brought to replace them. Among those arriving are five hundred homeless children from central Russia. The main characters of the story are identical Russian eleven-year-old twin brothers. One of them dies a violent death, but the surviving one accepts a Chechen orphan as his blood brother and moves back to Russia with him.

In the early stages of perestroika and de-Stalinization the story became a hit overnight. It uncovered the abuse of children and the atrocities ingrained in Stalinist nationality policy, fostering at the same time the notion that national hatred and prejudice were socially conditioned rather than innate. Today, the national strife in the northern Caucasus attests to the fact that the brotherhood between the Chechen and Russian boys is an exception rather than the rule, and that the great friendship of all Soviet peoples was a myth rather than reality. 'Nochevala tuchka zolotaia' is not without shortcomings. Some episodes are dragged out, and the conclusion lacks psychological justification. The author indiscriminately interferes with the natural flow of the narrative and often turns from artist into tribune. But the story is provocative and timely, and its message is strong, delivered in an articulate manner and with passion. In recognition, it was awarded the USSR State Prize for Literature.

Encouraged by this success, Pristavkin continued to follow the path set out in 'Nochevala tuchka zolotaia,' and he produced a novella 'Kukushata ili zhalobnaia pesn' dlia uspokoeniia serdtsa' (The Cuckoos, or a Sad Song for the Calming of One's Heart; 1989),[48] and the novel *Riazanka (chelovek s predmest'ia)* (Riazanka [A Man from the Suburbs]; 1991).[49] 'Kukushata' is an elaboration on Pristavkin's 'Nochevala tuchka zolotaia,' dealing with the same subject and relying on the same detail. The novella is a first-person autobiographical narrative, written between 1963 and 1984 and apparently put together in 1990. It resembles more a disjointed combination of casually compiled notes and observations than a well-structured and coherent work. No wonder Pristavkin's recent prose has been received with indifference in literary circles. The subject of 'Kukushata' is no longer a novelty, and its treatment is mediocre. It is another instance of thematic topicality, one of the main requirements of former Soviet publication policy, being not enough to produce an original work of art of acceptable quality.

Evgenii Evtushenko (b. 1933) is best known for his poetry, yet in the last decades his prose has received more attention than his poems.[50] Just like his verses, Evtushenko's novels are usually inspired by the circumstances of life and are a reaction to political and social events. Evtushenko's first novel, *Iagodnye mesta* (Wild Berries; 1981), is a deliberation on life in Brezhnev's Russia. His new novel, *Ne umirai prezhde smerti* (Don't Die before Your Death; 1993), is a reflection on Soviet life in the last years of Gorbachev's rule. The novel is a combination of fact and fiction, but the events described are rooted in reality.

The narrative is composed of a number of different plot lines. It includes a detective story; a sentimental story of unfulfilled love; recounting of the history of Soviet football (soccer); episodes from the personal life of important Soviet political figures, such as M. Gorbachev, B. Yeltsin, and E. Shevarnadze; as well as a chapter about the author's three great loves, written in confessional style. The autobiographical chapters, relating stories from Evtushenko's private life, are interesting and appear to be sincere. His attempts to justify his relations with the Soviet administration and security organs prior to perestroika, however, are in poor taste and not always convincing. Similarly the description of the author's role during the August 1991 anti-Gorbachev coup has an air of self-aggrandizement.

Two overriding themes are intended to provide compositional unity to the novel. One is the August 1991 coup, and the other is the notion of all-embracing fear which pervades the lives and paralyses the actions of an oppressed nation as well as of those who are in power. The evolution of different plot lines and the montage of disjointed episodes, in which different groups of characters participate, lead to the spontaneous gathering of most protagonists, including the author-narrator, at the meeting in support of President Yeltsin, on 19–20 August 1991, at the White House in Moscow.

The task of writing a novel about recent political and historical events is not an easy one. It becomes even more complicated when the author is the narrator as well as the hero of his own creation. In fact, Evtushenko is the only protagonist the reader can relate to. He is at the centre of most events, whereas most other characters appear episodically and are poorly developed. Political and cultural personalities appear under pseudonyms, and the uninitiated reader may have difficulty recognizing them.

The 1991 events in Russia is an important subject which requires serious treatment. Evtushenko's attempts to examine the recent past and make it the subject of prose fiction is commendable; however, these events are still fresh in the memory of contemporary readers, and it is questionable whether his approach, which lacks perspective, and combines tragedy with farce, can do justice to this subject.

Iurii Davydov (b. 1924) is a well-known historical novelist who usually creates in conventional realistic style and adheres to historical facts. The main focus of his attention has, until recently, been directed at the populist movement and the roots of Marxism in Russia. His two recent novellas, 'Zorovavel'' (Mr Zorovavel'; 1993)[51] and 'Zagovor sionistov' (The Zionist Conspiracy; 1993),[52] both nominated for the 1994 Booker Prize, are different in style and subject-matter.

'Zagovor sionistov,' set early in the nineteenth century, is a mixture of fact and fiction. At its root is a historical quibble which mirrors the tsarist approach to the so-called Jewish question. The story mocks the workings of the tsarist administration and ridicules the stupidity of its officials, who view the desire to open an inn for Jewish visitors to St Petersburg as a Zionist conspiracy. Davydov amplifies the personal human drama of his dejected hero by combining it with the issue of social injustice in tsarist Russia. Despite the fact that the language in the story is playful and humorous in tone, and events are related only impressionistically, the narrative addresses important historical problems. The message of the story is expanded by viewing past events from a contemporary perspective.

Some writers of the older generation continue their involvement in administrative and editorial work. Thus S. Zalygin (b. 1913), and A.

Anan'ev (b. 1925) are the chief editors of *Novyi mir,* and *Oktiabr',* respectively, and G. Baklanov (b. 1923) was the editor of *Znamia* until November 1993. Anan'ev continues to turn out voluminous novels and publish them in his own journal.[53] *Skrizhali i kolokola* (Tablets and Bells; 1989) is similar in subject and tone to his previous novel *Gody bez voiny* (Years without War; 1975–84), and it deals with the current situation in Russia. It is a combination of fiction, semi-journalistic prose, social analysis, and philosophic deliberations which culminate in an attempt to find a solution to Russia's economic and political ills. *Liki bessmertnoi vlasti. Tsar' Ioann Groznyi* (The Images of Immortal Power. Tsar Ivan the Terrible; 1992) and *Prizvanie Riurikovichei, ili tysiacheletniaia zagadka Rossii* (The Mission of the Ruriks, or the One-Thousand-Year Puzzle of Russia; 1993)[54] are historical novels in which the past is often contrasted with contemporary reality. Anan'ev's novels are full of images, ideas, and information, but their structure is baggy and they lack depth. His factual assessment of historical circumstances may be correct, but his interpretation of these situations is wanting.

Many writers of the older generation turn today to fictionalized autobiography and memoirs. S. Lipkin (b. 1911) is a well-known poet and translator. His novel *Zapiski zhil'tsa* (Notes of a Lodger; 1992) is a blend of reality and fiction, rooted in personal experience. It combines scenes of life in old Odessa with personal reflections of art, life, and society. S. Zalygin published an autobiographical novel, *Ekologicheskii roman* (Ecological Novel; 1993),[55] in which the author appears under the cover of a fictionalized first-person narrator who devotes most of his life to the struggle for the preservation of nature.

Bulat Okudzhava (b. 1924) relates in his *Uprazdnennyi teatr* (The Closed-Down Theatre; 1993)[56] the story of his childhood and family. His parents, highly placed officials in the Soviet bureaucracy, are purged, and most other relatives disappear. Life is a theatre in which every individual plays a role, but Okudzhava's childhood theatre collapses and the actors vanish into thin air. *Uprazdnennyi teatr* won the 1994 Booker Prize. Although Okudzhava deals sensitively and perceptively in this semi-autobiographical work with the social and moral dilemmas of the intelligentsia in post-revolutionary Russia, it is in many ways inferior to his earlier works. It is possible that the Booker Prize in this instance, as seems to be the case for V. Makanin, was awarded for a lifetime contribution to Russian literature and not for the best novel of the year.

It is clear that the new conditions in Russia have affected different writers of the older generation in different ways. Most of them, however, remain true to their past and continue to write in their old ways. The changes evident are mostly thematic and interpretative, and in most cases there is a visible decline in artistic quality. The recent works of most of the writers discussed here do not measure up to their best prose, produced in the years of stagnation. Creative freedom is a great stimulus, but not necessarily for those who have been fettered for decades by restrictions and have lost the ability to use it. Other well-known writers of the older generation, including I. Grekova and Grigorii Baklanov, have produced little of substance in the last six years, and nothing that merits positive critical attention. These writers represent a passing era. They are unable to change and are too old to adapt. It seems, then, that the future of Russian literature is today in the hands of the young.

4

The Intermediate Generation

The writers of the intermediate generation form a disparate group of individuals with different thematic, ideological, and artistic interests. Born in the late 1930s and 1940s, they grew in the shadow of Stalinism and matured in the days of the Brezhnev stagnation. They were too young to experience in full measure the effects of the Second World War, and their education and upbringing were influenced by the Soviet totalitarian myth. Over the years, they witnessed disparity between the communist doctrine and the realities of daily life in the Soviet Union, and many turned into cynics. Hence, their cultural, religious, and historical roots were feeble, and most of them were ready to acquiesce to the dictates of the system and work within the allowable creative perimeters. With the exception of Liudmila Petrushevskaia, whose stories were usually rejected by the editors of the major periodicals, they published in official Soviet journals, refusing to go underground or to join the dissident movement.

Prior to perestroika, many writers of the intermediate generation belonged to the so-called *sorokaletnie*, (literally, forty-year-olds), whose works were also dubbed 'Moscow school prose.' Despite certain parallels the works of the *sorokaletnie* differed from one another in many ways. The attention of writers such as Vladimir Makanin, Ruslan Kireev, and Anatolii Kurchatkin concentrated on Soviet *byt*, or the daily life of the city intelligentsia, and the rampant materialism and spiritual depravity of the new Soviet middle class. Vladimir Krupin's novellas were in the tradition of village prose, while the prose of Anatolii Kim was grotesque and surrealistic. Aleksandr Prokhanov's novels, on the other hand, dealt mainly with industrial development and Soviet expansionist policies in the Third World. As opposed to the writers of the old guard, who most often produced conventional realistic novels with characters and conflicts deeply rooted in Soviet life, many *sorokaletnie* experimented with time, space, and narrative techniques, and introduced a new vacillating and ambivalent hero into Soviet literature. This character is unable to cope with the complicated conditions of daily existence and continuously searches for a better understanding of the meaning of life, as well as of himself.

Today, most of these writers are in their late forties and fifties. Many of them suffer from a crisis of identity but are trying to adapt to the new realities of life. Their current creative output is determined as much by talent as by their political and social views. The new political situation in Russia has removed the need for ideological and aesthetic compliance, and latent opinions have come out into the open. In some cases, this new freedom has led to the expression of extreme nationalistic views; in other instances, it has resulted in the supplanting of previously adopted realistic forms by experimentation with genre, style, and narrative modes.

VLADIMIR MAKANIN

One of the best-known members of this generation is Vladimir Makanin (b. 1937). His first novel, *Priamaia liniia* (Straight Line), was published in 1965, but until the middle of the 1980s his prose received little critical attention. One of his best-known novellas, published in 1984 in *Novyi mir,* is 'Gde skhodilos' nebo s kholmami' (Where the Sky Met the Hills). It explores the relationships between social mobility, cultural disintegration, and artistic creativity. Today, Makanin is one of the few Russian writers who has maintained the level of his artistry as a prose writer beyond the Brezhnev era. By creating an existential myth, Makanin has, in his recent works, formulated a new conception of reality that is not fixed or static but fluid and unstable. He creates plots of impressive philosophical significance, and innovates without trivializing the issues discussed. Formerly, Makanin was usually concerned with the examination of the past and its effect on the present. Now, he also attempts to look into the future and to contrast it with contemporary reality. Yet there is a continuity in Makanin's choice of characters. Most are intellectuals with a propensity for philosophical discussion and are in search of a meaning for life. Many are lonely creatures exhausted by the dreary routine of daily existence.

Makanin's novella 'Laz' (Manhole; 1991)[1] was short-listed for the Booker Russian Novel Prize for 1992. It is a third-person narrative with no definite temporal setting or chronology but with a precise spatial frame. The action takes place simultaneously in two distinct worlds: in the manhole and on the surface. In the manhole, life appears to be normal. There are many stores, restaurants, and cafés; most important, there is an abundance of light. Cultural and intellectual life is vibrant. On the surface, by contrast, life is desolate. The streets are dark and empty. Thieves and robbers roam in search of victims. Chaos and anarchy reign. Life is ruled by fear, and one must try to find a hiding-place for oneself and one's family. The hero, Kliuchkarev, is the connecting link between these two realms. He is an intellectual with a wife and a sickly fourteen-year-old son. He lives in the city, but he also goes down to the manhole to visit those who appear to enjoy the good life. Kliuchkarev goes down into the manhole ostensibly to obtain indispensable supplies unavailable in the city; in fact, he is drawn into that world by his thirst for intellectual discussion and mental stimulation. He identifies with those in the manhole. For him, as for them, words are more important than actions.

It is evident from the story, however, that words are not enough to save the world. Abstract ideas, without practical deeds, are of little use, and intellectuals can do nothing but talk. The breakdown of social institutions makes apparent the split between different population strata. There is little in common between the so-called *narod*, or the masses that are above, and the members of the intellectual élite, who reside in the manhole. Without leaders, men of action, the masses ramble in the dark, but the intelligentsia, charged with the responsibility of leading the nation, consider themselves above the masses and mostly concerned with their own narrow and abstract issues. A bus driver in the city accuses the intelligentsia of failing to provide guidance, misleading the people, and causing their suffering. Clearly, there is too much light in the manhole, but not enough oxygen. The former is the symbol of intellectual wisdom; the latter represents real life. On the surface, on the other hand, there is complete darkness, both physical and spiritual. Both situations are equally bad. Too much light can obscure vision, just as total darkness does.

The story comprises several episodes: two trips by Kliuchkarev to the manhole, a trip to a friend in hiding at his dacha, and a trip to a morgue to recover the body of a dead friend. Except for Kliuchkarev, characters appear only episodically and help to expose the atmosphere of doom in the city and to uncover the terrible plight of the people. On the concluding pages, Kliuchkarev falls asleep on the street and has a dream. He is terrified by the fact that he is cut off from the manhole. In a convulsive dialogue with those in the underground, he asks for some supplies. They, in turn, demand information to satisfy their insatiable thirst for knowledge. But all Kliuchkarev gets from them are sticks to help the blind find their way in the darkness. When he awakens he sees a stranger pass by and soon disappear in the shadows of the night. Symbolically, the scene presents an invisible helping hand, and, perhaps, a religious image as the only hope for the future.

'Laz' can be read as being anti-utopian, as well as allegorical. It can also be viewed as an expression of the author's personal search for the meaning of his own existence. After all, he has more in common with those in the manhole than with the people on the surface. And yet, having apparently realized that the intelligentsia have failed in their bid to lead his own nation, he does not hesitate to satirize them, and produces a novella with a strong anti-intellectual flavour.

Makanin's attempt to transcend reality and venture into the future is further elaborated in his story 'Tam byla para ...' (There Was a Pair ...; 1991).[2] Here, a group of intelligent young people gathers regularly to drink, dance, and talk. The first-person narrator, who is also the hero, is always among them. He is much older than the rest, but he draws strength from their openness and the freshness of their ideas. The discussion often turns to the abstract notions of good and evil. One of the young men, Sasha, asserts that these ideas are like an endless labyrinth in which people lose their way. Life is too short for the individual to comprehend the distinction between virtue and depravity, and the struggle between them is eternal. None the less, with faith, stimulated by the need to believe, people should be able to rise above this labyrinth. While the nameless narrator is drawn to these young people, he is also envious of them. They do not hesitate to voice a new religious individualism and a readiness to establish a new relationship with the world beyond them. The narrator, on the other hand, is still steeped in old ways, unable to detach himself from the past, and is sceptical of their views. He is aware that faith is necessary but is not ready to accept it yet. He compares life to a treadmill – static and in continuous motion at the same time. People on the treadmill are passing through life continuously searching for an intangible transcendental reality.

One of the characters in the story, Olezhka, expresses an anti-intellectualism similar to that of the bus driver in 'Laz.' He asserts that the intelligentsia should come down to the level of the simple people and become equal to them. And if the intelligentsia are unable or unwilling to do so, they must be eliminated altogether. The narrator refuses to accept this view. He counters by saying that Russia has already experienced such a purge, alluding to the destruction of the Russian intelligentsia after the October Revolution. But Olezhka is unswerving. He begins to hate the narrator, and even tells him to get lost. 'Tam byla para ...' is not a philosophical treatise; rather, it is an exploration of the new spirit of pluralism and the ideas which engage young people today. It is also a story about the attempt to bridge the generation gap, and the difficult task of stamping out past experiences from one's subconscious. However, the final passage of the story provides, some glimmer of optimism in that the narrator finds joy in the discovery that, despite common flaws, there are still good people around and there is still hope for universal harmony.

'Dolog nash put" (Long Is Our Way; 1991)[3] is another anti-utopian vision in which the action is set in two distinct temporal and spatial confines. One part of the story, in which the narrator is an active participant, is set in contemporary reality; the other part, some two hundred years in the future. The hero of the first segment is the narrator's friend Il'ia Ivanovich. He is an engineer who abhors violence of any kind, and a schizophrenic overwhelmed by universal evil. The sight of cruelty or vileness makes him ill. He escapes the terrible reality of daily life from time to time by being admitted to a psychiatric ward. There he is treated and acquires some tolerance for the outside world, which enables him to survive temporarily. Nevertheless, he dies young, at the age of forty-eight, his first heart attack occurring when he watches a television program in which the problems of slaughterhouses are discussed.

Inspired by the experiences of his friend, the author-narrator sets the second part of the story in the future. He describes an allegedly perfect society, without wars, murder, or crime. Some people are involved in the production of food, similar in taste to real beef, by mixing grass with artificially produced protein. The factory in which this new product is manufactured is shrouded in secrecy. It is located on the steppe, beyond public view, and the people who work there are volunteers who have forfeited their right ever to leave this place. The hero, Nikolai, a young engineer, has invented a special piece of equipment to perfect the final product. He goes to the factory to help install it and asks permission to witness his invention in operation. It does not take long before he realizes that the food produced is not artificial at all but made from the meat of slaughtered cows. Extreme curiosity is Nikolai's undoing; his discovery of the secret makes it impossible for him to leave this place. Secrecy is uppermost in the minds of those in charge, and people who know too much pose a danger to their power. In the end, Nikolai tries to run away. He goes into the steppe every night to set a bonfire, hoping that a passing helicopter will notice the fire and take him back to the city. To his surprise he sees many bonfires on the steppe – people have been waiting there for years for someone to save them. They all want their freedom, and hope keeps them alive. Among those on the steppe are the people responsible for his detention. They live a double life. By day they pretend to obey the law and enforce the accepted rules and values, but at night they give vent to their innermost hopes and longings for liberty.

The hidden message of the story suggests that centuries of peaceful life have little affected the nature of people. The inherent evil in human nature can be concealed but not removed. The masses are still kept in the dark, ostensibly for their own good, while those who rule cultivate the big lie. The rulers of this professed perfect society, are just as cruel, secretive, and vindictive as the leaders of the Soviet state. People in this future society have, just as people today do, an insatiable thirst for freedom and knowledge. But their craving for total liberty is often fraught with dangerous consequences: because unimpeded access to information can pose a threat to those in power and freedom for one may mean slavery for others. The conclusion of the novella is far from optimistic: the world is full of people fighting for power; each one wants to control and dominate others, with little room for compromise. This struggle is assisted and encouraged by the prevailing universal lie, which ignores the basic ethical rules intended to make the cohabitation of people in this universe possible.

In 1993, Makanin published two narratives: the award-winning novella 'Stol, pokrytyi suknom i s grafinom poseredine' (Cloth-Covered Table with Carafe in the Middle)[4] and 'Kvazi' (Quasi).[5] Both narratives are set in Soviet reality; both delve into the philosophical origins of the Soviet state; and both explore the psychological effects on the human mind of life under communism. In 'Stol, pokrytyi suknom i s grafinom poseredine,' the aberrant ruminations of the nameless narrator uncover the working of the so-called Soviet lay system of justice, which is a fixture of daily life in the USSR. It is a perverted form of justice and a tool of social pressure, and its purpose is to intimidate the people, instilling in them a sense of guilt, and fear. It deprives people of their individuality and turns them into passive tools and accomplices of the state. The cloth-covered table is a symbol, unifying different members of a lay commission. Individually each of them is an insignificant creature, subdued by life and under constant threat of being interrogated by others.

But when members of the commission are together, around the table, they personify 'the people' and represent a force.

In 'Kvazi,' Makanin examines the essence of the Soviet ideological myth and views it as a quasi-religion. According to Makanin, anything 'quasi' is artificial and mortal – hence the disintegration of the Soviet state and the collapse of socialist ideas, both of which occur without any visible outside pressure.

Makanin's recent novellas are different from his earlier works. Their structure is loose, and characters are indistinct. Action becomes secondary to metaphysical deliberation, and human experience serves only to illustrate the author-narrator's philosophical reflections. The influence of Dostoevsky on the intellectual prose of Makanin is evident. Makanin uses Dostoevsky's ideas but sets them in a different reality. He narrates his stories in an unemotional and detached manner and often appears to be indifferent to the fate of his heroes; he seems to be more concerned with their ideas than with their personal lives and daily problems. Makanin's prose continues to be apolitical, but it has strong social ramifications, posing important questions about issues facing mankind on the path to social progress.

ANATOLII KIM

Anatolii Kim (b. 1939), a long-time resident of Moscow, graduated from the Gorky Literary Institute in 1971. His first published work appeared in 1973. Kim's art is rooted in his Korean and Asian heritage, but it is blended with his experience of a Russian environment. In his prose, Kim exhibits a predilection for the intuitive and the musical. His language is lyrical in tone and infused with romantic irony. His fictional world is full of exotic images and a reality that is often intertwined with the fantastic and mythical. He is always concerned with philosophical and ethical issues as they relate to the destiny of mankind and the natural environment. The relationship between words and deeds, good and evil, as well as life and death is always at the centre of his work.

Kim's novel *Otets-les* (Father-Forest; 1989)[6] is his most mature and ambitious work. It is one of the most important prose narratives written and published in the Soviet Union in the days of Gorbachev's perestroika. The novel is difficult to read and at times verbose, and requires much concentration, but those who master the text are rewarded by a wealth of insights, ideas, and accounts of human experiences and emotions. The novel is a parable and endeavours to provide an artistic and philosophical substantiation of Russia's nineteenth-century social history. The investigation of the fates of individual heroes leads the author to a psychological and ethical reassessment of the current generation of Soviet people. It appears from the novel that Soviet dogmatic ideology engenders oppression, tyranny, and the subjugation of body and soul by subverting the subtle balance between goodness and evil in human nature. It also unsettles the human psyche by corrupting the old values and traditions which have, for centuries, nurtured the human spirit. According to Kim, the prevalence of logical abstract ideals leads to the destruction of the people's identification with their natural surroundings and brings out in them the worst traits of their character. An ideal which is supposed to save mankind from slavery and lead to freedom instead enslaves people and breaks their spirit. The epigraph, and the author's opening remarks, set the tone for the novel. The epigraph proclaims the superiority of nature over human existence, and the introduction expounds the notion that fear of death is the motive for people's actions. Their unconscious instinct for self-preservation results in cynical deeds that deprive them of the ability to adhere to the truth.

The plot of the novel is constructed around the fate of three generations of the Turaev family: the father, Nikolai; his son, Stepan; and his grandson, Gleb. Their life stories cover the span of time between the 1880s and the 1980s. Their experiences are different, but all have difficult lives, marked by personal strife and suffering. All endure a continuous pain in their hearts that subsides only slightly under the soothing influence and the life-giving powers of the forest. Nikolai Turaev grows up in tsarist Russia, experiences the revolution and collectivization, and dies a lonely death on the streets of Moscow. His son, Stepan, endures torment and anguish and returns to the forest a broken man, after having survived the horrors of war and the concentration camp. Gleb becomes a scientist and mathematician in Moscow, but after fifteen years leaves his job and his family and escapes to the forest to contemplate suicide: 'Life has no meaning to him any longer. As a mathematician he can easily figure out that the energy of evil is much stronger than the energy of goodness ... that the energy contained in the nucleus of an atom presupposes the hidden desire of physical matter to destroy itself and *not to exist*.'[7] The three generations of Turaevs view their past from diverse perspectives and approach their future in different ways. To the young Nikolai, existence means suffering, and perfection can be attained only through suffering. But, as an old and dejected man, he wants neither suffering nor existence. Stepan does not question life and responds to the innate impulse of self-preservation and the urge to live. According to him, one has to live in order to learn the lesson of life. His desire to survive accompanies him in battles in war and in hospitals and prisons. But the young Soviet scholar, Gleb, rejects life because it is self-destructive: people abuse each other and ravage the environment, and life in a doomed world is futile anyway. Gleb's fate supports the proposition that at root the problem is the deeply embedded conflict between human nature and any social organization. When one's contribution to a social cause cannot satisfy the individualistic nature of one's character, one becomes alienated and turns one's back on society. But when the ethical foundations of society break down, a vacuum is created, and evil instincts in human nature, in the form of corruption, cynicism, or hedonism, come to the fore.

Nikolai Turaev is a thinker and amateur philosopher. He expresses many contradictory ideas, some of which are obviously supported by the author himself. According to Nikolai, happiness is possible only when the individual is totally free, but freedom is the unconditional acceptance of one's fate, as well as the total severance of all physical and emotional ties. It is apparent that absolute freedom leads to extreme alienation and loneliness, from which one can be saved only by death. The novel illustrates also that freedom is a burden as well as a responsibility, and that Nikolai, who is good at abstract philosophy, fails in his duties to those who are close to him. Freedom to receive implies the responsibility to give; that is the basic rule of human cohabitation. Having realized the prevalence of evil and the futility of existence, Nikolai rebels against God but, being unable to wage war against his invisible maker, resigns himself to passive submission and decides simply to ignore him.

The positive in the novel is expressed in the everlasting, life-sustaining, and unifying force of nature. The identification with nature erases, to a degree, the distinctions among the three generations of the Turaev family. They are all alienated, lonely, and forced to live a life of extreme personal solitude, yet all are subconsciously connected with the forest which reinforces the hidden unity between them. The novel suggests that the transformation of the souls of dying people into trees, and vice versa, is the foundation of the unity and harmony in the natural environment. Different elements of the natural world have the ability to communicate on a spiritual level, and, despite external enmity, people are united by a certain invisible bond which transcends time, space, or race.

The strength of the forest is manifested in its natural ability to reproduce itself. In the human environment, the death of an individual may mean the end of a family or a tribe; however, the forest is immortal and is perceived not as a collection of separate trees but as a unit with common roots.

The novel also suggests that people are essentially evil and subconsciously self-destructive. In its conclusion, however, there are vague allusions that faith in Christ can save mankind, and that a new generation, free of wickedness and capable of love, may come. Yet these inferences are rather declarative and not borne out by the experiences portrayed in the narrative. In fact many philosophical deductions propounded in the novel are of a controversial nature and require further elucidation. They are not based on logical deliberation, but are rather closely intertwined with the mythological essence of the narrative, rooted in the people's lore, and combined with fantasy and the grotesque.

The novel is constructed in the form of a loosely connected narrative, with many subplots and digressions. The action shifts continuously from place to place, and from one time sequence to another. There is a constant transition from reality to fantasy, myth, dream, and hallucination. There is a variety of first- and third-person narrators who are in the process of continuous change. Several different narrators may appear in the same paragraph, even the same sentence. Yet the voice of the author, and of the omniscient narrator, who are often one and the same, is always there. Stylistically, *Otets-les* is reminiscent of Kim's novel *Belka* (Squirrel; 1984), but its scope is much broader and all-embracing. Before glasnost, Kim's work was often criticized in the Soviet Union for its lack of social message and for the abstract discussion of such notions as evil, philistinism, and egoism. In his new novel, these issues are still addressed in an oblique manner, and only as they relate to the fate of individual characters, but the social ramifications of personal ills can be easily deduced from the picture presented.

Despite the fact that, in the days of perestroika, readers were primarily interested in politically and socially significant works and had little time for artistically important narratives, *Otets-les* generated a lively critical response. It is a book of intellectual inquiry, too serious to ignore. Most critics were impressed by the author's artistry but failed to agree on the interpretation of its philosophical meaning. Karen Stepanian accused Kim of extreme pessimism and the lack of trust in the positive origins of humankind.[8] But another writer claimed that the main thrust of Kim's judgment is not against the essence of individual man but rather against corrupt social institutions that operate with no regard for justice or morality, and help produce a generation of people devoid of spirituality or faith.[9] L. Bartashevich asserted that Kim had 'created a novel-parable, in which everything is generalized and intensified to the extreme, hence the power of evil is hyperbolized and a catastrophe is imminent,' yet the critic believed that 'nature, which is the general and eternal source of everything, can gradually heal the branch which lags in its development.'[10] Natal'ia Ivanova, on the other hand, regarded 'the idea of integrating the human being with the consciousness of the surrounding forest as a naive and utopian dream,' but what she did find important, and deserving further elaboration, was Kim's notion of the terrible heartache caused by extreme physical suffering and emotional stress.[11] Regardless of their critical interpretation, most reviewers agreed that the novel formed a new step in the development of Kim's creative talent, and, had it not been for the turmoil of perestroika, it would certainly have occupied a more important place in the intellectual debates of the Soviet intelligentsia.

In 1992, Kim came out with a new, thematically innovative novel which developed some of his former ideas but departed from the time and setting of his previous works. *Poselok kentavrov* (Hamlet of Centaurs),[12] set in ancient Greece, combines myth with elements of modern science fiction. Among the novel's actors are centaurs, wild horses, Amazons, space creatures, as well as real people, including the Greek geometrician Euclid. Each different herd, nation, or kind of mythological creature has its own territory and hierarchical social structure, and its members act according to diverse rules and values. Hunger for food and sex are the driving forces that move the centaurs. The thirst for power, and hate for their male counterparts, determines the actions of the Amazons. The ancient mythological world created by Kim is ruled by wild passion and a sense of belligerence which defies logic. Continuous warfare obliterates most of the centaurs, and the unceasing drive to subjugate others leads the Amazons to self-destruction.

The Russian critic Mikhail Zolotonosov[13] regarded Kim's new novel as an expression of extreme anti-feminism and a reflection of Russian marginal culture, which can deal with issues deemed unacceptable for discussion in the mainstream of civilized society. Indeed, the Amazons are painted in dark colours, and Kim exhibits little sympathy for their violent ways. They are rational creatures, with human traits of character, and are aware of their actions. Hence, they are responsible for their deeds and are judged by human, rather than animal, ethical standards. The centaurs, on the other hand – horses with human bodies, arms, and heads – are treated with compassion. They have no memory and, except for the few who have spent years in slavery among humans, have no ability to rationalize their actions.

Zolotonosov asserted that the main objective of the novel was to denigrate the Amazons. He suggested that Kim has the gods punish these proud, stupid, and brutal female warriors because of their anti-male sentiments and intentions. This narrow interpretation of the novel does little justice to its author and is a disservice to the reader. The narrative embodies the notion of an inherent duality in people. It is an allegory of contemporary society and human nature in general. It illustrates clearly that sexual passion without love can provide momentary pleasure and satisfy one's ego, but it fails to gratify the spirit. Kim resorts to the use of mythological characters in order to make his point. Even today, in the post-Soviet era, no established mainstream journal would accept for publication a novel in which sex is described explicitly and sexuality is one of the main subjects. To tone down the impact of sex, Kim creates a special language in which the centaurs communicate, but this device deceives no one. The actions of the centaurs explain their language. The novel shows also that the thirst for power is insatiable, and that the urge of nations to arm themselves in order to subjugate others carries within itself the seeds of self-destruction. Kim's hidden message is a warning to humankind. He cautions his readers against greed, and the unbridled passion for sex and power. He illustrates the failure of nations to gain security by arming themselves, and the futility of attempts to attain happiness at the expense of others. In this sense, Kim's new novel comes within the framework of his former concerns, and it can be viewed as a continuation of his *Otets-les*.

ANATOLII KURCHATKIN

Anatolii Kurchatkin (b. 1944), a native of Sverdlovsk, graduated from the Gorky Literary Institute in 1972. He is one of the *sorokaletnie* who are currently attempting to abandon their former realistic mode of presentation and adapt to the new conditions of the day. In one of his new novellas, 'Zapiski ekstremista (stroitel'stvo metro v nashem gorode)' (Notes of an Extremist [The Construction of a Subway in Our Town]; 1990),[14] he produces an anti-utopian vision in which a realistic beginning blends with an allegorical fantastic tale. The first-person narrator, a young philosophy student, and the son of a surgeon, is the main character and participant in the events described.

The story is set in motion by a tragic occurrence. One day, a man clinging to a street car is crushed by the oncoming traffic. The local transportation system is in a deplorable state, and a group of young people begins a campaign in support of the construction of a subway in the city. In fact the building of a subway has been in the plans for quite a while, but the negligence and apathy of the local administration have stalled the project for years. The campaign begins with demonstrations, followed by arrests and the expulsion of the instigators from the university. With time, it turns into a well-organized movement which receives wide support among the general public. It culminates with the resolution to construct a subway without the approval of, or help from, the city administration. Thousands of people go underground to clear the way for the new subway. They spend thirty years at the task and in the process build an underground city, completely isolated from the outside world.

The story of this underground city, constructed to house those who are building a mythical subway, is strikingly similar to the history of the Soviet state. In both cases a fantastic utopian idea takes hold of the extremists in charge. They isolate the people from outside influences, fearing that the people would otherwise be diverted from their idealistic mission. As in any segregated community, the struggle for power in the underground city is rampant. Those in charge believe that they are in possession of the whole truth, and those who dissent are terrorized and punished. The most dangerous crime is doubt. The slightest hesitation about the justice of the cause or about the possibility of reaching the final goal is punished. Only blind obedience is accepted. The extremists do not hesitate to blackmail their closest colleagues, with the purpose of intimidating all others. One of them is even executed, on trumped-up charges. It is all done for the alleged good of the cause.

Good people with progressive ideas often set in motion social and political movements with honourable intentions. With time, however, their notions may become impractical and remote, yet they continue to cling to them, becoming slaves of their own ideals. Such leaders instil their ideals with force, becoming despots and tyrants in the process. They fail to see the distinction between reality and myth, or between good and evil. Aleksandr Ageev suggested that 'at the root of any utopia there is always a pragmatic utilitarian goal,'[15] and he called this fantastic obsession with material objectives 'mystical materialism.' Hence the building of the subway can be compared with major Soviet construction projects, such as Magnitogorsk or the Belomor Canal. They are all part of the same illusion, which is ostensibly supposed to bring happiness to the people. It is well known, however, that material things can give momentary pleasure and contentment, but seldom emotional fulfilment or long-lasting happiness and peace of mind. The only distinction between Kurchatkin's utopia and the Soviet myth is expressed in the fact that whereas, in the novella, utopia is rooted in reality, Soviet ideology is derived from an abstract notion and aims at abstract goals. In both cases, those entrusted with the responsibility leading the masses pervert the objectives of the cause and place their personal interests above those of society. The irony of fate is obvious in both instances. Two years after the publication of Kurchatkin's story the Soviet Union ceased to exist; upon completion of the subway, its builders realize that they have laboured in vain: the subway is no longer needed by anyone, having been rendered absolete by the construction of a more efficient, aerial transportation system.

Most of those who survive the underground ordeal and return to the surface are dejected and cannot adapt to the new life. Many return to the underground city or commit suicide. They have wasted their lives; their myth has been destroyed. The narrator, now an old man, is the only survivor of the original five extremists, the leaders of the campaign. He has a hard time adjusting to his new life. Lonely and despondent, he goes to visit the graves of his parents and thinks his survival is a sad joke that someone has played on him. Everyone in his family, including his son, who has returned to the underground, is dead, while he remains. He is often visited by young people who ask him to relate the story of the extremists' movement and complain that life is aimless and empty.

The conclusion of the story is pessimistic and paradoxical. The old myths and illusions are destroyed, and those who have adhered to them are defeated. Yet the young people in the 'normal society' are depressed and unfulfilled. They need an aim, an objective, or a new illusion. Dostoevsky has suggested that the final result is always less important than the process of attaining it. When there is no definite purpose in life, existence becomes aimless, and people become open to corrupting influences. But when good ideas are set into action with the help of intimidation and force, the results are even more tragic. Kurchatkin does not offer any solution to this dilemma. There is only a hint that democracy, communication, tolerance, and mutual understanding can bridge the gap between the vagaries of human nature and the complexities of social interaction.

'Zapiski ekstremista' is a departure from Kurchatkin's realism. He creates a social and anti-utopian fantasy that follows the example of Aleksandr Kabakov's *Nevozvrashchenets* (No Return; 1989)[16] and is followed, in turn, by V. Makanin's 'Laz,' and other similar works in a genre that is becoming quite popular in Russia today. Artistically, however, 'Zapiski ekstremista' does not compare favourably with Kurchatkin's earlier stories. It provides food for thought, but it lacks profound characterization or psychological insight.

Al'bina, the heroine of Kurchatkin's new novel *Strazhnitsa* (A Guardian for Gorby; 1993),[17] is a mentally unstable woman. Overwhelmed by an early-childhood ominous dream, she is haunted by a premonition that something terrible will happen and is obsessed with the notion that she must protect Gorbachev and the Soviet people from danger and political pitfalls. Al'bina's mental state is made worse by her family situation. She cohabits for many years with an unloved and unfaithful husband, and becomes involved in a passionate love affair with an Afghan war veteran half her age. Furthermore, Al'bina is an ardent supporter of Gorbachev, while her husband, a highly placed party official, is against perestroika and Gorbachev's reforms. As the story progresses, her mental and physical state deteriorates. She cannot accept the fact that her young lover is no longer interested in her, nor can she cope with the gradual decline in Gorbachev's power and his final fall from grace. In the end the Soviet Union disintegrates, and Al'bina, the mother of two grown sons, still in her forties, dies in unexplained circumstances in a mental institution, from what appears to be cancer.

Kurchatkin's attempt to merge a tragic family drama, the story of an emotionally unstable woman, and issues concerning the political situation in the Soviet Union in the years of perestroika is not very successful. He tries to cover too much ground, and in consequence is unable to do justice to any of the elements he includes. The evolution of Al'bina's mental state is illustrated poorly. Family life is treated superficially, and the actions of some characters are puzzling. Political events are only alluded to in the narrative but are explained at length in footnotes. The time has apparently not yet come for turning Gorbachev and Yeltsin into fictional characters. A certain time interval is necessary in order to gain a proper perspective of the historical dimensions of the 1991 events in Russia.

LIUDMILA PETRUSHEVSKAIA

Liudmila Petrushevkaia (b. 1938) is one of the writers of the intermediate generation whose name became widely known to the Russian reading public in the mid-1980s. A native of Moscow and a graduate of

Moscow State University, she began writing prose in 1963, but she had little opportunity to publish her works in the days of Brezhnev. With the exception of some plays and an occasional story, her writing was rejected by editors because it portrayed the darker side of Soviet life and the grim existence of those dispossessed and downtrodden by the difficult conditions of daily life in the Soviet Union.

In 1987, Petrushevskaia began to publish regularly in the main Soviet journals,[18] as well as in the West. Her first collection of prose, *Bessmertnaia liubov'* (Immortal Love), came out in 1988. Petrushevskaia draws her characters from the twilight zone of Soviet city life of the intelligentsia. Most are single women, widowed, or divorced. Many are betrayed and bitter, cruel and cynical, or defeated by the circumstances of life. Some are abused, ignored, and exhausted by their continuous struggle for survival, while others are unethical hypocrites, concerned only with their personal well-being. The atmosphere in Petrushevkaia's stories resembles their setting. The action usually takes place in cramped communal apartments, where home is no longer a place of rest. Instead of providing an escape from external pressures, oppressive living conditions degrade the inhabitants and often lead to family disintegration.

One of the stories that has attracted much critical attention is 'Svoi krug' (Our Crowd).[19] Written in 1979, but not published until 1988, the story is an indictment of the Soviet intelligentsia, its petty betrayals, hypocrisies, and lack of morals. It is presented in the form of a relentless monologue by a divorced woman who suffers from a fatal congenital disease and is already in the process of going blind. Being aware that her condition is dire, she desperately tries to provide a secure home for her seven-year-old son. On the concluding pages of the story, the woman abuses and beats the boy in the presence of a group of old friends, including her former husband. She hopes to elicit compassion for the boy and make sure that the child is removed from her care, even before her death. On the surface, this act may appear to be an expression of extreme selflessness and altruism; however, under closer scrutiny it may turn out that this pathetic attempt to arrange for the security of her son may, in the long run, do him more harm than good. The psychological ramifications of parental maltreatment can vary, but the memory of his abusive mother may haunt the boy for the rest of his life.

In the opening paragraph of the story, the narrator confesses in a haughty tone: 'I am a harsh person, rough, always with a smile on my full red lips, always with a mocking grin to all ... I am very smart. What I do not understand does not exist at all.'[20] In the last sentence of the story, contemplating her actions, she repeats: 'It is better that way for all. I am smart. I understand.'[21] The arrogance of the narrator is evident, but because of her wretched state the reader excuses her well-intentioned cruelty. The narrator is ill, but otherwise little different from her friends, with whom she meets regularly for years and shares values. The narrator's manipulation is an act of desperation, but it is also an indication that social decay and moral disintegration sap the human body and exhaust the resources which stimulate understanding and love.

In 1989, Petrushevskaia published a prophetic anti-utopian story, 'Novye Robinzony (Khronika kontsa 20 veka)' (The New Robinsons [A Chronicle of the End of the Twentieth Century]).[22] There are allusions in the story to Daniel Dafoe's *Robinson Crusoe*, but it is a monologue by a young woman, the daughter of a man who decides to escape, together with his family, from the city into the remote wilderness, deep in the Russian countryside. They escape from some undefined environment to some unidentifiable place. The village they arrive at is reminiscent of the abandoned settlements described in the prose of F. Abramov and V. Astaf'ev. The newcomers work hard to provide for themselves and survive in these harsh conditions. It does not take long, however, before they have to move on, when armed outsiders come in and plunder the village. The family moves deep into the forest and lives in total isolation. When the father puts on the radio and hears no sound, he is happy that no one is on their trail. They have managed to escape again.

The title of the story is symbolic. The escapers have become new Robinsons not because they have lost their way, but because they have exercised their free will and decided to run away. They are prepared to sacrifice their material well-being in order to retain their independence and freedom. The atmosphere in the story is chilling. It alludes to the fact that those in power abuse and oppress the ordinary people, who are left with one choice: to submit or to escape. A spirit of dejection and hopelessness permeates the story, yet the inner goodness of the new Robinsons provides some reason for hope. They have nothing to spare, and manage with very little. They can hardly provide for themselves, yet take in two abandoned infants and care for them. In his discussion of 'Novye Robinzony,' E. Sidorov disagreed with those who assert that harshness and helplessness are the main traits of Petrushevskaia's prose. In fact, he suggested that, in her stories, 'there is light and love of life. Most importantly she always overcomes aesthetically her material. Had it not been for this artistic recreation the subject-matter could indeed impart dejection.'[23] That is, of course, not the opinion of conservative

critics who assert that neither Petrushevskaia nor her heroes have compassion for the suffering of others.[24]

'Pesni vostochnykh slavian' (Songs of the Eastern Slavs),[25] and other
stories by Petrushevskaia published in 1990, continue in the tone of so-
called harsh realism, but they dispel, at least in part the notion that her
prose is naturalistic and aspires to complete fidelity to life. These stories
are a mixture of realism fantasy, a combination of the real and surrealistic. They emphasize the brutal aspects of family life, the dark side of
human nature, as well as the realities of psychological disintegration
under the pressures of daily existence. 'Pesni vostochnykh slavian'
begins with an introduction which states that '"sluchai" – an occurrence
– is a peculiar genre of city folklore.'[26] It is followed by seven stories providing accounts of most incongruous occurrences in which the absurd
becomes the norm rather than the exception. The Moscow stories, as
they are called, are full of horrid events, hideous crimes, and characters
on the brink of mental collapse. People perceive fantasy and delusion as
reality and act accordingly.

Petrushevskaia's main interest is always in the situations and occurrences described. The individual is only important to her as playing a
role in the events portrayed. Petrushevskaia usually tries to withhold
her authorial voice by remaining detached and letting the characters and
events speak for themselves. Yet here, more than in any of her previous
stories, her compassion for those who suffer is apparent. She illustrates
it partially by juxtaposing the vacuousness and degeneration of the outside world with the potential for goodness, vigour, and dedication hidden deeply in human nature. In 'Novyi raion' (New District), a guilty
conscience haunts a man who has murdered his wife. Paradoxically,
despite the fact that he admits to his crime the evidence is insufficient for
his arrest. He remains free, but without inner peace, and is continuously
tormented by his guilty conscience. In 'Mest'' (Vengeance), a woman is
driven to suicide by her guilty conscience over the alleged murder of a
friend's child. However, upon learning on her death bed that the child is
still alive and well, she is relieved and happy and can now rest in peace.
In other stories, such as 'Sluchai v Sokol'nikakh' (An Occurrence in
Sokol'niki), 'Materinskii privet' (A Mother's Greetings), and 'Ruka'
(Hand), it is difficult to distinguish among what is real, what is affected
by the characters' morbid state of mind and what is the product of the
author's imagination. Most characters are either mentally unstable or
seeking respite from the horrors of reality by escaping into the
unknown.

Two other stories, 'Novyi Gulliver' (The New Gulliver) and 'Medeia' (Medeia),[27] published in *Aprel'*, are similar in subject and tone to 'Pesni vostochnykh slavian.' In 'Novyi Gulliver,' the narrator, a man with influenza who is confined to a hospital bed is overwhelmed by the idea that the cockroaches in the hospital are small human beings, ready to swarm and overtake everything dear to him, including his life. 'Medeia' is in the form of dialogue between a cab driver and his woman passenger, who narrates the story. We learn from their brief exchange that the taxi man is devastated: his mentally unstable wife has killed his beloved fourteen-year-old daughter, and he cannot forgive himself for failing to protect her. The murderess is confined to a psychiatric ward, but the passenger suggests that the husband's loving attention could assist in her recovery. The story underscores the shocking paradox of family relations: the man could have saved his daughter by loving his wife. Love is indeed a great healer and can help save one from oneself, but it is also an expression of emotions which often defy logic. The husband cannot force himself to love his wife and give her the tender affection she requires. She, in turn, in a fit of jealousy and vengeance, kills the object of his adoration, failing to see, in her morbid state, that her daughter is her own flesh and blood as well.

'Vremia noch'' (The Time: Night)[28] is another stinging indictment of the Soviet intelligentsia. The bleak picture of reality and the depressive atmosphere in the story are intensified by the corroding effect of poverty on family and human relationships. An introductory note to the story indicates that the daughter of a deceased poet has called the author, offering her mother's prose manuscript entitled 'Zapiski na kraiu stola' (Notes from the Edge of the Table). Sometimes later, the notes arrive in the mail. Thus, the story is composed of notes, observations, and comments by Anna, the poet in question. They are interspersed with dialogue, flashbacks, reminiscences, and entries from Alena's, Anna's daughter's, diaries, which she has read without the latter's knowledge or permission. The narrative is fragmented. The action covers a long stretch of time, and there is a constant shift from place to place, and from the present to the past.

'Vremia noch'' opens with a scene which sets the tone. Anna and her grandson, Timosha, visit some old friends but find that they are not welcome. Anna works in an editorial office, but she is destitute, and Timosha is always hungry. Soviet ideology advocates equality, but, as is too often the case everywhere, those who are well off shun their less fortunate old friends. What follows is a nightmarish account of family misery and unhappiness. There are no positive characters in the story, and no hint of some inner goodness. Reality is gloomy, and life is bleak. Children are born out of wedlock, and mother and daughter are jealous of each other. Poverty destroys even the maternal instinct. It is hinted in the story that people can become destitute because they fail to live up to certain social norms, but degrading poverty can turn humans into beasts. In that sense there are many parallels between mother and daughter. Both have numerous affairs with married men, and both resent their old mothers. Both demand and expect from each other deeds of which neither is capable herself. The children, on the other hand, are helpless without parents, yet they hate them and do not want them around.

The story is narrated as the stream-of-consciousness outpouring of an aching heart. Narration is terse and intense. We view reality through the eyes of Anna, but her crippled perception provides a distorted picture of life. There is no shred of optimism in the conclusion, just an example of one of the great paradoxes of family life: families have often a hard time staying together because everyone craves privacy; yet, when there is no one around, the individual can be destroyed by the loneliness and depression that inevitably set in. When Alena and her children want to return to her mother's cramped apartment, Anna initially refuses to let them in but then relents. One day, Anna returns home and, hearing no sounds from within the apartment, becomes frantic, fearing that they might have poisoned themselves while she was away. Indeed, Alena and her children are gone, probably on their way to another adventure in living, and Anna realizes suddenly that she is facing old age in solitude and dejection. The imagery of 'Vremia noch'' is just as depressing as the story itself. There are no scenes of nature, or of internal or external beauty. The experiences and associations of the heroines are destructive, and life crushes them. There is nothing these unfortunate creatures can do to save themselves but submit to their fate.

In other stories, Petrushevskaia continues her exploration of the murky sides of Russian city life. In 'Po doroge boga Erosa' (In the Ways of God Eros; 1993),[29] the charming, slender, and unfaithful wife, Olia, abuses her husband, driving him thus unwittingly into the arms of her unattractive friend, Pul'kheria. By a strange twist of fate, Pul'kheria, who is always looked down upon by Olia, is now the cause of her friend's marital problems. There is little talk in the story about real love, but, for one, this new infatuation is an escape from mental abuse, while, for the other, it signifies the flight from loneliness.

The brutal pressures of family life drive Olia's husband to the verge of insanity. Sania, the hero of the story 'Ustroit' zhizn'' (To Arrange a Life; 1990),[30] on the other hand, is driven by family strife to alcoholism and the pursuit of a young widow who shows no interest in his affection. The woman is tactful. She does not want to offend Sania, a friend of her deceased husband, but she discourages his advances. Her youthful mother, however, sees in Sania a kindred spirit and pressures her daughter relentlessly to show favour to this man. The mother interferes in her daughter's affairs, but instead of helping her cope with her difficult life, destroys her stability and peace of mind.

In 1993, Petrushevskaia published a number of very brief stories for children, under the general title 'Nu, mama, nu' (Come on, Mother; 1993).[31] Although intended for small children, the stories contain an adult message. Each story provides a lesson in moral education. Some advocate selflessness, compassion, and love. Others decry greed, egoism, and the lack of honesty.

Petrushevskaia presents her readers with an array of episodic occurrences and situations from the daily life of Soviet city-dwellers. Her prose is compressed, and her stories have little plot, but they provide a wealth of material. Her prose is truthful to life, but she is selective in the choice of subject-matter. There are some positive characters in her stories, people endowed with generosity of spirit and commitment to fellow humans, but there is not a single happy family in her recent works. Petrushevskaia does not preach. She does not criticize the actions of her heroes, nor does she investigate the psychological motivation behind their actions. She presents, instead, an accumulation of facts which speak for themselves.

Most of her narrators are women who participate in the actions described, but some are portrayed as bystanders who tell a story as if they observe it from the sidelines. They view events from different perspectives and often speak with different voices. The language of Petrushevskaia's prose is intentionally stripped of figurative and ornamental devices in keeping with the harsh reality of her subject-matter. One critic suggested that her prose is 'a peculiar kind of *skaz* with special traits of a non-literary narrator. It represents a combination of two different styles. Official-business and ordinary-conversational styles form the language of oral expression, which is full of incorrect phrases, and is subsequently attached to a peculiar official, business-like situation.'[32] Petrushevskaia, thus, makes ample use of unorthodox literary patterns and ignores accepted language norms. According to Natal'ia Ivanova, grotesque is one of the characteristic features of Petrushevskaia's prose in general, and of her language in particular: 'She creates in the genre of intentional verbal absurdity in which sounds form words and words shape phrases, in accordance with the principles of the grotesque.'[33]

The prose of Petrushevskaia is in the tradition of Soviet *byt* literature of the 1970s. But she takes it a step farther by rejecting the interference of ideological editorial scrutiny and censorship. In fact, some of her stories, published in the days of perestroika, were written in the 1970s. As is the case in Iu. Trifonov's novellas, in Petrushevskaia's works the struggle for a room, an apartment, a place to live, is synonymous with the struggle for survival. In Trifonov's prose, however, there is still some hope for a better future. Social institutions are criticized, but not completely denounced, and the plots are placed within a certain historical perspective. Trifonov contrasts the narrow-minded egotism and the ethical shallowness of his negative characters with the inner grace, nobility, and selflessness of those who oppose them. Petrushevskaia's stories, on the other hand, are limited in scope, and her magnifying lens is focused on a restricted area. The spirit of pessimism overshadows the inner goodness of some of her characters, and the positive in human nature is most often the result of self-abhorrence, self-pity, or a guilty conscience, which usually follows criminal activity or an immoral act. That is not to say that there are no instances of parental devotion, integrity, or self-sacrifice in Petrushevskaia's stories. Indeed, there are such examples, but they are the exceptions rather than the rule. Petrushevskaia sympathizes with the predicament of her characters. She identifies with their suffering, but she does not spare them. She realizes that happiness and contentment are rare commodities, bestowed as much by individual character traits as by the social environment and conditions of life.

ANDREI BITOV

Andrei Bitov (b. 1937) is one of the most gifted contemporary Russian writers, and one of the few reluctantly permitted by Soviet authorities to publish simultaneously in official Soviet publications as well as in the West. He was isolated by the Soviet regime, but not banished or exiled. Bitov's prose is autobiographical, intellectual, intricate, and playful. His stories are well constructed and balanced. His style is graceful and has a peculiar lyrical quality, and his plots combine a variety of interconnected thematic threads. Bitov's prose is precise, stimulating, and infused with irony, but it is also challenging, and not to everyone's taste. It is full of allusions and it offers a multitude of different perspectives, and it is open to a wide range of different interpretations. Bitov the writer often places himself at the centre of his narratives and discusses issues of literary activity and the complexity of the creative process. He concerns himself also with the relationship between people and nature, and he places his plots within the general framework of historical and cultural evolution.

The current situation in Russia has exerted a peculiar effect on Bitov's talent. He is not involved directly in political activity, but continues to teach, serves on a number of editorial boards, and writes introductions to the works of young aspiring authors. Except for his recent 'Ozhidanie obez'ian' (Waiting for the Apes; 1993),[34] however, he has published little fiction in the last six years. It appears that, after one has spent years in the literary underground, the newly acquired freedom can create problems. Bitov admits that what he does 'best, is write books. And it is writing that has proved to be the most difficult thing of all, given the new opportunities.'[35] He claims that, before glasnost, he lived in his inner world and was internally free, but that was a freedom of degradation. Today, Russian people 'easily swap a slave's freedom for the slavery of being free that exists in the democratic world.' Bitov decries the situation and says, 'We have no ideas, and there are no longer any new ideas,' yet he believes that literature can help solve the problems of society. He thinks, however, that it is up to the younger generation to look into the future and express their new experiences in artistic form. Bitov's 'present is bound too strangely with the past.'[36]

A footnote to 'Ozhidanie obez'ian' explains that it is the concluding part of the novel Oglashennye (The Announced), which also includes 'Ptitsy ili novye svedeniia o cheloveke' (Birds or New Information about Humans; 1975) and 'Chelovek v peizazhe' (The Man in the Landscape; 1987). 'Ptitsy' is a loosely connected narrative composed of dialogue, description, and meditation. One of the protagonists of the story is confounded by the fact that people overlook the grave danger to their existence by failing to view themselves as biological creatures. He compares the nature of rational man with that of other living species, and he asserts that the morality of the predatory animal is much higher than that of humans. The insignificance of man in relation to the omnipotence of the forces of nature, and the delusion that man is in control of his own destiny, is one of the main ideas expressed in 'Ptitsy.'

'Chelovek v peizazhe' is a short narrative composed of a dialogue between the first-person authorial narrator and a landscape painter who is also a notorious alcoholic. Their conversation gravitates from issues of creativity and aesthetics to problems of nature and history. The narrator muses about the essential duality of people and the complexity of the artistic process. He is concerned with issues of the relationship between idea, perception, reflection, imagination, and the record of reality, as well as the disparity between the artist's initial intention and the final product of his creation.

It is difficult to summarize the content of Bitov's stories because they are almost plotless, and the reality they portray is vague. The characters are ill defined, and the location is often obscure and in a state of constant change. 'Ozhidanie obez'ian' is no different. It is set in the 1980s and ends in the days of the anti-Gorbachev coup in August 1991. The action moves from place to place and back and forth in time, but most of it is set in Abkhazia and Russia's south. Among the appearing and disappearing characters are representatives of various Soviet nationalities. Some are serious and reputable individuals; others are vagabonds and criminals. The heroes of 'Ptitsy' and 'Chelovek v peizazhe' also occupy a prominent place in the narrative.

The authorial lyrical 'I' is the only real character in the narrative. But even he is a double, and in constant struggle with himself. He is in a perpetual state of self-analysis and introspection. He reflects on the difficulty of artistic creation, and on the interconnection between life and art, and is also concerned with issues of ecology, pollution, national strife, and the ramifications of the recent changes in Russia for the future of the arts and the artist. Bitov alludes in the narrative to the fact that freedom does not necessarily bring happiness, and that glasnost made him dumb and killed the writer in him.

The title of the story refers to a paradox in nature as well as in history. The apes supposedly live a free life somewhere in the Caucasus, in a country where humans have no freedom. The expectation of finding the apes, however, is an illusion; they never arrive. But the narrator does not want to part with his illusion. If what is real in life is elusive, an illusion is better than nothing. The narrator suffers and is full of pain. He has a hard time coming to terms with reality. Life is difficult, and artistic creation arduous. On the last page of the narrative, there is a vague hint of hope. During the August 1991 coup in Moscow, angels hover over tanks and barricades, and entreat God to help those who have lost their way in this turbulent and mutinous world.

Stylistically, 'Ozhidanie obez'ian' is similar to Bitov's earlier works, but the author's tone of despondency in the story is new. It is not a call for a return to the past, but an expression of sadness with the current state of affairs in Russia. The narrator is depressed because he is unable to write, and because the newly granted freedom is abused by many. The author searches for new values, but personality change does not come easily and is accompanied by internal strife. Bitov's state reflects the plight of those who refused in the past to acquiesce in the demands of the former regime, yet reject today the new opportunistic possibilities of adaptation. Like any honest individual, Bitov wants to remain himself. It is a difficult task in times of social discord.

VIKTORIIA TOKAREVA

Viktoriia Tokareva (b. 1937) is a writer of the intermediate generation who continues to create in the old spirit. True, the social background of her realistic prose is different today, but the nature of basic human relationships has changed little. Her recent story 'Ia est'. Ty est' On est'.' (I Am Here. You Are Here. He Is Here; 1991)[37] is, in many ways, similar to her earlier prose and fits well within the Soviet *byt* literature of the previous decade. It is a story about the fragile state of the family institution, and the unfulfilled love of a middle-aged woman. It is also about loneliness, jealousy, and the realization that true love can be achieved only through self-sacrifice.

The main character, Anna, is a young widow, in her mid forties, and the mother of a surgeon, Oleg. Lacking fulfilment in her marriage, she has always dreamt about a new grand passion and, before her husband's death, refused to bear another child in order to keep herself available in case of any eventuality. When her husband dies unexpectedly, she suddenly realizes that her dream is an illusion. Most good men are married, and those available do not deserve her care. That is when she channels her attention to her son and smothers him with affection to the point that he is forced to marry in secret. No woman, in his mother's estimation, deserves the love of her son. When Oleg brings his young wife home, Anna is angry, jealous, and suspicious of her daughter-in-law, Irochka. It is not long before the young couple is forced to move elsewhere. For half a year there is no communication between mother and son, but then something tragic happens: Irochka becomes crippled in a car accident, and there is no one to look after her. Oleg turns to his mother for support, and Anna finds new meaning in life in her commitment and devotion to Irochka's recovery. Oleg, in the meantime, succumbs to the pressures of his superior at work, an aggressive married woman whose husband is on an extended business trip, and becomes involved in a love affair.

The story is ironic. Once Irochka is well on the way to recovery, her previously devoted husband, Oleg, seeks fulfilment somewhere else. And Anna, the lonely widow, realizes that Irochka, her daughter-in-law, is the only family member who will stay with her for good. The human quest for authentic experiences and meaningful existence is endless, but only those who identify with the suffering of others can attain tranquillity and real satisfaction. The issues of infidelity, permissiveness, and the urge for instant gratification of the ego are not new to recent Russian literature, but problems created by the corruption of social institutions and the lack of moral principles are combined in this story with the new materialism generated by the possibilities of perestroika. Acquisitiveness, the urge for monetary gain and foreign travel, which are often combined with sexual escapades, undermine with new force the very institution of marriage and foster the false notion that momentary pleasure can lead to meaningful and lasting satisfaction.

The action in the story covers one year in the life of the Moscow intelligentsia in the days of perestroika. There is much dialogue in this third-person narrative, but little characterization or psychological analysis. Secondary characters are poorly drawn and appear only episodically in order to provide the necessary background rather than to act in their own right. Tokareva attempts to cover more ground than is suitable for the confines of a relatively short story. Hence, some issues posed receive no adequate treatment, and the author relies on melodramatic contrivances. Tokareva's prose flows smoothly and is infused with a tinge of humour, but there is little optimism in the story. The ending is inconclusive: there is little happiness in sight for any of the protagonists. Perhaps only Anna reaches a new level of maturity: instead of pursuing her illusory and unattainable dreams, she accepts life for whatever it has to offer.

Family life, which is closely related to the issue of love, occupies an important place in the prose of Tokareva, as well as in her personal life. She asserts: 'I have been married for twenty-five years. I can't imagine life without a family. A woman without a family is without a master, like a stray animal. It's a tragedy. In this sense I am patriarchal, traditional. But I am always waiting for perfect love. It keeps me going, makes me dress well; and I wait, hope. That's why I write my stories ... draw my male ideal. I am patient.'[38] It is not difficult to see that Tokareva herself is the prototype for the character of Anna, even though, whereas Anna has already concluded her futile search for perfect love, having realized that 'it is all in the past,'[39] Tokareva still believes in and hopes for the possible, but improbable. In any event, the story does not provide any answer to the question 'What is perfect love?' and whether such love is possible at all. Instead, the reader is urged to agree that, even if perfect love is seldom attainable, hope is the best substitute for it.

VLADIMIR KRUPIN

Political change affects different writers in various ways. Vladimir Krupin (b. 1941), a native of the Viatka region in northern Russia, has always been close, in style and spirit, to Russian 'village prose.' In his 'Kolokol'chik' (Handbell; 1981) and 'Sorokovoi den" (The Fortieth Day; 1981), he idealizes the old ways of the Russian village, makes derogatory remarks about non-Russian minorities, and alludes to the superiority of the Russian people. In 1990 Krupin was appointed editor of the conservative journal *Moskva*[40] and became one of the more vociferous members of the Russian ultra-nationalist camp.

Krupin's recent prose is similar in subject and style to his earlier works, but his Russian nationalistic sentiments are no longer subdued, but on the surface. His 'Proshchai, Rossiia, vstretimsia v raiu' (Farewell, Russia, We Will Meet in Heaven; 1991)[41] is a narrative in the form of a long dialogue between two old philosophizing peasants. Their language is colourful, and the discourse is full of humour. The main subject of their conversation is the current difficult political and economic situation in the country. The first-person narrator claims that Orthodoxy will save Russia, while his friend, Kostia, asserts that a new Stalin is needed to put things in order again. The narrator is more apathetic and restrained, while Kostia is aggressive and belligerent. He criticizes Gorbachev and Yeltsin, who, according to him, deceive the people: 'The tsar did not lie. So they killed him, and Russia perished.'[42] There is a sense of urgency and despair in the voice of Kostia. His deep concern for the fate of Russia is overwhelming, but his language is witty and comical, rooted in the lore of the Russian countryside.

The life of the Russian peasant has never been easy or frivolous. It has been in the tradition of 'village prose' to criticize these difficult conditions. But, in the past, criticism was impersonal, moderate, and, in most cases, under the surface. The rule of those in power was never questioned, and no solutions to the problems addressed were ever offered. Today, all this has changed. It is no longer necessary to hide. The protagonists speak for the author and express his ideas. Krupin strongly believes that only a combination of Orthodoxy and a strong hand can save Russia. In his view, however, Russian Orthodoxy is under constant pressure from the Catholic Church, and other cults and sects. They have recently come out of hiding, and today occupy the airwaves and television screens. According to Krupin, 'democracy is alien to Russia ... only thieves, swindlers, prostitutes, and sexual minorities are happy with democracy.'[43]

Krupin is certainly a talented writer. He deals with a milieu he knows well, but his preoccupation with extra-literary issues, his journalistic epithets, and the proliferation of political invectives in simple peasant speech diminish the effectiveness of his recent prose.

ALEKSANDR PROKHANOV

In the early 1980s, Aleksandr Prokhanov (b. 1938) was one of the leading apologists for the Soviet invasion of Afghanistan and an ardent supporter of exporting Soviet-style revolution to the Third World. Sensitive to political change and supportive of those in power, he always placed his talent at the service of the regime. In his novels published between 1982 and 1984, and set in Afghanistan, Kampuchea, Mozambique, and Nicaragua, respectively, Prokhanov denounced American imperialism and extolled the peaceful and progressive foreign policy of the Soviet state.[44] With the advent of perestroika, Prokhanov, the opportunist, adapted to the new conditions of the day and became a fervent proponent of so-called Soviet, and later Russian, *gosudarstvennost'* or statehood. He became the editor of the weekly *Den'*, and joined hands with the most extreme pro-communists and Russian nationalistic forces, which call for the overthrow of Yeltsin and the establishment a dictatorial regime in Russia.

In his novel *Mesto deistviia* (Scene of Action; 1979), Prokhanov portrays industrial development in a remote Siberian town which unsettles the lives of its inhabitants. In his *Shest'sot let posle bitvy* (Six Hundred Years after the Battle; 1988),[45] he returns to the theme of industrialization. At the centre of V. Rasputin's or Iu. Bondarev's prose, dealing with technological progress, are issues connected with the construction of hydro-electric stations; Prokhanov deals with the construction of a nuclear power plant in the town of Brody, located in central Russia.

The plot of the novel is constructed around an artificial and naïve conflict. The main character, Fotiev, is a romantic dreamer. He arrives at the construction site with the purpose of introducing a new method of management, called 'Vektor.' It is supposed to identify the weak spots in the production chain and make work more efficient. This new system is never explained, but the reader is to believe that human labour is the only factor that determines the quality of production. At first, Fotiev is given an opportunity to introduce his new method. But, when he becomes infatuated and begins an affair with Antonina, a trade union official and lover of Gornostaev, the acting head of construction, his troubles begin. Gornostaev wants to stop the experiment and remove Fotiev from the site.

The subject of the novel is a serious one. After the Chernobyl disaster, the issue of nuclear energy became extremely sensitive in the Soviet Union. Yet, Prokhanov, who supports the preservation of the Soviet Union and socialism, does not question the feasibility of expanding nuclear installations, or their effect on the country's ecology. Nor does he blame the government for the Chernobyl catastrophe. Instead, remaining true to himself, Prokhanov continues to advance ideas which support his own ideological and political views. Thus, one of the heroes, who undoubtedly speaks for the author, accuses the West of the Chernobyl calamity. He asserts that, in the West, 'they knew that an accident was imminent and they were happy about this misfortune. They prepared it and waited for it ... The enemy was close. He managed to penetrate into our ministries and trusts; infiltrate the sciences ... and stealthily put forth destructive plans which were doomed to failure.'[46]

Making use of the relative relaxation of glasnost, and in response to Gorbachev's policies, Prokhanov attacks the Brezhnev regime but defends socialism and the Soviet state. He promotes Russian nationalism by claiming that the construction of the plant in Brody is a truly Russian enterprise. He places the novel within a mythological context, referring to the mysterious foreign hordes who appeared some six hundred years previously in the region of Brody, only to be rebuffed by the Russian forces. This historical and fantastic legend serves as a contrastive device for comparing the past with the present and amplifying the current dangers to the Russian people and the Soviet state. Scenes from the Afghan war and the Chernobyl débâcle are scattered throughout the novel. Most positive characters, including Fotiev, are war veterans or Chernobyl survivors. Risking their own lives, they have selflessly fulfilled their duty. In Brody, they oppose the bureaucracy and support

Fotiev's plan, which allegedly promotes the rule of the people. Prokhanov idealizes the former Afghan warriors and suggests that they will help protect and build a better Russia.

Prokhanov's new novel is no great masterpiece. The plot lacks compositional unity, and various subplots and digressions overshadow the delineation of the main conflict. The characters are unidimensional and poorly drawn. Prokhanov's descriptive skills are adequate, but he lacks the creative imagination to produce a truly artistic text. Hence, his novels are verbose, his language is dry and lacks expressiveness, and his characters are indistinct, lacking psychological depth and charged with the task of promoting the author's ideas, which are of questionable merit. No wonder few are convinced by the author's message, which is always on the surface.

In 1991, after the anti-Gorbachev coup, Prokhanov published another novel, *Angel proletel* (An Angel Flew By; 1991).[47] It is a continuation of the previous narrative, featuring the same set of characters and the same location. But three years after the appearance of *Shest'sot let posle bitvy*, the situation in the Soviet Union has changed drastically, mirrored by the change in tone and spirit of the new narrative. Here, the 'Vektor' system, which is to save Russia from chaos, is rejected, and Fotiev leaves for Moscow. The antagonism between the workers and the bureaucracy reaches new heights: workers organize strikes and demonstrations, which result in confrontation with the army and internal security forces. The scene in which the people face the army defiantly is reminiscent of the scenes at the White House in Moscow during the coup of August 1991. But Prokhanov takes the reader a step farther. After one of the workers is run over by an armoured car, the commander, an Afghan veteran, kills himself, apparently in remorse. The novel ends inconclusively, but no upheaval can stop the launching of the new nuclear plant in Brody. In the last few pages, the author indulges in a lyrical outburst in which he decries the destruction of Russia and expresses his fear and anguish for its future. The novel appeared in print when the Soviet Union was already in its final stages of disintegration. As there is no need any longer to defend socialism or the Soviet state, Prokhanov instead vehemently attacks Gorbachev and his administration and denigrates national minorities.

In 1993, Prokhanov published another novel, *Poslednii soldat imperii* (The Last Soldier of the Empire).[48] Its main character is a Russian social scientist who turns down an invitation to come to the United States to work for the Rand Corporation. The narrative is rabidly anti-American and reminiscent of Prokhanov's prose of the early 1980s. Many scenes are autobiographical and set in Afghanistan, Angola, Mozambique, Nicaragua, and Kampuchea. In this work, Prokhanov decries the collapse of the Soviet empire and the disintegration of the Soviet state.

The subject and the setting of Prokhanov's recent novels are different from those in his works of the early 1980s, but their tone and style are the same. These novels are in the hazy domain of prose, where artistry, journalism, and politics are irrevocably merged. They are topical and opportunistic, and the prose is often flatly journalistic, subverting any serious aesthetic consideration the author might have given to his creation. None the less, the Russian nationalistic conservative press extolled the merits of Prokhanov's prose. We read in *Sovetskaia Rossiia* that 'the image of Fotiev is Prokhanov's greatest achievement in the novel. It is an expression of a Russian type of our epoch of destruction and devastation. He is a Russian man who has preserved the naivety of the soul, the purity of his world view, and the compassion for the suffering of others ... The novel ... is the first song of our new tragic epos.'[49] It is clear from this evaluation that, as was the case in the former Soviet Union, politics rather than artistry determine the critical response to a work of art.

IURII ARAKCHEEV

Diadia Vania is a conventional literary almanac started in 1991 and published by the Chekhov society in Moscow. Its editor is the former secretary of the Moscow City Writers' Union, V.M. Shugaev. In the first issue of the almanac, most of the space is devoted to literary essays, reminiscences about departed literary personalities, and documentary prose. Among its contributors are established authors such as Iu. Nagibin, S. Esin, and V. Shugaev. One of its authors, Iurii Arakcheev, is a mainstream middle-aged writer and a member of the former Writers' Union. His narrative *Istoriia odnogo razocharovaniia* (The History of One Disappointment; 1991)[50] is a journal version of his forthcoming novel *Postizhenie* (Comprehending). It begins with a factual account illustrating the practical results of Bolshevism in Russia, its effects on the workings of Soviet institutions, and the mentality of those in power. It is followed by self-examination, and the investigation of the roots of Marxism-Leninism and its consequences for Russia.

In the beginning of Part one the first-person narrator, a correspondent of *Pravda*, introduces the reader to a dinner-party scene somewhere in a remote district of Kazakhstan. The guest of honour, the district party secretary Romaniuk, is an arrogant braggart. He conducts business in a state of intoxication, bullying and berating his subordinates and settling scores with some minor local officials. He reinforces his authority through intimidation and terror. The narrator, who is present at the party, is disconcerted and deeply offended by the behaviour of Romaniuk. The scene he witnesses revives his old simmering doubts about the propriety and legitimacy of the Soviet system of government, and he decides, once again, to re-examine the classics of Marxism-Leninism.

In Part two, the narrator analyses the works of Lenin and concludes that there is little logic in them. Instead of arguing with his opponents, Lenin berates them, removing them from power by force and aiming at dictatorship rather than democracy. In Part three, the narrator investigates the essence of fascism and concludes that Hitler's advent to power was a consequence of the Bolshevik Revolution in Russia. He compares Marx and Lenin to Dostoevsky's Great Inquisitor, who makes use of lofty ideals in order to enslave the masses. According to Arakcheev, the Soviet system has created a multitude of inquisitors, of Napoleons, of different sizes. They have brought into existence socialism for themselves and equality for all others. Romaniuk is one of these inquisitors. In his district he is powerful and dominant and uses tactics similar to those applied by the early Bolsheviks.

The Epilogue, written five years after Gorbachev's ascent to power, is not very optimistic. The author does not blame individuals for the misfortunes of the Soviet people. Instead, he condemns the system and laments that there is no sign as yet that those in power are ready to relinquish it. Arakcheev's narrative is not a novel in the accepted sense; rather, it is a combination of fact, fiction, self-exploration, philosophical investigation, and social analysis. It is also a confession of a disappointed man who has been compelled to serve a god he does not believe in. The narrative is intense and sincere, and it represents the views and emotions of a generation of non-dissident intellectuals who have been superficially supportive of the Soviet system. They were forced to acquiesce to those in power and to bury their doubts and resentment deep inside.

Three years after the publication of the novel and the collapse of the Soviet empire, Arakcheev was disenchanted again. He continued to adhere to some of his old liberal opinions, but rejected the current system of government and opposed the leadership of Yeltsin. The metamorphosis in the views of Arakcheev is a reflection of a wider malady that today afflicts some members of the Russian liberal intelligentsia. Disappointed with the lack of stability and the course of economic reform, many seek the guidance of new political leadership and grope for new values.[51]

The discussion of the prose of middle-aged writers illustrates clearly the effects of the recent political changes in Russia on their creative output. Most try to adapt to the new conditions of the day and take advantage of the new freedom of expression and publication. Yet the results are different in each case. Makanin, for example, creates anti-utopias and widens the scope of philosophical investigation. Bitov explores the vagaries of artistic creation and the effect of freedom on his art. In the stories of Petrushevskaia, ordinary collisions of everyday life assume the expression of extreme harshness, callousness, and human suffering. The prose of Kim and Tokareva has changed little, but the subject-matter of their works reflects the new spirit of the times. The style of Krupin's recent stories is similar to that of his earlier works, but the author's ideological and religious views are now on the surface. The prose of Prokhanov has always been infused with political substance; whereas previously he worshipped Soviet idols today, he pays homage to the new gods of Russian statehood and nationalism.

It is apparent, therefore, that the former uniformity of Soviet literature was just a pretence. Perestroika has uncovered the hidden cleavages between the former *sorokaletnie* and has driven them farther apart. Today, except for age, they have little in common.

5

The New Writers of Perestroika

Glasnost and perestroika, followed by the abolition of censorship and the disintegration of the USSR, have opened the way for a number of new names on the Russian literary scene. Some of them are the product of perestroika and belong to the younger generation; others are mature writers, previously unable to escape the vigilant scrutiny of censors and editors. Still others managed to publish something many years ago, then disappeared from sight for years. Many new authors have simply been hiding in the underground and writing 'for the drawer.' These writers belong to different age groups and work in a variety of distinct styles, themes, or genres. Yet all of them bear the imprint of the times. Their views reflect their past experiences as well as their current social, aesthetic, and ethical attitudes.

The new writers of this transitional age are subdivided here into three distinct groups. To the first group belong authors who follow in the traditions of Russian conventional realism. The third group includes those who identify mainly with current Russian post-modernism. In between is the second group, composed of writers whose works combine traditional realistic narrative modes with elements of post-modernism. This division, however, is arbitrary and what distinguishes writers assigned to one stream from those relegated to the other two is relative, and sometimes vague. Some authors combine elements of conventional realism with post-modernist devices, as well as with components of the avant-garde and conceptualism in one and the same work. Others, in response to the new free-market conditions in Russia, use diverse narrative techniques in different works. Thus, the same writer may one day produce a realist work of prose and, the next day, a post-modernist or avant-garde narrative.

A. *In Traditions of Realism*

SERGEI KALEDIN

Sergei Kaledin (b. 1949) made his literary debut in the days of perestroika, at the age of thirty-eight. His first novella, 'Smirennoe kladbish-
che' (The Humble Cemetery; 1987), is a physiological sketch with an
unusual setting – a city cemetery. It introduces the Soviet reader to a new
cast of characters and types: social outcasts, derelicts, and alcoholics.
The cemetery is a place of eternal rest. Burying the dead is a social service, but it is also a job for those who work there. In 'Smirennoe klad-
bishche,' the murky world of those who make their living at the
cemetery assumes a life of its own. The author is a good observer. He
illustrates clearly that the harsh realities of the graveyard do nothing to
mitigate the abusive, greedy, and cynical nature of those who work
there.

Kaledin is good at identifying conflicts and settings that are new to
Soviet literature. His novella 'Stroibat' (Construction Battalion; 1989)[1] is
a realistic narrative that can be categorized as so-called *zhestkaia proza*, or
harsh prose. It deals with a subject that, until recently, was very sensitive
and secret – namely, the Soviet military in times of peace. Before perestroika, Soviet writers described the army in glowing terms. Kaledin
destroys the old stereotypes and takes the reader to a remote town in
Siberia in which a military construction battalion is stationed.[2]

Military service in a construction unit is usually reserved for those
who are physically unfit or otherwise handicapped, as well as for former
criminals and delinquents. National minorities, often poorly versed in
Russian, form a big part of these detachments. The atmosphere in the
battalion, as portrayed by Kaledin, is reminiscent of the environment in
correctional institutions for juvenile delinquents. Soldiers are subject to
the same kind of physical, mental, and emotional abuse. There is the
same hierarchical structure, clannishness, and rule of the strong. Those
in the first year of service irrevocably submit to the tyranny of older soldiers and in subsequent year's abuse and terrorize newer conscripts.
Alcoholism, narcotics, thievery, and individual and group fights provide
a temporary distraction from the harrowing conditions of daily life in
the service.

This general background introduces the reader to the main conflict,
which unfolds only on the last pages of the story. A fight between two
gangs – one composed mainly of former criminals, the other many of

those who are soon to be discharged – breaks out, and the servicemen who guard the punishment cells try to interfere in and end the fight. In an ensuing skirmish, one of the guards is accidentally killed by the Jewish soldier Fishel. Although no suspects have yet been identified, all those to be demobilized are detained for a few days for questioning. During this period, Konstantin Karamychev, a Russian from Moscow, denounces Fishel. He does not act out of spite or ethical considerations. After all, Fishel is on his side and has killed the guard to protect Konstantin and his friends. But Fishel's fate means little to Konstantin. Even one day of extra army service he regards as an unnecessary sacrifice. The outcome of this collision is a reflection of the general situation in the battalion, and it amplifies the atmosphere of intolerance, hatred, abuse, and exploitation of representatives of national, mostly Muslim, minorities by the Slavic majority. The author idealized the weak Fishel, the only Jew in the battalion, presenting him as an ethical model for others. The strong Konstantin, on the other hand, is portrayed as a self-centred egoist with no social conscience or personal integrity.

Most Soviet critics who commented on the novella focused little attention on its artistic quality. They ignored the hackneyed language, which is full of slang. However, they were overwhelmed by the harsh reality, and by the effect military service has on the young conscripts. Vasil' Bykov decried the fact that the military establishment has tried for years to suppress the truth about the distressing state of affairs in the Soviet Army, and he suggested that 'the truth of Kaledin's novella is not invented. It is realistic and veritable, and that is the reason for its artistic strength.'[3] The conservative *Nash sovremennik*, however, was not impressed; it criticized *Novyi mir* for having published the story in the first place and defended the Soviet armed forces from allegedly unjustified attacks, suggesting that the situation described is not typical and in poor taste.[4] Indeed, Kaledin devotes most of his attention to the general environment in the battalion, leaving little room for detailed characterization or psychological analysis. The general effect of the narrative is, however, unmistakable. The story is intense and sincere and poses important questions about a social malady of great magnitude.

Kaledin's next narrative, 'Pop i rabotnik' (The Priest and the Worker; 1991),[5] is different. It is based on the author's personal experience, his desire for a general rapprochement with the church, and an eagerness to better understand the motivation that leads to religious zeal among the faithful. The main conflict in the story is a figment of Kaledin's imagination, but the leading characters have real-life prototypes. One of them is the author himself. The action is set in a village parish some one hundred kilometres from Moscow. The priest, Father Valerii, lives in Moscow but comes regularly to the village to conduct services. The *starosta*, or lay elder, Vera Ivanovna, an old, sick peasant woman, has boundless dedication to the church. She is selfless, honest, and benevolent, taking in and caring for the ill, the infirm, and others in need. She jealously guards church property and does not trust the priest's wife, who wants to take charge of the parish's money. The author-narrator is a church employee, Babkin, a city fellow, ostensibly driven out by his wife. In fact, he has a *dacha* in the vicinity of the church, and accepts the job with the obvious intention of studying firsthand life in the parish community. In the end, when Vera Ivanovna is taken by an ambulance to the hospital, she entrusts Babkin with the secret of where the church money is hidden. But when Babkin goes to retrieve it, he is attacked by the young Tol'ka, an alcoholic with a criminal record. He is one of those who are being taken care of by the compassionate Vera Ivanovna and perform some odd jobs around the church.

The action in the story takes place some time in the first half of 1987. The church is still under the control of the State Committee for Religious Affairs, and there is still much suspicion within each parish. Most churches have been infiltrated by KGB informers, and Vera Ivanovna trusts Babkin, the outsider, more than she does anyone within her own parish. This is a sad commentary on the real state of affairs in the Soviet church. In fact, in an interview about the novella, Kaledin admitted that, in his attempt to get closer to religion, he found only one real Christian – Vera Ivanovna, who is imbued with a mystical spirit of dedication and selflessness. She is the only mainstay of Orthodoxy among the members of this parish community.[6]

Kaledin's narrative is carefully constructed, containing numerous digressions and much dialogue. Despite the fact that the actions described take place not far from the capital, the language is the vernacular of remote provincial Russia. 'Pop i rabotnik' lacks the intensity of Kaledin's earlier stories, and the melodramatic, inconclusive ending does little to alleviate the situation. The reader is left guessing about the destiny of Babkin, the health of Vera Ivanovna, and the fate of the money. But, as in the case of Kaledin's earlier stories, external intrigue is less important than the social and spiritual ramifications of the narrative. One is made to appreciate that the transition from atheism to religious affiliation and the acceptance of faith is not a simple matter. It is just as difficult as the rejection of religion forced upon those who grew up with it. Furthermore, one is made aware that, even among those who belong to the church and appear to be faithful, there are few who have not been infected with the germ of egoism and materialism and are ready and able to follow the word of God. It may take years, if not generations, before the Russian church can rid itself of the remnants of its 'socialist' past, and people turn to religion not to escape from socialist atheism but rather in response to an inner urge to fill the spiritual void.

LEONID GABYSHEV

The labour-camp theme in Soviet literature is well represented by works of writers such as A. Solzhenitsyn and Varlaam Shalamov. Leonind Gabyshev (b. 1952), one of the new authors under perestroika, introduces the reader instead to the world of young criminal offenders. Born in the city of Omsk, in Siberia, Gabyshev is a graduate of a Volgograd construction trade school. His young age notwithstanding, he has managed to work in a variety of jobs and trades, as well as spend five years incarcerated for a criminal offence. His first published work, the novel *Odlian, ili vozdukh svobody* (Odlian, or the Air of Freedom; 1989),[7] is rooted in autobiography. The main action in the novel takes place some time in the late 1960s and early 1970s at the Odlian correctional labour camp for juvenile delinquents, somewhere in the Ural mountains. In a flashback we are told the story of the young convict Kolia Petrov, the son of a former militia chief, who by the age of fifteen had become an experienced thief and hooligan.

The author paints a horrid picture of physical, mental, and sexual abuse, leading to desperation, and even suicide. The cruelty of the inmates knows no bounds. Even the weak, who are usually abused and humiliated, become vicious and cruel when the opportunity to abuse someone else arises. The camp does not correct, nor does it educate. Instead it cripples the sensitive nature of the young, leading them to conclude that, if one wants to avoid abuse, one has to beat and abuse others. One must be a slave or a torturer, as no middle road is possible. Correctional institutions for juveniles are controlled by internal 'mafias,' which are the mainstay of the camp administration. Control over the inmates is maintained by constant beating, which is administered by the so-called thieves and 'horns' – the former self-appointed strongmen, and the latter, appointed by camp management to control and intimidate the mass.

The original version of the novel, published in *Novyi mir*, portrays a world with no redeeming features, in which everything is gloomy and depressing. It is a strong indictment of the Soviet penal system. The version published in 1990 in book form contains a new chapter in which we are told that the hero's jail term has been reduced for good behaviour, and that he has turned into an exemplary worker and a champion of justice. He dreams about a former girlfriend, whom he allegedly still loves, and decides to lead, in future, a decent and honourable life. It is a positive ending, befitting a socialist-realist work.

The novel, written in 1982–3 and published in 1989–90, created an uproar among the Soviet reading public. The subject was still new and exciting, and literary critics responded accordingly. All were touched by the newly uncovered taboos of Soviet life, until recently hidden from the ordinary Soviet citizen. But once the initial enthusiasm wore off, everyone realized that *Odlian, ili vozdukh svobody* was not a great work of art; as a result, its success, based on its topicality, was short-lived.

The novel is a third-person narrative interspersed with much dialogue in which the voice of the author-narrator merges with that of the main protagonist. While the theme is interesting, the prose is pedestrian and unimaginative, and the characters poorly developed and soon forgotten. The experiences of the hero are related in great detail, but no psychological investigation is undertaken to explain the motivation of his actions. None the less, the novel is valuable for its thematic relevance and the author's sincerity. It exposes the indifference of the Soviet system of justice and its failure to protect the young who come into conflict with the law. The tone makes it clear, and the author corroborates this view, that society rather than the individual criminal is responsible for the existing situation. Gabyshev asserts that, despite the fact that, since 1900, the population of Russia only doubled, the number of prisoners today is eight times higher than that at the beginning of the century.[8] Since no official statistics relating to crime and justice have ever been published in the USSR, one can only surmise that, by eradicating the so-called remnants of bourgeois consciousness, which were closely identified with faith and religious ritual, the Soviet state undermined the spiritual foundations of the masses, thus helping to create a new class of youthful criminals.

OLEG ERMAKOV AND THE AFGHAN WAR EXPERIENCE

In 1991, the Soviet Union commemorated the fiftieth anniversary of the Nazi onslaught. Since 1941, works describing events taking place during the Second World War have occupied a dominant place in Soviet litera-ture. Close to 20 per cent of all prose fiction published in the USSR after 1945 portrayed the devastation and horrors of war, but it also glorified the heroic exploits of Soviet soldiers and officers. Furthermore, it was supposed to instil in the young a spirit of patriotism and dedication to the Soviet fatherland.

Today, the Second World War has faded into history. The few surviv-ing veterans are old and feeble, and gradually the thematic treatment of the Second World War has been relegated to historical fiction. In contem-porary fiction, it has been replaced, in part, by the recent war in Afghan-istan. But, since the nature of the two wars is different, so is the literature describing them. In the 1941–5 war, there was a clearly identifiable front line and a major enemy who was an invader. The cause of the Soviet Army was just, and the defence of one's motherland was a moral obliga-tion and a legal duty. Hence, despite artistic and interpretative distinc-tions in the works about the Second World War by writers as diverse as V. Bykov, Iu. Bondarev, G. Baklanov, and V. Kondrat'ev, the main objec-tives of the war were never questioned, and the justice of the Soviet cause was never in doubt.

The case of the war in Afghanistan is different. Despite the fact that hostilities there lasted twice as long as those during the Second World War, little was known about its background and history. It was, in a sense, a secret war, taboo to the Soviet people. It was a war without a single front line, a readily identifiable enemy, or a clear objective. Soviet soldiers were invaders and strangers in a foreign and hostile country. The vague notion that, by supporting the Afghan revolutionary Marxist regime, Soviet soldiers were fulfilling important international obliga-tions convinced few participants of the justice of their cause.

One of the first writers to deal with the subject of Afghanistan was A. Prokhanov. His novel *Derevo v tsentre Kabula* (A Tree in the Centre of Kabul; 1982) provides a slanted account of the existing situation. There is nothing in the novel to indicate that the Soviet troops are intruders; rather, the novel suggests that they are in Afghanistan to help and pro-tect the local population. In another novel, *Risunki batalista* (The Draw-ings of a Battle-Painter; 1986), published in the days of glasnost, Prokhanov does describe some battle scenes between Soviet soldiers and Afghan anti-communist warriors, but the main emphasis is political and ideological. It glorifies the dedication and determination of Soviet sol-diers and advances the notion that war develops a number of positive human qualities in them. The war in Afghanistan is presented by Prokhanov in the context of a global confrontation between American and international imperialism and the progressive revolutionary forces, supported by the Soviet Union.

By the end of the 1980s, the Afghan disaster was no longer a secret to anyone in the Soviet Union. After a period of long negotiations, the last Soviet soldiers finally abandoned Afghanistan in February 1989. This is when truthful and objective narratives, portraying the Afghan débâcle, began to appear. Most of these works, written by young war veterans of the lower ranks, demobilized after the war from active service, are based on personal experience. The authors relate stories about army service under the conditions of war and provide horrifying accounts of combat, viewed through the prism of their own perception.

Oleg Ermakov (b. 1961) stands out most prominently among the writers belonging to this group. A native and resident of the Smolensk region in central Russia, he made his literary debut in 1987, at the young age of twenty-six, with the publication of a short sketch in the December issue of *Oktiabr'*. His first stories 'Kreshchenie' (Baptism; 1989) and 'Zheltaia gora' (The Yellow Mountain; 1989),[9] followed by 'Blagopoluchnoe vozvrashchenie' (Safe Return; 1989)[10] and 'Afganskie rasskazy' (Afghan Stories; 1989),[11] immediately attracted the attention of critics and the reading public. Ermakov's early stories are limited to the portrayal of isolated episodes in the life of Soviet soldiers in Afghanistan. 'Kreshchenie' and 'Zheltaia gora' deal with issues of ethical adaptation to conditions of extreme cruelty and brutality. In 'Kreshchenie,' Ermakov introduces a conflict similar to the one presented by V. Kondrat'ev in 'Sashka' (Sashka; 1979). Kondrat'ev's hero refuses to obey an order to kill a German prisoner of war. Ermakov's protagonist refuses to follow the example of his fellow soldiers and shoot an Afghan rebel, who has taken part in the murder of their Soviet colleagues.

Examples of moral courage, however, are few and far apart in the new literature about Afghanistan. The general picture which emerges from Ermakov's fiction is one of callousness, violence, abuse, and tyranny – not only in scenes of warfare on the battlefield, but also in those depicting life during the temporary suspension of hostilities. Life in military encampments in Afghanistan has little in common with the idealized and romanticized notion of brotherhood-in-arms. It is reminiscent, rather, of the conditions depicted in Kaledin's 'Stroibat' (Construction Battalion; 1989), where the law of the jungle reigns, and the older and more experienced servicemen mercilessly abuse and terrorize the new conscripts, while officers and commanders look on coldly and indifferently.

'Afganskie rasskazy' comprises six impressionistic sketches about the effects of an aimless war on those who are directly involved in it, as well as on those who remain behind in the hinterland. The first sketch sets the tone. In it, two nameless young people, apparently in love, dream about a beautiful future together. They intend to dedicate their lives to a worthy cause by teaching school in a remote Russian village. He treats lightly his forthcoming army service. After all, two years is a short period of time, and ever after they will live happily together. In the last sketch, she, a village teacher, anticipates his return to her as he is already on his way back from Afghanistan. Instead, she receives a letter notifying her of his death. Between the introductory and concluding sketches, the stories depict the life of Soviet soldiers in the combat zone. Each story has a different set of characters and relates a different incident, scene, or fate. The cumulative result is disheartening. Precious life is lost for a cause few understand or appreciate. The war brings out in its participants the worst traits of character. The net effect on those who survive is corruption of the flesh and spirit. One seldom encounters in these stories expressions of patriotism or calls for the victory of world revolution. The soldiers are little interested in the general war effort. Ermakov's Afghan stories are realistic in conception but moderate in tone. Shocking details are rendered with circumspection, which invests them with an air of sincerity. He presents well the general atmosphere of gloom and the sense of futility which have a negative psychological effect on the servicemen.

'Kolokol'nia' (Belfry; 1990)[12] is another of Ermakov's Afghanistan stories. It is a first-person narrative in which the surface realism is intercut with a dream-like, nostalgic flashback to the narrator's life in his native village. There we are introduced to his grandfather as well as to his unnamed wife and son. As the narrator prepares to join the army in Afghanistan, he and his son are baptized, since, according to the grandfather, one does not go to war without submitting to the religious rites of baptism. In the few war scenes described, the reader is exposed to accounts of aimless cruelty. War for an obscure cause, and without a clear objective, breeds resentment, evil, and hatred towards everyone and everything.

The village church was destroyed and desecrated in the days of Soviet rule by the same government that today sends its young people to a useless and, perhaps, criminal war. The bell tower, its bell missing, is at once a reminder of the past and the only symbol of hope for the future. This symbolism is also manifest in the act of baptism which signifies spiritual renewal. The grandfather still retains some values from the past, and he passes them on, through a renewal of identification with the church, to his grandson and great-grandson. Interestingly, there is no mention in the story of the narrator's parents. Those born and raised in the days of Stalin and Brezhnev are apparently viewed as lost souls, incapable of redemption. The religious dimensions of the story take the reader onto a new plane. Disillusioned with the atheistic doctrine of a government which has deceived its sons, many young people find themselves in a social and spiritual vacuum and turn to the church in their search for new values and hopes.

Ermakov's first novel, *Znak zveria* (Sign of the Beast; 1992),[13] is similar in style, subject, and tone to his earlier stories. It is a realistic third-person narrative, interspersed with some lyrical digression, flashbacks, and much dialogue, and interwoven with some first person portrayal and meditations. The effect of *Znak zveria* on its readers is cumulative. It provides a broad canvas of events in Afghanistan, as they are perceived by the private Cherepakha. The narrator is a good observer. He does not preach, nor does he judge anybody; rather, he presents seemingly disconnected episodes from the life of a Soviet artillery detachment – accounts of combat, movement from place to place, relations with the local population, and the interaction with Afghan pro-Soviet military units. He also describes life within Soviet army detachments, emphasizing the interrelationship between different levels of military personnel. Each chapter is set in a different environment, in which different characters collide in different ways. The major conflict is the war itself, and its solution is beyond the reach and understanding of the simple soldier.

Unlike the Second World War, in which everyone was fighting for a common cause, in Afghanistan each soldier or officer fights his own private war for survival, attempting to reach his own limited objectives. The Soviet soldier in Afghanistan finds himself in a world full of enemies. He is confronted by armed Afghan partisans, and by a civil population who hate the invaders; he is suspicious of his ostensible allies, the Afghan pro-Soviet army, and also faces constant adversity within his own military unit. Even the environment is hostile, with a difficult climate and unfriendly mountainous terrain. In the end, life in conditions of enduring abuse and tension takes its toll. It leads some to passive submission; others resort to more resolute steps, such as suicide and desertion.

The thirst of the Soviet military force engaged in this futile endeavour seems endless and insatiable. It requires new sacrifices every day and takes its toll on both body and soul. The novel exposes convincingly the corrupting effect war has on the young conscripts. They become addicted to drugs and alcohol. They rob the local population and steal from each other. The few female members of the service unabashedly sell their bodies for money to any officer who will pay the price. The war brings to the fore the most negative qualities in human nature, and the worst animal instincts often guide the actions of those engaged in military service. Furthermore, brutality in an army comprising many different nationalities takes on a more pronounced ethnic tinge. Ermakov does not dwell on the psychology of his characters, but the motivational factors which induce them to act are evident. Everyone is utterly alone in this hostile world. There is no one to rely on. The soldiers count continuously the days remaining to the end of service, in hope that good luck and sheer chance will spare them.

Ermakov is certainly a talented writer. His style is personal and unobtrusive, and he writes with an economical use of words, and he describes a harsh and tragic reality with due restraint and objectivity. Despite some compositional artificiality, and the lack of thorough psychological analysis, he draws characters that are believable and true to life. He avoids the use of clichés and shuns figurative speech, but employs metaphoric language in his description of nature. Ermakov's hero appears in different works under different names but is essentially the same man, with the same outlook on life. The conflicts and descriptive detail in different stories are also similar, and the plots are always confined to definite time limits. The action usually begins with the commencement of service and arrival in Afghanistan and ends with the discharge from active duty and the return to the Soviet Union. An acute sense of time is present in all his works: everyone is biding time in the hope of survival. The discharge from army service and the return from Afghanistan are portrayed as an ascent from hell. But in real life the alleged newly acquired freedom is an illusion because there is little positive in store for the injured and brutalized souls and bodies of the Afghan veterans. Ermakov's plots are traditional and realistic, but the structure of his recent novel is somewhat disjointed. The characters find themselves in conditions of utmost physical and emotional tension, yet the conclusion of the novel is anti-climactic: the soldiers are discharged and return to the Soviet Union, and one may make the erroneous deduction that all the strain, accumulated over the years of service, suddenly evaporates.

Ermakov has made a name for himself in Russian literature while still under age thirty. He is not a professional writer or journalist. In fact, he works at an institution which predicts the weather. It is not my intention to predict his future, but one wonders whether Ermakov will be able to expand his horizons beyond the Afghanistan débâcle. Since he is already repeating himself by dealing with similar conflicts and descriptive detail in different works, it is possible to surmise that the well of autobiographical experience will soon become exhausted. It remains to be seen whether, in the future, his creative imagination will be able to match his language and narrative skills.

The grim picture of the Afghan war, described by Oleg Ermakov, is reinforced in the documentary prose of Svetlana Aleksievich. She has taped interviews with more than sixty individuals whose fates have become entangled with the Afghanistan calamity and produced a narrative entitled *Tsinkovye mal'chiki* (Boys in Metal Coffins; 1990),[14] about the effects of war on its survivors. The book includes interviews with servicemen of different rank, as well as with mothers and wives of those killed in combat.

The dehumanizing effect of war is evident in the reminiscences of most veterans. It is difficult to kill for the first time, but later the thirst for blood becomes natural and difficult to ignore. The Afghan experience unsettles the mind of its participants. It fractures their mental equilibrium and destroys the established balance of social and ethical values. After the war some remember fondly their experiences in the shadow of death, which they view as an extreme form of freedom in life, void of all moral and physical chains. But most veterans try to forget their horrible past because dwelling on it interferes with their adaptation to the new conditions of peace. However, those injured and crippled can never forget or forgive because their future has been ruined by their past. The memory of Afghanistan will always be with them. Some veterans attempt to escape from their past by seeking redemption and spiritual renewal in faith. Several Afghan veterans have enroled in the Zagorsk theological seminary with the purpose of joining the ranks of the clergy.

It is clear that the end of the Afghan war marks the beginning of its literary investigation, and it may take years before autobiographical and documentary emphasis is supplemented by deep psychological and historical analysis. The current literature about the war in Afghanistan is limited to a narrow personal perspective. It does not deal with broader issues of historical and political significance. It avoids addressing the internal situation in the country, and it does not portray or discuss the enemy on the battlefield. An all-embracing and psychologically impressive picture of the Afghan war requires knowledge, creative imagination, artistic skill, and, most important, time.

In the meantime, however, there are already signs that supporters of the old regime are trying to suppress the truth about the terrible past and to muzzle those who bring it out into the open. Thus, under the pressure of those who support the old Soviet myth, several Afghan veterans interviewed by Aleksievich have denied the accuracy of the statements attributed to them and have taken the author to court, accusing her of calumny. The proposed trial, in the Belorussian capital, Minsk, is in fact a trial against the freedom of speech, and a sign that the fledgling democracy in the former Soviet Union is still in danger.[15]

ALEKSANDR TEREKHOV

Early in 1988 the weekly *Nedelia* (The Week) published the story 'Durachok' (The Little Fool) by the then unknown writer Aleksandr Terekhov (b. 1966). In his literary debut, Terekhov exhibited a degree of maturity and skill usually not demonstrated by young novice authors. A native of the Tula region, and, at that time, a student of the faculty of journalism at Moscow State University, Terekhov worked, prior to army service, as a correspondent for a provincial newspaper. He currently lives in Moscow and is a contributor to the journal *Ogonek* (Small Light).

'Durachok' is based on the writer's personal experience, and it deals with the so-called *dedovshchina*, or the abuse of young conscripts by their older peers in the Soviet army. The story generated much critical attention in unexpected non-literary quarters. The military press, as well as various war veterans' groups, have accused Terekhov of slander and betrayal. 'Durachok' was followed by two other narratives, 'Zema. Ironicheskii dnevnik' (Zema. Ironic Diary; 1989),[16] and 'Memuary srochnoi sluzhby' (Memoirs of a Conscript; 1991),[17] dealing with the same subject.

Terekhov is not the first to expose the difficult lot of the Soviet soldier, and the ruthless conditions of army service in the USSR. This theme was initiated in Soviet literature in the early days of glasnost by Iurii Poliakov, in his 'Sto dnei do prikaza' (One Hundred Days before the Order; 1987). But, whereas Poliakov provides a prosaic and fictionalized account of the difficult lot of Russian soldiers, Terekhov claims that he writes about himself, and for himself, and without any initial intention to publish his confession.[18] Furthermore, despite his young age, Terekhov is a more accomplished craftsman than Poliakov. He uses army vernacular in moderation and is still able to retain his appreciation for good taste. Nor does he generalize: he describes the cruelty and brutality of some, pointing, at the same time, to the good human qualities in others. In 'Zema,' which was initially intended to be part of a larger narrative, Terekhov derides and brings down to the ordinary human level the figure of the commander – an old general. Following the example of Dostoevsky, in *Zapiski iz mertvogo doma* (The House of the Dead; 1862) he hints that the purpose of a uniform is to cover up human imperfection in general, and the fallibility of each individual in particular. Terekhov illustrates how the harsh reality of army life can turn an individual into a passive tool and an object of abuse at the same time. The duties and responsibilities of a soldier in the Soviet army are ill defined, and it may appear from the story that conscripts serve their immediate superiors rather than the state.

'Memuary srochnoi sluzhby' comprises a number of sketches, scenes, and character outlines that provide a realistic picture of the daily life of the simple soldier. Each episode centres on a different conflict and helps form the general panorama of army life. The picture that emerges is depressing. *Dedovshchina* is a strict system of social stratification, determined by the length of time one spends in the army. *Dedy* (grandfathers) are soldiers in their last months of service, soon to be discharged. By virtue of their self-imposed, alleged superiority, and according to unwritten rules never sanctioned by anyone but respected by most, including officers, they are free to abuse and humiliate any soldier who dares not to submit. Terekhov illustrates, in his story, the irony of daily army existence. At first, young conscripts suffer from ill treatment and abuse, but, when newer conscripts arrive, they vent their anger and frustration on the newcomers. The first year of service, full of humiliation, deprivation, and loss of human dignity, turns many soldiers into cruel and callous beasts, and those who refuse to submit or betray are punished and suffer terribly. No wonder some are driven to desertion, even suicide. There is no justice for the simple conscript, just terror. The message of Terekhov's stories is clear: the romantic notion of brotherhood-in-arms is a sham. Instead of preparing young people for a productive life, army service cripples them in body and spirit. The weak often break down and are later in life unable to cope with the problems of daily existence; those who are strong continue to exhibit the brutality to which they have become accustomed in army life.

'Zimnii den' nachala novoi zhizni' (The Wintry Day of the Beginning of a New Life; 1991),[19] another novella by Terekhov, is set in a different environment. Army barracks are here replaced by a dormitory, and, instead of being soldiers, the actors are students. The action takes place in the late 1980s in Moscow. The author presents an unidealized picture of Soviet student life and illustrates the effect of glasnost and perestroika on the Soviet school. Old values are questioned, and social decay and corruption penetrate the bastions of higher education. Depravity, thievery, and debauchery are no longer hidden under the surface and are the order of the day. The hero, Grachev, appears to be a decent young man. He is for freedom and against dogmatic ideology, but he is also an eccentric and a dreamer, obsessed with the fear of rats, real or imagined, which allegedly infest the dormitory. This fear develops into a phobia, symbolizing the fear of life. Grachev studies geography, but he is also an amateur writer. He composes a novel about revolutionaries who realize, in the end, that they have wasted their lives, as does Grachev. He is overwhelmed by the injustice and degeneracy that surround him. All his life he tries in vain to escape evil. He wants to be honest, but he lives in a world in which there is little room for his positive aspirations to flourish. There is no escape from the dormitory, just as there is no way to flee the army barracks. The dormitory is a microcosm of society in general. In the end, Grachev breaks down. On the final pages of the novella we encounter him in a hospital ward of what appears to be a mental institution.

Terekhov writes in the tradition of Russia critical realism. His new themes often shock the Russian reader, but his plots and his approach to the treatment of his heroes are conventional. He relies in his works on psychological portrayal, internal monologue, and dialogue. His language is intense but soft, modulated with irony, and includes the colloquial vernacular of the population strata described.

Terekhov is one of the youngest Russian writers to appear on the literary scene in the days of perestroika. He submitted his first story to a respectable publication while still in his early twenties. It is surely an extraordinary occurrence for Soviet literature. 'Young' writers in the Soviet Union have usually been in their forties. No wonder Terekhov feels lonely among his older colleagues. He does not share their scepticism and cynicism. He feels that most of those who have matured in the 1960s have succumbed to communist pressures and have compromised their integrity. According to him, they have no right any longer to aspire to cultural or spiritual leadership and should remove themselves from positions of influence. Terekhov comes into Russian literature with a new consciousness, which while still influenced by Soviet education is little tainted by practical life experience under communist rule – hence, his idealism and his initial belief in the possibility of the victory of justice. But as the fate of some of his characters illustrates, it is difficult, if not impossible, to be part of a social structure and avoid its influence.

Only time will reveal the future course in the development of Terekhov's talent. One hopes that his liberal optimism will foster the creation of new, accomplished works of art, unblemished by his lack of tolerance for his older colleagues. V. Rasputin, much admired by Terekhov, also started out as an idealist, but unfortunately turned from a talented creative artist into a rabid conservative nationalist pamphleteer.[20]

MARINA PALEI

Marina Palei is one of the new talented Russian female prose writers whose name became known in the early 1990s. She is a resident of St Petersburg, and a medical professional for whom literature is not a hobby but rather a calling. She has tried her hand at poetry and criticism, but has finally settled on prose fiction. Her first work to appear in a major journal, the novella 'Evgesha i Annushka' (Evgesha and Annushka; 1990), was published in *Znamia*.[21] It attracted wide critical attention, and received positive reviews.[22] The story, set in a small communal apartment, is told in the first person by an inconspicuous female narrator, apparently a medical student. The main characters are two old women, Evgesha and Annushka. At the centre is the selfless, submissive, and charitable Annushka, a former factory worker now 'resting from life' in retirement. Poverty does not break her spirit; on the contrary, it makes her more compassionate to the suffering of others. Evgesha, a retired nurse, is six years younger and still active. She is proper, disciplined, hard-working, and, above all, just. Life has been difficult for both women. Neither has children, but both treat their distant relatives with affection and understanding. Annushka lives a virtuous life and dies as a saint, refusing to be a burden on others and making appropriate preparations for her own demise.

The structure of the story is somewhat fragmented, but compositional unity is provided by ethical and spiritual harmony. There is no major central conflict in the novella, just an illustration of the progression of simple but difficult life. The story can be read as an indictment of the Soviet system, which fails to provide its citizens with decent living quarters and its old people with adequate means for survival. But such an interpretation oversimplifies the issue. The social message of the story is hidden deep under the surface. The narrator's compassionate tone alludes to the reality that suffering may ennoble. She treats her characters with respect, and as Annushka does, believes in the goodness and honesty of people, and in the need to have compassion for fellow humans.

The author's medical background is also apparent in the story 'Otdelenie propavshikh' (The Ward of Those Ruined; 1991).[23] The action is set in an obstetrical ward of a hospital in a remote Russian provincial town. Other than the two male ward physicians, all of the characters are female. The older doctor displays some compassion for his patients, but the younger one, who has just arrived from Leningrad, is cynical and abusive, and enjoys his power over women in trouble. We learn about the life of this obstetrical ward from the brief dialogues between the doctors and their patients. The picture that emerges is one of backwardness, ignorance, and suffering. Most women, unable to protect themselves from their abusive partners, come to seek abortions, the only means of birth control available to them. Palei appreciates the difficult lot of these women, but she does not moralize. Nor does she blame anyone for their distress and helplessness. The picture presented evokes pity and sympathy for those in need.

In 'Kabiriia s Obvodnogo kanala' (Cabiriia from By-Pass Canal Street; 1991),[24] Palei presents the life story of a woman whose sex drive is portrayed as an insatiable craving for life. The story is an expression of optimism and hope, of overcoming adversity and most difficulties of daily existence. Despite her poor health, the main character, Raimonda, gives vent to her inner thirst for life and lives to the fullest. Her sexual drive is presented as a force able to return her to good health from a condition in which death is imminent. The implication is not that Raimonda's behaviour is ethical, but rather that sexual temptation is stronger than reason. In the story, Palei addresses the issue of female sexuality, a subject taboo until recently in Russian literature. However, intimate scenes are not described, and infidelity and other vices are mentioned only in passing.

The story 'Reis' (The Trip; 1993)[25] relates the emotional outburst of a woman obsessed with her former husband and lover. Although she has been separated from him for nine years, his image continues to dominate her consciousness. The nameless first-person narrator buys a return plane ticket to Montreal in order to be able to travel and talk to her former husband, who is booked on the same flight. Much is left unsaid in the story, and we know little about the actual relationship of these two people. Yet there are hints that the heroine carries a gun and, before embarking on her return flight to Russia, might have killed her former husband at Mirabel airport.

The story is told in the form of an internal monologue alternating with dialogue between the narrator and the invisible man. It sounds like the mad ravings of a desperate woman. Reality is presented through the prism of the narrator's deformed perception, reflecting the psychological state of mind of an individual who is hurt by fate and craves recognition. The stream of consciousness that springs from her morbid disposition is a combination of the real, the surrealistic, and the imagined, indiscriminately interwoven.

Marina Palei presents in her prose life from a woman's perspective. Most of her narrators are female, as are her main characters. Except in 'Reis,' the narrator's role is limited. Palei exhibits thematic variety in her stories. Her prose is realistic, yet stylistically diverse. Her most recent story is a departure from her former narrative mode. In it, she delves into the surrealistic, employing complex language and sacrificing clarity for external effect. It remains to be seen whether this change is temporary or is an indication that Palei is ready to experiment with prose and move in a modernist direction.

ANDREI MATVEEV

Ekstsentr-labirint (Eccentricity-Labyrinth) is a new journal began as a joint venture of Leningrad and Sverdlovsk writers. The title of the journal, and its place of publication, reflect, in a sense, the unstable conditions of the day. The original names of the cities in question have been changed since to St Petersburg and Ekaterinburg, respectively, and the monolithic, highly centralized Soviet state has ceased to exist. According to one of the journal's editors, Vladimir Kharitonov, the complicated, irregular structure of a labyrinth, which refers in many ways to the current state of affairs in Russia, symbolizes 'the entanglement of human fate, the contradictory state of the universe, and the might of omniscient divine wisdom.'[26]

The novel *Istoriia Lorimura ili obretenie very* (The Story of Lorimur, or the Discovery of Faith),[27] by the aspiring author Andrei Matveev, which appeared in *Ekstsentr-labirint* in 1991, affirms Kharitonov's assertion. It is a story about young people who have rejected the values inculcated in the days of Brezhnev's stagnation and have become internal émigrés in their own country. In the first half of the novel, the narrator tells the story of his friend Lorimur. In the second half, he recounts his own life experience. Lorimur is a selfless truth seeker in quest of a higher spirituality that transcends the mediocrity and mendacity of daily life in Brezhnev's Russia. He is ostensibly imbued with some mystical powers and exercises great influence over those who come into contact with him. Lorimur escapes the life he abhors by joining some eastern cult, and spends most of his days in the region of the Himalayan mountains. He is killed in enigmatic circumstances, during the early stages of the Afghan war, but his body disappears in mysterious fashion from the cave where it was last seen. The narrator's path is different. He rejects official ideology but cannot rid himself completely of the effects of Soviet brainwashing. He withdraws from life and takes a job in a zoo, closer to nature and away from social decay. The influence of Lorimur on the narrator is overpowering, but, instead of turning to a foreign religion, the latter seeks an answer to his problems in Christianity.

Matveev's novel is the story of a lost generation. It is a tale about those who have become alienated from the mainstream of Soviet life and have refused to acquiesce to the demands of the regime. In the end, the spiritual vacuum created by the repudiation of official ideology is filled by ardent faith. It is interesting to note that, structurally, the novel is set between two important milestones in Soviet history: the Prague Spring of 1968 and the Afghan war, which began in 1979. The change in the character of Lorimur begins after his return with his parents from Czechoslovakia in 1968, and it concludes with his mysterious Christ-like disappearance during the Afghan war. The novel makes clear that young people in Soviet Russia have been greatly affected by these two events: in particular, repression resulting from the Prague Spring, and the rout of socialism with a human face that ushered in the era of Brezhnev's stagnation, fostering total submission and destroying all hope for freedom, and, in turn, resulting in the Afghan war, which laid bare the vacuous essence of official Soviet ideology and hastened the disintegration of the Soviet state.

The novel, narrated in the first person, begins with a story within a story; the second half is narrated in confessional style. Lorimur's diaries form the basis of much of the narrative. Notes, reminiscences, dialogue, and opinions expressed by various characters are loosely connected, but the novel is held together by the image of the omniscient narrator, who is also the protagonist.

Matveev is a writer of promise, but his talent and skills are descriptive rather than analytical. He addresses important philosophical and psychological issues in the novel, but his analysis often lacks depth, and the actions of his heroes are not always as convincing as one might wish. The search for faith and spirituality is a complex endeavour, and great skill is required to describe it convincingly. In Matveev's novel, the reader learns what the heroes are seeking but is not sure of the actual essence of their discovery – a point further obscured by the fact that the search for God Matveev treats not as an abstract venture but as a practical effort to fill a void in the hearts and minds of his heroes.

IRINA POLIANSKAIA

Irina Polianskaia, a native of the Cheliabinsk region, is a professionally trained actress and a graduate of the Literary Institute in Moscow. Her prose is conventional, but her style is highly individualistic. Her language is poetic and complex and requires careful reading, and is infused with a musicality of expression, containing unexpected metaphors, word play, and exact comparisons. Most of her stories are told in the first person by a female narrator, and the focus of the author's psychological investigation is chiefly her female characters. Her first stories appeared in *Avrora* (Avrora) and *Literaturnaia ucheba* (Literary Studies), but her best-known work is the novella 'Predlagaemye obstoiatel'stva' (Proposed Circumstances).[28]

The novella is a family drama in three parts. Part one is set in 1957, when the Stratonov family – father, mother, and two small daughters – is still together. Then, Stratonov, a scientist, abandons his wife, Marina, a teacher, and marries his assistant, Natasha. Parts two and three take place some fifteen years later. The daughters, Gelia and Taia, are now students, and their mother is leading a lonely life, full of despair. After the family breaks up, there is no communication between father and children.

The narrative structure is complex and original: first-person narration by Gelia, Taia, and Marina is intertwined with third-person narration. Much of the story is related in direct speech by Gelia to her sister, Taia. The family history is unravelled with the help of numerous flashbacks, internal monologue, and quotations from letters. Gelia's determination to learn the truth about her family's past is propelled by the discovery of old letters and notes hidden by her mother.

There is a sense of tragedy in the story, of irreparable loss. A family that appears to be essentially good is destroyed for no apparent reason. The story intimates that, as hard as people try, they cannot avoid the snares of fate, and everyone is responsible for the consequences of his or her actions. The theme of time dragging people into the unknown is also addressed. The young people rebel against the inevitable submission to the dark forces of destiny and voice a desire and determination to remove the causes of human suffering and family trouble.

'Predlagaemye obstoiatel'stva' appears to follow the tradition of Soviet *byt* literature, but only on the surface. In *byt* literature, the emphasis is mostly on extramarital affairs, infidelity, and the moral decay of family and society. There is nothing of that kind in Polianskaia's novella: no love scenes, family squabbles, or infidelities are described; rather, we see the family conflict through the innocent eyes of the children who are eager to understand their own background. The author devotes her attention to the investigation of the impact of family break-up on mother and children. They appear to suffer most, through no fault of their own. The novella does have some shortcomings: characterization is inadequate, and some conflicts remain unresolved; we learn little about what moves the male characters. But, as Alla Latynina suggested, the extraordinary sincerity of lyrical confession helps the reader follow this slow-moving narrative and holds his or her attention.[29]

Most of Polianskaia's short stories concentrate on a single incident or episode. They are rich in subtle insights, and many have social and psychological ramifications. The story 'Kak provozhaiut parokhody' (How You See Steamers Off; 1988)[30] is a sentimental account of unrequited love by a teenage girl for a passing sailor. And the story 'Igra' (The Game; 1988)[31] relates an accidental encounter between two girls who communicate and understand each other perfectly well without uttering a word. The story 'Chistaia zona' (Clear Zone; 1991)[32] is a first-person narrative by a nameless woman admitted to a hospital for what appears to be cancer surgery. The focus in the story is not on the patient's physical condition, but rather on her state of mind and her moods. Through her postoperative ruminations, we realize that her father, an eminent scientist involved in secret research for the Soviet government, has been incarcerated by Stalin's henchmen. It appears that many residents of the region in question have been exposed to dangerous levels of radiation and, now, many years later, are paying the price.

In the story, Polianskaia investigates the state of mind of a woman in extraordinary circumstances. We know little about her life in the external world she inhabits, but we become familiar with her inner world and her emotional experiences. We witness how the change in her physical condition alters her perspective on reality and affects her mental state and temperament. The title of the story, 'Chistaia zona,' has symbolic meaning; it refers to the operating room, where everything is sanitized and where the patient, removed from the daily realities of this world, faces the surgeon's knife. It pertains also to the ostensibly clean, restricted area of the research camp, isolated and removed from the outside world. Paradoxically, the interrogator in charge of the heroine's father's case is a namesake of Gogol's fallen hero Bashmachkin. This eppisode symbolizes the fact that the cream of society has been locked up in prison, while those at the bottom of the social ladder, and incompetent to lead, were in charge.

Polianskaia is an author of promise. Her approach is episodic, even impressionistic, but sincere and insightful. The structure of her stories is original, and her perspective is subtle. She treats her heroines with understanding and compassion. On the surface, her plots appear to be simple, but they reveal the underlying complexities of human nature and human relationships. Her language is complex, and not always easy to follow, but those who master it are rewarded with multiple perspectives and insights.

ALEKSANDR ROSLIAKOV

The independent literary almanac *Konets veka* (The End of the Century) first appeared in January 1991 in Moscow. It publishes former samizdat literature, as well as contemporary prose by authors such as V. P'etsukh, V. Makanin, and V. Aksenov. One of its early contributors, instrumental in the preparation of the first issue and responsible for the choice of its title, is Aleksandr Rosliakov (b. 1954). Despite the fact that he had published two collections of prose (*Chuzhoe i svoe* [Someone Else's and One's Own] and *Piat' shagov* [Five Steps]), his novella 'Such'i petli' (The Loops of a Bitch; 1991)[33] had been rejected by most established journals in Moscow.

'Such'i petli' begins with a scene in which a woman is hitting a dog on a leash. The bitch runs in circles, trying to avoid punishment. Five other dogs stand idly by and watch the spectacle. The Russian word *such'i* has a double meaning: it may refer to the Russian *suka*, a bitch, as well as to *suk*, a bough or a thorn. In this case, both interpretations are applicable. The introductory passage is a metaphor for the fate of the heroine who, like the dog, is tethered by the thorny loops of life. She faces iniquity alone, while the world looks on with indifference at her degradation.

The novella recounts the confession of a prostitute, who tells her life story to a film-maker. She begs him not to use her in one of his forthcoming films since she still hopes to begin a new life, and fears that being seen in incriminating circumstances may hurt her future. It is a touching story of the use and abuse of a young trusting soul. She tries to protect her virginity but is, little by little, pushed down by circumstances of life into the abyss of corruption and moral decay. Despite the fact that the main protagonist is a prostitute, sex is not the primary subject of the story and intimacies and sex scenes are not explicitly described. In this work, the fate of the fallen woman is emblematic of the unpredictability of fate and the reality that good intentions do not always lead to similar results. The heroine fails in her positive endeavours because she is trusting and not ready to cope with her callous and cruel environment.

The narration comprises long paragraphs of vernacular and slang, interspersed with racy dialogue and philosophical digressions by the first-person narrator. The narrator and the heroine are nameless, and no specific reference is made to time or locale, with the result that the situation described can apply to Soviet society in general. There is a certain intensity in the story. Having lost faith in humankind, the heroine is, at first, hesitant to tell the truth, but, after a while, is willing to find relief from her pain in confession. The fact that she is drunk and desperate adds a touch of sincerity to the story, but the reader is predisposed to accept her account at face value because no other perspective is offered. The message of the story is simple but forceful: it is difficult for an honest single young woman to preserve her dignity in an evil world.

In addition to the writers discussed, a number of new authors of the realistic stream have already managed to make a mark on the literary scene. One of them is Liudmila Ulitskaia (b. 1938), a writer of plays for the stage and screen who has recently begun to produce prose fiction. Her novella 'Sonechka' (Sonechka; 1992)[34] was short-listed for the 1993 Booker Russian Novel Prize. It is a perceptive account of a love triangle in which the submissive and selfless heroine is pleased with her husband's newly found happiness. Ulitskaia does not moralize: she sees good in everyone and treats her characters with subtlety and understanding.

Works by Iurii Buida, Genadii Golovin, and Ol'ga Novikova were nominated for the 1994 Booker Prize. Buida's 'Don Domino' (The Domino-Players 1993)[35] is a tragic tale about people at a remote railway station, deep in Russia's hinterland. The station serves some secret purpose, allegedly for the good of the country. But people there are kept in the dark, and anyone who seeks the truth is destroyed. A mysterious train, racing through the night to an unknown destination, symbolizes the vile force that oppresses the people. The hero, Ardab'ev, nicknamed

Don Domino, serves the state selflessly. He asks no questions because only ignorance can give him peace of mind. But, in the end, he realizes that the motherland has deceived him, and he blows up all the installations and commits suicide. The story is an allegory and a strong indictment of the Soviet regime. By forcing people to forget their past and renounce any hope for the future, the state drives them into bondage. The story has some artistic shortcomings – character portrayal is obscure, love scenes lack intimacy, and narration is often monotonous – but the message of the story is unmistakable: any system that serves a futile cause is, in the end, bound to destroy itself and ravage its subjects in the process.

Golovin's 'Pokoi i volia' (At Peace and Liberty; 1993)[36] is a first-person autobiographical account interspersed with insightful digressions about love, life, nature, and the creative process. The narrative occupies the hazy domain where fact, fiction, and biography merge. The author expresses his love for animals and faith in the goodness of ordinary people, and believes that poverty is no deterrant to happiness. Although the story does not lack interest, its message is not always convincing. Except for the author-narrator, most of the characters, including his beloved wife, remain obscure.

Ol'ga Novikova's first novel, *Zhenskii roman* (A Woman's Novel; 1993)[37] attempted to provide a picture of life in the Soviet writers' community and of the workings of the publishing business in the USSR. The noval's heroine is the honest, hard-working, but naïve editor Zhenia Selenina who, after two unsuccessful love affairs, finally finds a man worthy of her attention. The subject of the novel is not new. Iu. Trifonov dealt at some length, in his novellas, with similar issues, and with greater ease and subtlety, and, most important, in a language and style that are vastly superior to Novikova's pedestrian prose.

Except for Terekhov, who is still in his twenties, most of the writers discussed here are in their thirties and forties. They became known to the reading public in the late 1980s and early 1990s and had published nothing prior to perestroika. Most of these writers follow the traditions of Russian conventional realism; however, some – for example, Marina Palei – have recently begun to experiment with style. Others – for example, Kaledin and Terekhov – make attempts at thematic diversity. In general, however, variety does not come easily to most young Russian writers. Thus, Oleg Ermakov, one of the better-known young writers, has gained prominence for his narratives depicting the Afghan débâcle;

however, his recent attempts at thematic diversity are a failure. His short narrative 'Freski goroda Goroukhshchi' (The Frescos in the Town of Goroukhshchi; 1993)[38] is set in the Middle Ages. It is rich in religious overtones, and its main characters are mythological and historical figures. Yet the narrative lacks clarity, its structure is confusing, and it fails to excite the reader. Similarly, the experimental 'Chaepitie v preddverii' (Tea-Drinking at the Threshold; 1993),[39] in which Ermakov attempts to explore the relationship between reality, dream, and artistic creation, lacks the lucidity, sensitivity, and emotional authenticity of his Afghan stories. Artistic variety is one of the signs of creative maturity, but it may take years for young writers to master the art of diversity.

B. Eclectic Prose

MARK KHARITONOV

One of the most important literary events of 1992 was the award of the First Booker Prize for the best Russian novel of the year to Mark Kharitonov for his *Linii sud'by, ili sunduchok Milashevicha* (Lines of Fate, or Milashevich's Little Trunk; 1992).[40] Kharitonov (b. 1937) was born in Zhitomir, Ukraine, but grew up and spent most of his life in Moscow. A little-known essayist, translator, and prose writer, he began writing fiction in the 1960s, yet his first collection of stories, *Den' v fevrale* (A Day in February; 1988), did not appear until the days of glasnost. *Linii sud'by* was written in 1981–5, but its author could find no one willing to accept the novel for publication until 1992, when one of the editors of *Druzhba narodov* happened upon the recently published *Den' v fevrale*, liked it, and invited Kharitonov to contribute something to the journal.

The main subject of *Linii sud'by* is literature, as well as the experiences, emotions, ideas, and fates of those directly connected with it. The main character of the novel, the literary scholar Anton Andreevich Lizavin, is doing research for his dissertation on the creative work of Russian provincial writers from his native region of Nechaisk. In the process, he comes across the prose of Simeon Milashevich. Intrigued by his discovery, Lizavin spends years searching libraries, archives, and his native places for information. His efforts are rewarded by the discovery of a mysterious little trunk containing unknown stories, notes, diaries, and observations by Milashevich.

The novel covers a time span of more than fifty years, from early in the century until the 1970s. Each of the novel's eighteen parts contains numerous short chapters, those devoted to the experiences, prose, and ideas of Milashevich alternating with those dealing with the life of Lizavin and his academic exploits. In addition, many characters are introduced episodically and are identified by one peculiar character trait or external feature only. These minor characters appear on the scene unexpectedly and disappear just as suddenly, but all are in some way connected with the lives and fates of Milashevich and Lizavin.

The novel comprises alleged fact, fiction, and fantasy, interspersed with a heavy dose of abstract philosophy. The discovery of Milashevich's trunk gives Lizavin access to the former's creative laboratory and uncovers, at least in part, the philosophical motivation that underlies his life and art. In fact, as the plot develops, the parallels between the world-views of Milashevich and Lizavin expand, and it becomes apparent that exposure to the literary heritage of Milashevich has an effect on Lizavin's intellectual make-up. Kharitonov attributes to Milashevich a number of traits and details characteristic of his own experience and beliefs. Both Kharitonov and Milashevich are preoccupied with the search for a new vision of life and a higher meaning of existence. The language of both is metaphorical and difficult to follow, and both have difficulty finding publishers for their works.

Milashevich's philosophy is not articulated clearly, but his so-called provincial idea is close to the author's heart and is elaborated most clearly in Kharitonov's unpublished novella 'Provintsional'naia filosofiia' (Provincial Philosophy), written in 1977 and intended to be the second part of a trilogy.[41] Milashevich idealizes Russian provincial life and opposes those who believe that the revolution will do away with the backwardness of the provinces. According to Kharitonov, Milashevich's idea of provincialism is not defined by geographical boundaries but is instead a spiritual realm and an approach to life based on the balance and harmony characteristic of Russian provincial life. Milashevich's intention is to erase the distinctions between big cities and the provinces and to foster provincial values all over the country. These views are developed and often challenged in the novel in an ongoing intellectual debate conducted by Milashevich, Lizavin, the narrator, and some other characters.

The notion that spiritual leadership belongs to a certain segment of the population is not new to Russian and Soviet history. Some parallels exist between Milashevich's philosophy of provincialism and the ideas propounded by the writers of Soviet 'village prose.' The October revolution and the subsequent Soviet experience have discredited the naïve utopian ideas of Milashevich and the notion that it is possible to create a perfect society. None the less, Kharitonov believes that these ideas, which he considers advanced for their time, testify to the foresight of his hero.

Religious faith is another concern of Milashevich; however, as a non-practising Christian, he first seeks redemption through revolutionary emancipation. His notes on religion are rational and challenging, characteristic of a searching agnostic rather than a committed atheist. It is possible to surmise that, since the novel was written before glasnost, Kharitonov toned down the religious theme in order to avoid antagonizing prospective publishers.

The novel is composed on three different levels – a story within a story, within a story. At the root of the narrative is the story of Lizavin and his discovery of Milashevich and his trunk. On another level is the life story of Milashevich, which is replete with elements of a detective novel. On the third level are myriad stories composed of, and based on, the notes and manuscripts found in the trunk. On the surface these three levels may appear to be separate, but in essence they are closely intertwined. Since Milashevich's prose is highly autobiographical, and his ideas exert great influence on Lizavin, the content of the little trunk forms the intellectual foundation and the starting-point for most philosophical deliberations. Like Lizavin, Kharitonov is a scrupulous researcher. He constructs his small chapters with meticulous care and patience, assigning to each of them some special idea. But the chronology is confusing, and spatial dimensions are vague. Progression in the novel is not measured by the development of occurring events; instead, the intention of the author is to move the plot by following the development of ideas.

Stylistically the novel represents a blend of realistic fiction with elements of post-modernist prose. Third-person narration by different raconteurs is interlaced with quotations from letters, notes, documents, as well as excerpts from the manuscripts of Milashevich. Aphorisms or pithy statements as epigraphs to chapters, and usually taken from the little trunk, set the tone for the portrayal of actual events or for intellectual dialogue. Paragraphs with no formal end, followed by other paragraphs which begin without a capital letter, allude to the interconnection and continuity of all phenomena, and of life itself. Narration in the form of verse hints at the unity between the poetic and prosaic in literature, as well as in life. Much of the novel reads like stream of consciousness, from the minds of Lizavin, Milashevich, and the omniscient narrator. Their internal monologues often merge and form a philosophical dialogue whose objective is to discover the path to faith, and the meaning of life.

Linii sud'by is a serious novel. It presents a wealth of philosophical insights and subtle observations, and it challenges the reader to become involved in the intellectual debate. Yet one wonders: how does the award of the Booker Prize to the novel reflect on the current state of literature in Russia? Alla Latynina saw in the novel parallels with Marcel Proust and Herman Hesse,[42] and Karen Stepanian predicted that the novel will become a classic of Russian post-modernism.[43] Konstantin Kedrov, on the other hand, saw in the novel 'a compromise between traditional realism and the new literature. The bitter philosophy of Mark Kharitonov is adequate for his entangled style, ... which is not very easy to overcome.'[44]

Linii sud'by is a provocative novel with a an inventive plot. It is full of subtle detail and elaborate ideas, but the narrative is disjointed and its style is intricate and difficult to follow. The novel is a combination of disconnected fragments, but the author attempts to present, through this confusing artistic edifice, a unitary vision of the world. It is a novel about literature, and is for the literati and not for the ordinary reader. To master its text, one needs erudition and a lot of patience. Thus, despite its merits and acclaim, the novel is unlikely to gain the wide public recognition a literary classic deserves.

After the appearance of *Linii sud'by* Kharitonov published in *Znamia* the short story 'Ochered'' (The Queue; 1992).[45] It is a narrative about Soviet daily reality in which the queue has become a natural fixture. Since there is no reference to place, time, or merchandise sold, the queue becomes the embodiment and microcosm of the Soviet system itself. Written in the form of a monologue by a woman narrator, the story explores the psychology of the individual raised in the shadows of this eternal queue. This individual is obedient, deprived of personal freedom, and a perfect subject for state oppression. He defends and worships the system because it feeds and provides him with a sense of security.

VIACHESLAV P'ETSUKH

Viacheslav P'etsukh (b. 1946) is one of the better-known Russian writers of the late 1980s and early 1990s. Born to a Russian mother and a Polish-

Ukrainian father, he is a graduate of the Moscow Pedagogical Institute, and a professional teacher of history. He began writing in the 1970s, and even published some minor works before perestroika, but his name became known to the broad reading public only after the advent of glasnost. The subject-matter of P'etsukh's stories is usually the several topics that concern him most – namely, Russian history, human nature, and the relationship of life and literature. He sets his plots in contemporary reality, as well as in the Russian historical past, sometimes mixing them together. But intertextuality and the reliance on models from Russian classical literature are a deeply ingrained aspect in most of his works. P'etsukh's prose is marked by thematic and stylistic variety. Reality is often combined with fantasy, and in most cases serious subjects are dealt with in a humorous manner. P'etsukh satirizes Soviet life and society, and irony is the hallmark of his prose.

The novella 'Novaia moskovskaia filosofiia' (The New Moscow Philosophy; 1989),[46] regarded by its author as a novel, is one of P'etsukh's best-known works. It is a story for which the author is deeply indebted to F. Dostoevsky. Not only are the structure and subject-matter similar to that of *Prestuplenie i nakazanie* (Crime and Punishment; 1866) but even some characters from Dostoevsky's novel appear in P'etsukh's narrative. The action in the story covers four days in the life of the inhabitants of a Moscow communal flat. The plot is set in motion by the disappearance of an elderly woman who occupies a small room in the apartment. Even before the reasons for her disappearance are established, the other residents become involved in an intense struggle for the living space which has been vacated by the old lady. In the end it is discovered that the old woman is dead. Frightened by a harmless, but inventive, prank of two teenagers, she dies and sits unnoticed for thirty hours on a bench in the nearby park.

The incident forms the necessary background for the vigorous philosophical discussion between the main characters, Belotsvetov and Chinarikov. The first is a pharmacist, and the latter an Afghan war veteran, once a student of philosophy but now a janitor. The subject of their argument is the relationship of good and evil in human nature, but the story contains numerous digressions.

On the surface, the narrator appears to be removed from the author; in fact, he expresses the writer's ideas. He meditates on the relationship of artistic creation with real life and suggests that even the most fantastic and improbable creations of the writer's brain have some time, somewhere, happened before. The importance of literary creation for the well-being of mankind is underscored by the assertion that, 'in the process of the ethical development of people, literature has been assigned genetic significance, because it expresses in a concentrated manner the spiritual experience of mankind ... without literature man cannot become a complete human being.'[47]

The title of the novella is, in a sense, ironic. The new Moscow philosophy, expressed in the notion that Russia is 'charged with the mission of furthering spiritual development,'[48] is not new at all. It is contrasted in the story with the alleged old philosophy about the backwardness and uselessness of Russia propounded by the nineteenth-century Russian thinker P. Chaadaev. The 'new philosophy' is an old idea promoted for centuries by those who have advanced the notion of Moscow as a third Rome and advocated vigorously by Russian and Soviet nationalists.

P'etsukh understands that, in drawing heavily from *Crime and Punishment*, he invites comparisons with the nineteenth-century Russian classic. To avert possible negative criticism, he acknowledges that his innate capabilities are not equal to those of Dostoevsky, yet he asserts that his task is more difficult than that of his famous mentor. Today's protagonists are petty and self-centred, and 'the St Petersburg variant of the drama has been executed in strict accordance with the rules of art, while this chronicle is an attempt to re-create life, according to the laws of life itself.'[49] Indeed, Dostoevsky's characters are well rounded, and their ideas seem convincing and well motivated. Raskolnikov kills for an ideal, and Dostoevsky devotes many pages to the task of discrediting his hero's philosophy. Dostoevsky disapproves of groundless murder because it undermines his religious ethic. However, while some inhabitants of the flat in P'etsukh's novella may still have a conscience, none has any ethical principles whatsoever. Their philosophical discussions are about abstractions and are little related to their activities. The author of *Crime and Punishment* makes it clear, from the very beginning, where he stands in relation to his protagonists. P'etsukh stands aside, leaving the dialogue between Belotsvetov and Chinarikov open-ended. By turning tragedy into a farce, he attempts to remain non-committal. It appears thus that the novella is not about a new Moscow philosophy but rather about the lack of one. The main difference between *Crime and Punishment* and the story in question is thus in the quality of art rather than in the distinction between the human traits or character features of the heroes.

It seems clear that 'Novaia moskovskaia filosofiia' was intended by P'etsukh as a parody of *Crime and Punishment*, rather than as a serious comparison. One wonders, however, why P'etsukh, otherwise serious about Russia's history and its cultural heritage, has chosen one of the best nineteenth-century Russian classics for the subject of his derision.

The title of P'etsukh's story 'Anamnez i epikriz' (Anamnesis and Epicrisis; 1990)[50] is symbolic. It relates directly to the names of two cats residing in a hospital ward but refers indirectly to the diagnosis and recommendations for the treatment of all social ills. In a sense, the hospital ward is society in microcosm. It is inhabited by six patients, including the narrator, each of different social background. The narrator listens to the arguments between different patients and ponders the nature of the Russian people. According to him, they are different from the people of all other nations. Most people – even cats – live in peace with one another. The Russians, on the other hand, fight each other continuously, allegedly because there are many different species in the Russian nation, each with different interests and concerns. According to P'etsukh, a unifying idea is required in order to bring all Russian people together. He suggests that, since the Russian language is common to all of them, they should entrust their fate to it. B. Sarnov pointed out that P'etsukh's story has some parallels with 'Istoriia bolezni' (Case History) by Mikhail Zoshchenko.[51] That may be so, but P'etsukh is much more ambitious than his venerable predecessor. He portrays the actions of the patients of a single hospital ward, but refers by implication to the illness of a whole nation. His proposed remedy to save Russia is, of course, utopian precisely because there is no readily available solution to the current predicament of the nation. By trivializing the discussion of important issues, P'etsukh illustrates the futility of human endeavour. His humour is not an expression of ordinary wit; rather it is bittersweet, and reminiscent of N. Gogol's laughter through tears.

'Aleksandr Krestitel'' (Aleksandr the Baptist; 1991)[52] is another story which combines a serious subject with a concocted idea treated in a playful manner. The story is set in 1920, in a small Russian provincial town. The local *Cheka* investigates an alleged murder. The citizen Aleksandr Saratov has been set on fire and burnt to death in the market square. At first, it is suspected that the murder is an anti-revolutionary act. It transpires soon that Saratov, a local man, has been preaching a new faith, and has proclaimed himself to be the new saviour. He is certain that the *Cheka* intends to arrest him anyway, and he convinces his followers to put him on the cross. But since there are no nails to be found anywhere in town, it is decided to burn him instead. Three days later, his followers remove his body from the casket, in order to create the impression of his resurrection.

Saratov's idea have their roots in Dostoevsky and in Russian tradition. Saratov asserts that the essence of God is present in every human being, and he promotes the notion of man-godhead: 'Faith – according to him – means the awareness of the mutual dissolution of man and God. Faith means the surrender of self to the lord who is in everyone.'[53] Saratov believes in the apocalypse, but rejects the notion of immortality. He claims that the Russians are a chosen people because they are capable of extreme suffering. As in his other stories, P'etsukh satirizes here the state of affairs in Russia: he advances the notion of Russia's unique place in the world and its being predestined to carry its spiritual message to humankind, but he does so with humour, and in a language full of archaisms suited to the subject-matter. Again, the author trivializes an important subject and tries to create the impression that he does not take his heroes seriously.

On the surface, P'etsukh appears to be detached from his narrator and protagonists, while, in fact, there is a close affinity between their ideas. P'etsukh refuses to consider himself a philosopher. He asserts that 'his works have no direct relation to philosophy, but are rather an expression of play in philosophy.'[54] Indeed, P'etsukh is no philosopher, but he is concerned with philosophical issues that have affected the Russian historical past and determine the course of life of his contemporaries. His philosophical discourses are wide-ranging parodies, and his commentaries on Russian life are full of tragic irony. It is possible to surmise that P'etsukh involves his characters in important philosophical discussion with the purpose of engaging the reader in the discourse and thereby enabling the reader to arrive at his or her own conclusions. Interestingly enough P'etsukh addresses in his works many issues that are close to the hearts of many writers of the Russian conservative nationalist wing. Yet he claims that he 'feels no sympathy to the so-called *pochvenniki*, because in many instances they replace in their works talent for good intentions.'[55]

P'etsukh is one of the most prolific of contemporary Russian writers. In the last few years he has published several collections of prose, including *Veselye vremena* (Merry Times; 1988), *Novaia moskovskaia filosofiia* (The New Moscow Philosophy; 1989), and *Ia i prochee* (I and Other Things; 1990). A number of his stories and novellas have recently appeared in a variety of journals and almanacs, including *Znamia*, *Oktiabr'*, *Druzhba narodov*, *Volga*, *Konets veka*, and *Pravda*. However, recently it has become obvious that P'etsukh is beginning to repeat himself. His new stories have little impact on the reader and are soon forgotten. His new plots may be inventive, but his methods and ideas are the same. Since characterization is not P'etsukh's forte, he devotes most of his attention to long monologues and descriptive passages, with the result that his narratives are often tedious.

P'etsukh's new novella, 'Zakoldovannaia strana' (Enchanted Country; 1992),[56] is a good example of the weaknesses described above. It is set in a Leningrad kitchen in 1983. Two poor women, who have not paid their rent for years, are awaiting a joint visit from a pest exterminator and an official from the internal revenue department. The discussion in the kitchen centres on such issues as the nature of the Russian people, and the essence of Christianity and its comparison with communism. The bulk of the story is a long monologue by the first-person narrator in which Russian history from time immemorial is outlined and an attempt is made to provide philosophical substantiation for the nature of the Russian people. The discussion of such weighty issues at an accidental kitchen gathering may perhaps be a comment on the intellect of ordinary Russians. Yet, the long, dull monologue leads one to wonder whether these simple working women are adequately equipped to deal offhandedly with such serious historical and philosophical matters. It is obvious that the author has got carried away with his own eloquence. He is the main character in this novella, as well as in most of his other works. Regardless whether he is an omniscient narrator, a character participating in the action, or an allegedly objective observer, he is always at the centre.

In other stories, such as 'Sorok chetyre goda s samim soboi' (Forty-Four Years with Oneself; 1992),[57] the first-person author-narrator is engaged in self-exploration, and the analysis of his relationship with his own double. In 'Emigrant' (The Émigré; 1989),[58] the narrator decries the fact that there is no room, anywhere in the world, for people with independent ideas, and, in 'Chistaia sila' (Clean Strength; 1989),[59] he examines ways in which people acquire moral values and wonders whether values corrupted by life experience can be passed on, in their unadulterated form, to the next generation.

P'etsukh is a versatile writer. Some of his stories are realistic; others are steeped in fantasy. Some are set in contemporary reality, others in tsarist Russia. In some stories, the focus is on history, literature, and philosophy; in others, the complexities of human nature are the focus. But his style is recognizable, despite shifts in narrative means. His prose is playful, full of paradoxes and absurd collisions. The narrator and the characters meditate, contemplate, and talk a lot, but there is little action.

In most stories, the message is not expressed directly but rather is concealed under the cover of humorous and farcical incidents. P'etsukh ridicules the established order of things and shows little respect for representatives of state and social institutions. In his view, there is no difference between criminals and politicians: 'Both manipulate without restraint the fates of God's children, with the purpose of satisfying their own narrow interests.'[60] P'etsukh's prose is eclectic, and he does not shy away from the use of hyperbole, surrealism, and the grotesque. His intertextuality, reliance on outside sources, black humour, parody, and authorial self-reflexiveness can be regarded as cognates of post-modernist art; however, P'etsukh should be viewed as a modern writer with old roots and conservative traditions. His world may be fractured, but it is not fragmented or abstract, and his stories have definite temporal and spatial dimensions.

ANATOLII KOROLEV

Anatolii Korolev, a resident of Moscow, published his first collection of prose, *Ozhog linzy* (The Burn of a Lens), in 1988. His next publication, 'Genii mestnosti' (The Genius of the Place; 1990),[61] attracted considerable critical attention, and heralded the appearance of a new and promising writer on the Russian literary scene. It chronicles a fictionalized sequence of important historical and cultural events which evolve in connection with, and as a reflection of, the development of a park named after Hannibal and located in the centre of St Petersburg. The narrative is rooted in reality and exhibits the author's versatility and erudition. It displays also the musicality, suppleness, and ironic bent of his language.

Historical events are also at the root of Korolev's most important publication, his recent novella 'Golova Gogolia' (Gogol's Head; 1992).[62] Historical facts form the background for a serious philosophical discussion of the relationship of good and evil, power and corruption, and the place of God and faith in the evolution of the human predicament. 'Golova Gogolia' combines reality, fantasy, and philosophical allegory. Its realistic frame contains its phantasmagoric detail and intellectual discourse. The author himself assigns his narrative to the 'genre of documentary mythology, with elements of black humour.'[63]

The tone of the novella is set in its first paragraph. In his sketch 'Kazn' Tropmana' (The Execution of Tropman; 1870), I. Turgenev relates the story of the execution of the hideous French criminal and murderer Tropman. Turgenev did not witness the final act of legalized murder;

instead, he turned his eyes away in abhorrence, and act for which Dostoevsky berated him. According to Dostoevsky, no man has the right to
turn a blind eye when evil is perpetrated. This short introduction is followed by a sequence of episodes in which real historical personalities
interact with fantastic and demonic figures. The events described illustrate the wicked nature of people, and the prevalence of evil in human
relationships. Thus, the unearthed Gogol is faced by the KGB officer
Nosov, the man in charge of the cemeteries in town. Nosov steals
Gogol's boots, an act of vandalism that symbolizes for Gogol an assault
on his art, which he considers immortal. Gogol decries the fact that 'the
wide reading public celebrates the victory of ... freedom from the law,
equality in sin, and brotherhood in violence. And that it has become possible now to assail and repudiate even the arts.'[64] The image of Gogol is
transformed into other images, but the message which transpires from
these dialogues is clear: nothing in this world is sacred. The bestial wickedness that permeates the earth contains the seeds of a new beauty,
based not on goodness, but on evil, because this universe of jealousy and
violence is in the process of becoming more accomplished and perfect,
and hence more beautiful.[65]

The roots of this all-pervading evil are traced back to the French Revolution, when murder was committed in the name of freedom and equality. Furthermore, murder is raised to the level of aesthetic norm, the
objective of which is 'to excite the imagination of the spectator's heart
and mind, by providing him with a peculiar work of art, unknown until
now.'[66] The heroes of the Revolution realized that there could be no rule
of justice or harmony, yet they also knew that the passionate love of freedom could never be extinguished. They were victims of their own evil
machine, the guillotine, which expressed the aesthetics of terror. The
parallels between the French Revolution and that of 1917 in Russia are
obvious. In both cases, no sacrifice was too great in the struggle for the
unattainable goal of freedom and equality. People might be killed, but
their ideas will live on, and many revolutionaries might have been
purged for no reason, but they continued to believe until their last gasp.

Another episode in the novella is set in May 1945, just after the end of
the Second World War. It deals with the transfer, upon the demand of
Stalin, of A. Hitler's jaw from Berlin to Moscow.[67] In the story, Stalin is
juxtaposed with the image of the Devil, and there is little difference in
their views. According to Stalin, love causes suffering, and fear fosters
love. Only by loving Stalin can the people rid themselves of their fear of
him. The influence of Dostoevsky on Korolev's thinking is evident, but

the latter manipulates Dostoevsky's views for his own purposes. Ivan Karamazov speculated that, if there is no God or immortality, then everything is permitted. Stalin and Satan, on the other hand, doubt the existence of God because nothing is denied them and they are free to perpetrate evil without fear of perdition.[68] Stalin justifies his wicked actions and blames God for all evil. Since Stalin has free rein, he asserts that God 'has betrayed and deserted the people.'[69] Both Stalin and Satan are aware of the fact that power corrupts, but again Stalin blames God for the people's trouble, saying that it is the 'absolute power of the maker that corrupts everyone,'[70] including the maker himself.

Korolev asserts that he had written the novella 'with the sole purpose of investigating the question whether suffering and pain are the responsibility of God or of the people' and he concludes that the story has evolved into a theodicy which intimates that 'evil does not originate from God. It is just a deficiency of goodness which God permits.'[71] Korolev's interpretation of his novella is not to everyone's liking. The Russian priest Mikhail Ardov chided Korolev for his attack on Gogol and for Korolev's alleged lack of 'artistic mastery and elementary taste.' He asserted that Korolev's attempt at theodicy uncovers the latter's ignorance on issues of Christianity.[72] There is no question that Korolev shows little reverence for established authorities, but this attack on his creative integrity is unjustified. Artisistic mastery and creative imagination should not bear the brunt of opposition to the thematic message of a work of art.

Korolev's novella is an important work of art in which the author has taken an innovative approach to the treatment of eternal and monumental issues. In it, he exhibits a superior creative imagination and combines historical documentary material with elements of mythology and fantasy. The novella is also a successful example of experimentation with the use of genre, style, and structure to treat a subject that requires precision, brevity, and clarity. To his credit, the author attempts to address issues without trying to provide definite solutions to them.

None the less, the reader may question some of the author's inferences. The novella leads to the conclusion that evil is the main driving force in the historical process of modern times but ends with an idyllic scene of Christ in the Holy Land. This scene symbolizes the possibility of redemption, and a new beginning for all, including the villains residing in the Kremlin. The postscript leads one to question the appropriateness of the proposed ending. Here, Korolev connects the notion of the destructiveness of Russia, expressed by V. Rozanov in the novella's epigraph, with the events in Russia in the summer of 1991, and he asserts that Russians are still eager to suffer and that violence is part of their destiny. In the end, the writer provides the reader with the commandments of the newest testament: they proclaim 'that there is no God ... and, even if he exists, Satan is equal to God ... that God is boring, and Christ is insipid ... that Evil is all over and it becomes a Blessing ... and that, if Evil in the world is destroyed, then Goodness will also disappear ... because those who do not know Evil will never be able to see its distinction from Goodness.'[73]

Korolev's final statement is a logical conclusion to the intellectual discourse in the novella, but it refutes the symbolic intent of the scene depicting Christ in the Holy Land. Korolev places the current predicament of Russia within the context of European and Russian culture and history. He disagrees, of course, with Stalin's idea that absolute power corrupts God, and he promotes instead the notion that, by providing people with the ability to make a conscious choice between good and evil, the maker protects man's freedom, dignity, and spirituality, without which humans would be mere beasts.

'Golova Gogolia' is a provocative and challenging narrative. Its subject-matter is in the Russian classical tradition, while its style has many parallels with the innovative and experimental Russian prose of the early 1990s.

ALEKSANDR KABAKOV

Aleksandr Kabakov (b. 1943) is a writer whose name is closely associated with the genre of the anti-utopia in current Russian literature. Born in Novosibirsk and educated as a mathematician, he worked for a rocket manufacturer, and later as an editor with several Soviet literary magazines. He began writing in the early 1980s but published nothing until glasnost.

Until 1987, anti-utopias were taboo to the Soviet reader for obvious reasons. In attempting to put into practice its communist utopian ideology, Soviet society created, in fact, the conditions of anti-utopia. The ideal of utopia was thus closely related to the reality of anti-utopia, the consequence of a dream that could never be fulfilled.[74] Perestroika changed the existing situation, and the publication of Evgenii Zamiatin's *My* (We; 1924) and George Orwell's *Animal Farm* and *1984* opened the path to this, until recently, forbidden genre. Kabakov was quick to capitalize on this opportunity. He lifted the veil of secrecy from this subject and paved the way for other writers, such as V. Makanin, A. Kurchatkin, and L. Petrushevskaia.

Kabakov's *Nevozvrashchenets* (No Return; 1989)[75] was the first dystopia to appear in the days of perestroika. A well-conceived but poorly written narrative, it achieved immediate success not because of its artistic perfection, but rather because of the author's ingenuity and the topicality of his subject. The narrative is set in two distinct and alternating time sequences: 1988 and some five or ten years later. In the end, the two levels converge as time catches up with events and what appears in the beginning to be fiction becomes reality. The action takes place in Moscow. The narrator, the main character of the story, works in a scientific research institute as an extrapolator, able to predict the future. Two security officers who are familiar with his work approach him and ask him to create a story describing the situation in the country five years hence.

Kabakov's foresight is astonishing. His extrapolator predicts the disappearance of the Soviet Union and the establishment of a different kind of dictatorship. He sees many former Soviet republics becoming independent, and life in Russia as full of chaos, violence, and suffering. The economic situation is dreadful, and crime is rampant. The new regime conducts a campaign of so-called levelling, destroying former communist officials and their families. In 1988, when the first cracks in Gorbachev's perestroika became evident, *Nevozvrashchenets* was viewed by many as a warning to the Soviet people of what might happen if perestroika failed.[76] The novella can also be read as a satire on the Soviet system, and on perestroika itself. Through the character of the extrapolator, Kabakov satirizes the Soviet system of state planning and ridicules those who claim that their familiarity with the allegedly universally applicable philosophy of Marxism arms them with clearer insights into the future than those obtainable by mere mortals.

Several years later, Kabakov published the novel *Sochinitel'* (The Scribbler; 1991).[77] It is a mixture of reality and fantasy, combined with elements of a political detective novel and a melodramatic love story. The action is set in 1990–1, and it takes place in a variety of foreign locations, as well as in Russia. On one level, the nameless scribbler writes a movie script in which he himself is an active participant. He is married but carries on a passionate love affair with a married woman, a television commentator. On the other level, the work of the Soviet intelligence service is described. Three former Soviet citizens are apprehended in foreign countries by Soviet security agents and are secretly brought back to Russia, together with their female companions. One of them is a deserter from the Soviet Army in Afghanistan; another is apparently a Soviet defector from Afghanistan; and the third is a Soviet refugee in Germany. Back in the Soviet Union, they are trained for a special mission – an attack on one of the country's leaders, with the purpose of destroying or intimidating him. They are promised that, after the successful completion of their mission, they will be reunited with their women and set free.

The allusion to Gorbachev and his reforms, as well as to his relations with the KGB, is obvious. The novel was written prior to the August 1991 coup, but the parallels are striking. Security officers use intimidation, blackmail, and force in order to achieve their political objectives. Soviet publication policy is also alluded to when writers, refusing to acquiesce, are victimized. Here, Kabakov uses narrative devices similar to those in *Nevozvrashchenets*. In both cases, the author-narrator is a writer who creates a plot in which he is an active participant. However, while the plot of *Sochinitel'* is inventive, it is also convoluted and relies on stock sex scenes and other details intended to shock, rather than to impress, the reader. As well, the characters are flat and soon forgotten, and the language dry and full of foreign words which are hardly part of literary Russian.

'Bul'varnyi roman' (A Cheap Novel; 1990),[78] another novella by Kabakov, is somewhat different and is similar in tone to Soviet *byt* literature of the previous decade. It contains no scenes of violence or political infighting. As in Kabakov's other works, the author-narrator appears as a minor character. In order to add authenticity, he interferes in the flow of the narrative and admits that some episodes are a figment of his imagination; in so doing, he absolves the characters of direct responsibility for their actions. The story opens with a passionate love scene, which is followed by the history of the Pirogov and Ignat'ev families, who are neighbours. Both Ignat'ev and Pirogov spend tortured nights, obsessed by dreams: Ignat'ev dreams about Pirogov's wife, Liudmila; Pirogov dreams about a two-storey town house in which the Ignat'evs live as well. Ignat'ev appears to be the better man. Even though he has never been unfaithful to his wife, he has developed an irrational and uncontrollable passion for Liudmila. Pirogov, on the other hand, is unfaithful to his spouse, and his fervour is calculated, driven by greed. The story's ending is little connected with the main plot. In it, Kabakov ventures into vague philosophical deliberations related to the unpredictability of life, which defies explanation and takes its own course, regardless of people's intentions, illusions, or rational plans.

Kabakov's prose is timely, reflecting the decline in the fortunes of Gorbachev's reforms and the beginnings of the disintegration of the Soviet state. Kabakov attempts to bridge the Soviet past with the unpredictable future of Russia. However, even though his stories are innovative, topical, and experimental, they are not great literature as his characterization and psychological analysis are inadequate. Author, narrator, and hero are often fused together, which obscures the main thrust of his story. It is interesting to note that Kabakov himself is no great fan of the kind of literature he produces. He asserts that he prefers the anti-establishment literature of the Soviet era to the writings of new contemporary authors, which he claims, may be pleasant to read but lacks what he calls 'real blood and tears ... It is difficult to live on a diet, after having eaten real meat.'[79] The real meat, according to Kabakov, is a literature with dramatic tension and social concerns, rather than a prose which sacrifices substance to form and word play. It remains to be seen whether Kabakov will be able to produce the kind of literature he likes to read.

MIKHAIL KURAEV

The literary debut of Mikhail Kuraev (b. 1939) took place during the early days of perestroika, when he was close to fifty. His novella 'Kapitan Dikshtein' (Captain Dikshtein; 1987) is, however, different from the mainstream Soviet literature of that period. It escapes the intrusion of publicism and topicality, characteristic of most fiction of that time, and it proffers a fantastic narrative, placed in a historical frame and executed in the traditions of modern experimental prose.[80] The 1921 Kronstadt rebellion against Bolshevik rule forms the historical background of the novella, but the plot is essentially moved by the transformation of the main hero, who faces the inevitability of assuming the name of another character. The roots of Kuraev's playful and ironic narrative art can be traced back to N. Gogol and A. Belyi, but the device of constructing a plot in which one prisoner assumes the name of another one who is dead was also used by S. Zalygin in his novel Posle buri (After the Storm; 1980–5).

The novelty and freshness of 'Kapitan Dikshtein,' which remains Kuraev's best work to date, have been acclaimed by Soviet and Western critics alike. It also raised high expectations which have, unfortunately, not been justified as yet. Kuraev has published a number of stories and novellas in the last few years, but most of them fall short of the artistic level reached in his debut.

'Kapitan Dikshtein' was followed by *Nochnoi dozor* (Night Patrol; 1988),[81] a fictional account of the nostalgic ruminations and self-justification of a former guard in the Soviet internal security forces.

'Malen'kaia domashniaia taina' (A Little Family Secret; 1990),[82] a story apparently written in 1966, was reworked for publication. The action is set in Leningrad in the 1960s, and the characters are old people, most of them close to seventy. The two heroes are the old widow Mariia Adol'fovna and her former suitor, the old bachelor and retired veterinarian Vladimir Petrovich. Mariia Adol'fovna is on a visit to Leningrad from the provinces, where she has been staying since her evacuation during the war. The title of the story refers, however, to a secret in the family of Mrs Teben'kova, a distant relative of Mariia Adol'fovna. Teben'kova manipulates the old couple and encourages them to marry, for she believes that their marriage will benefit her own family life. The old couple goes through with the nuptial rites, but the marriage remains a mere formality. Vladimir Petrovich is self-obsessed and refuses even to attend a small party in honour of the newly-weds, arranged by the Teben'kovs. Mariia Adol'fovna, angry at this lack of attention, leaves her husband and returns home to the provinces.

The psychological make-up of the main characters is presented in a subtle and perceptive manner. We know little about the past of Vladimir Petrovich, but his actions come as no surprise. He is an old bachelor and a victim of habit. It appears from the story that companionship in old age is important for survival but is seldom an adequate substitute for peace of mind and self-respect. The story casts light on the fretfulness of old people, who are set in their ways and unable to change. Yet the reader does not perceive the story as an intense family drama but, rather, as a farce. The confusing structure, poor handling of time, and the uncalled-for intrusion of the narrator often divert the reader's attention from the main course of events.

Another novella, 'Petia po doroge v Tsarstvo Nebesnoe' (Petia on His Way to Heaven; 1991),[83] set in 1953 in Russia's far north, in Soviet gulag country, concerns itself with the fate of a mentally handicapped boy. Petia, the hero, craves recognition and is in awe of those in power. When Stalin dies, he wonders why all free people are sad, while the always grim and dejected prisoners are happy. In his naïve childish way, Petia pretends to be an adult traffic controller. Even though he often interferes with the activities of local officials, people refuse to chasten the boy and he is the object of everyone's affection, as one who has been maltreated by fate. However, this warm disposition to Petia does little to protect and save his life. When two prisoners escape from the camp, Petia, ever ready to assist those in charge, follows in pursuit of the escapees and is accidentally killed by a frightened soldier who has lost his way in the taiga. The irony of the conclusion is evident: the post-Stalin amnesty sets the escaping prisoners free anyway, while Petia loses his life in his well-intentioned service to the oppressive regime. Thus, the Stalinist system is denounced for fostering the oppression and murder of innocent victims, as well as for failing to protect the young and handicapped.

The novella is a third-person narrative with numerous authorial digressions. It comments, in a derisive and censuring tone, on the general situation in the Soviet Union as well as on the historical background of the location described. The story of Petia is touching and pathetic; however, instead of exploring his inner world and psychological conditioning at greater length, Kuraev takes the easy way out, concentrating on external detail, making use of melodramatic devices such as suspense and surprise, and engineering a tragic conclusion that lacks intensity. Commenting on Kuraev's recent stories, S. Taroshchina asserted that 'they have led ... to the sad notion that in the days of the recurrent social psychosis, and the triumph of publicism, even many good writers lose their elementary literary skills.'[84]

In 1992, Kuraev published two stories, 'Druzhby nezhnoe volnenie' (The Tender Excitement of Friendship)[85] and 'Kuranty b'iut' (The Bells Ring),[86] which are in many ways similar to his earlier prose. They have inventive plots but lack dramatic tension, and they explore the historical background but eschew deeper psychological investigation. The recent stories, however, have a new metaphysical dimension. In fact, an introductory note to 'Kuranty b'iut,' the subtitle of which is 'metafizicheskoe chtenie' (metaphysical reading), contrasts metaphysics with dialectics. Its hero, the leading metaphysician of a Russian provincial town, contemplates the parallels between the relationship of different parts of the human body and between different components of humanity in general. He muses about the predicament of the overseer of the bells of the Peter and Paul fortress in St Petersburg who wants to become the custodian of time by controlling the movement of the clock.

The unattractive wife of the middle-aged first-person narrator of 'Druzhby nezhnoe volnenie,' Malkhov, leaves her husband for his best friend. The narrator contemplates his unhappy life and his family's lineage, and reflects on the current situation in Russia. His conclusions are depressing: life is futile, but few understand it. He views his personal predicament as a reflection of a general social malady. He understands that 'to live according to one's *principles* is inconvenient, but life that is *convenient* leads to discord.'[87] The narrator is desperate because Russia is in a mess, heading in an unknown direction, and he is too old to live and see this new, allegedly better, life. One senses the author's voice in this dejection. Now in his mid-fifties, Kuraev grew up and matured in a system that cultivated the socialist myth about a beautiful future. Today that myth has been destroyed, but the good life is still a dream.

Kuraev's recent novel *Zerkalo Montachki* (Montachka's Mirror; 1993),[88] is a sprawling narrative without a single compositional centre or protagonist, but, rather, with an array of diverse characters who reside in a communal apartment in Leningrad, among whom is Mr Montachka. The action in the novel is set in the early 1960s, but the life stories of most characters cover the early years of Soviet Russia, and even pre-revolutionary times. The realism of the novel is juxtaposed with the fantastic notion that one's mirror image can disappear. The novel goes on to deliberate on the disparity between reflection and perception and to examine elements of demonology and sources of evil, as well as the duality of people and nature. The novel is evidence of the evolution of Kuraev's power of imagination, but the abundance of subplots and minute detail obscures the author's main idea.

Kuraev's excursions into metaphysics are daring but often poorly integrated with the plots of his stories. The different narrative voices are frequently indistinct, and it is difficult to separate the inflections of the first-person narrator, the omniscient narrator, and the author himself. Despite the shortcomings cited, Kuraev's prose has redeeming features. His plots cover a wide range of social, metaphysical, and personal issues, and his language is ornate and metaphorical. He blends a variety of different perspectives on issues of historical and political significance, with subtly detailed portrayals of personal dilemmas in the framework of dramatic irony. He makes a conscious attempt in his stories to combine realistic portrayal with experimental modernist narrative techniques.

TAT'IANA TOLSTAIA

Tat'iana Tolstaia (b. 1951), a native of Leningrad, many years has lived in Moscow. She first appeared in print in 1983, two years prior to Gorbachev' ascent to power, but she became well known in Russia, as well as in the West, only in the days of glasnost. Tolstaia has come into Russian literature with her own personal style and an array of characters outside the mainstream of Soviet life, ranging from the ordinary to the grotesque and bizarre, most of them memorable. Her stories feature the mentally imbalanced, social misfits, lovelorn women, and disillusioned and deceived dreamers. Most are hurt by nature or abused by the harsh realities of daily life. They are doomed to isolation, unable to communicate with each other, and, hard as they try, they cannot loosen the grip of habit and break through the closed circle of their unfortunate fate. Tolstaia's prose is cultured and non-committal. She does not preach or prescribe; nor does she reproach her characters for their failures. She is a sensitive and compassionate observer who accepts human imperfection. Her language is playful, rich in vivid metaphors, striking colours, and artful parallels, and her plots interweave fantasy with prosaic reality, rooted in Russian lore.

Tolstaia's first collection of prose, *Na zolotom kryl'tse sideli* (On the Golden Porch; 1987), published in English translation in 1989,[89] has received critical acclaim, both in Russia and in the West. In 1988, Tolstaia published a new story 'Somnambula v tumane' (Sleepwalker in a Fog),[90] similar in style and spirit to her earlier works. The hero, Denisov, thrice married before, is at present in love with Lora. Her father, a zoologist ousted from his job in an academic institute for alleged ideological sins, is a sleepwalker. Denisov is a failure – whatever he attempts ends in disappointment. He wants to become an inventor, but is incapable of invention. He makes an attempt to write poetry but cannot. He is overcome by fears and doubts. As he daydreams over a map of the world, he doubts even the existence of Australia. He is alarmed by the fact that life is passing by rapidly, while he is unable to leave a mark in this world. Denisov fails in his endeavours because his attempts to gain public recognition are motivated by crude calculation. He is a product of a vacuous and corrupt social environment, and his actions are moved by selfishness rather than ethical and spiritual considerations. Tolstaia juxtaposes in the story the temporary blindness of the sleepwalker with the ignorance, lack of vision, and self-centredness of those who are blessed with good health and normal eyesight. Their blindness is not temporary; it is a state of existence in which the illusory is a substitute for the real, and in which people communicate verbally but fail to appreciate the needs and aspirations of others. Everyone is in a fog, unable to make a clear choice or see the light of day.

There is a sense of ambivalence in most of Tolstaia's stories. On the one hand, she displays affection for the downtrodden, lonely, and alienated; on the other hand, under the surface, she seems to castigate them for their passivity and inability to cope with the pressures of life. But nowhere, including in this story, does Tolstaia offer any solutions to the problems faced by her heroes. 'Somnambula v tumane' contains many striking metaphors, descriptive details, and digressions, but little plot beyond a sequence of events to illustrate that there is not much point in seeking solutions to insurmountable problems. And yet, in the end, Tolstaia tries to provide the reader with a glimmer of hope. In the last paragraph we read: 'The sleepwalker is running along impassable paths, ... as though he sees what the seeing cannot, as though at night he grasps what is lost during the day ... Surely he will keep running till he meets the light?'[91] To the reader, who is faced with the grim reality of daily existence, this poetic expression of hope is inadequate. As K. Stepanian asserts: 'A sleepwalker, running to meet the light – as a symbol of hope? In our extraordinary times, when so much is being decided? It is not serious.'[92] Hope, of course, is often an emotional craving for something unattainable, but it can also be a strong desire for something tangible. It is a force which can help overcome the sinking feeling of depression, invigorate the human spirit, and foster positive activity. Stepanian expects too much from a work of art, of course. Its objective is to reflect the human predicament rather than to provide practical solutions for the problems of daily life.

The concluding paragraph of 'Somnambula v tumane' relates to the experience of a single individual, but its social ramifications are evident. And, in that sense, it marks a change from the emphasis in Tolstaia's earlier stories. She abandons, at least in part, her detachment from the outside world and becomes more engaged with the real. She comprehends that the personal and social elements of human existence are intricately intertwined, and that the full realization of each personality is possible only in an environment in which the two are in harmonious balance. This growing social awareness in Tolstaia's prose is apparently a response to the new political realities in the Soviet Union, as well as to her direct exposure to Western civilization. In 1988–93 she travelled extensively and spent much time teaching, lecturing, and giving interviews in the United States. She can no longer remain a detached observer of the political scene, and frequently becomes embroiled in controversy. Her verbal outbursts criticizing life in the United States, which often outrage her American hosts, speak of her naïvety and lack of understanding of how American society functions.[93]

Tolstaia's activities other than writing prose affected her creative output in several different ways. First, in comparison with the five previous years, 1989–94 are indeed lean years. Moreover, the influence of politics on her later fiction is obvious to anyone familiar with the subject-matter. Tolstaia's new concerns are apparent in the story 'Limpopo' (Limpopo; 1990), published first in Paris and only later in Russia.[94] It is narrated by an unnamed woman who is a witness and participant in the events described. The action takes place in two different time sequences. It begins in the days of 'stagnation,' and it ends apparently in the days of perestroika. Lenechka, a school friend of the narrator, is a naïve idealist out to save humanity but unable to find a place for himself in the real world. He meets Judy, a black African student, who comes to the Soviet Union to study veterinary science. Lenechka is eager to consummate his affair with Judy. The intended product of their mixed-race love will be a new Pushkin – a new and superior individual, symbolizing the higher unity of races. But Lenechka's adventure ends in failure. Pursued by communist nationalists who are against mixed marriages, including his uncle Zhenia the diplomat, the couple, along with their friends, are forced to escape to a provincial town full of grotesque creatures. Their idealized romantic love ends as a tragic farce. Judy dies of pneumonia, and Lenechka goes mad over her loss. What begins as a realistic story about life in Soviet Russia in the days of Brezhnev turns into an allegorical tale about the Soviet system and its bureaucracy. The Soviet administration is satirized, and its officials are ridiculed.

In the story, Tolstaia addresses a variety of important issues such as racism and moral decay, but she does not investigate them at any length. The characters in the story are drawn sketchily and are soon forgotten. Only the language, rich in metaphors and colloquial expressions suited to the exotic topics of the manic conversations in the mythical provincial town, is reminiscent of Tolstaia's earlier prose. Similarly, the pessimistic atmosphere that pervaded Tolstaia's early stories is present here as well. The main characters are destroyed, their great plans never brought to fruition. Truth seekers and dreamers, like Lenechka, are misunderstood and doomed to perish. Life is futile because people are victims of their own delusions. There is no question that 'Limpopo' is artistically inferior to Tolstaia's earlier stories. It is too early, however, to judge whether this decline is circumstantial and temporary or a sign of the transformation in her talent. Some Russian critics have reacted swiftly to these new developments in Tolstaia's prose. Thus, for example, M. Lipovetskii asserted that he 'reads "Limpopo" and thinks ... that after "Peters" ... it is a fiasco ... There is not a single live character in the story, only grotesque masks.'[95]

In 'Limpopo,' Pushkin is a symbolic figure, and a positive role model. In Tolstaia's next story, 'Siuzhet' (Plot; 1991),[96] he reappears as one of the characters who drives the plot. The story is based on the amusing conjecture that Pushkin was not killed in the duel with Dantes but, rather, destroyed his opponent. Many years later, on a trip to Simbirsk, the old Pushkin is assailed by a little boy, who turns out to be the future Lenin. The old Pushkin dies soon, but Vladimir Ulianov goes on to become the minister of interior in the tsarist government. When he dies, on the estate of Gorki, he is replaced by Dzhugashvili – the future Stalin. The story is a parody with fantastic elements, but its message is clear: it alludes to the fact that the Soviet state continues and perfects old tsarist institutions. Lenin introduces his ruthless ways of policing, and Stalin follows in his mentor's path. Symbolically, from early childhood, Lenin detests Pushkin, the freedom-loving spirit of his verse, and the culture he represents. We are told that, as Pushkin grows old, most people lose interest in his works. Indeed, great artists are seldom appreciated by their contemporaries. The young want change, regardless of what is to follow.

'Siuzhet,' an interesting artistic experiment, is different from most stories by Tolstaia. In it, the Russian historical past forms the basis of the plot, and most characters are based on real-life prototypes. It remains to be seen whether the new political, historical, and social motifs in Tolstaia's recent stories will become dominant in her prose or she will return to the kind of literature that made her famous in the first place. In the meantime, it is possible only to surmise that her vivid imagination and her elegant, musical prose are better suited to the portrayal of the inner world of individual human experience than to the investigation of social maladies.

ALEKSANDR·IVANCHENKO

A native of Sverdlovsk, and a resident of the Ekaterinburg region, Aleksandr Ivanchenko (b. 1945) is one of the most talented Russian provincial writers. His name became known to the wide reading public only in the days of perestroika. His first collection of prose, *Iabloko na snegu* (The Apple in the Snow; 1986), contains stories about childhood, rooted in autobiography and supplemented with fiction. These stories constitute a refreshing chronicle by a sensitive and impressionable observer. His second collection, *Avtoportret s dogom* (Self-Portrait with a Great Dane; 1990), published in Sverdlovsk, includes a novel under the same title,[97] and two novellas, all written prior to perestroika. Ivanchenko's most recent novel, *Monogramma* (Monogram; 1992),[98] short-listed in the 1992 Booker Prize competition, was also published in Ekaterinburg.

Ivanchenko is a meticulous craftsman, famous for his stylistic versatility. His creative diversity is best illustrated by the collection *Avtoportret s dogom*. The three narratives included are so different from one another in style and subject-matter that it is difficult to believe that they could have been written by the same author. Thus, 'Tekhnika bezopasnosti – I' (Safety Engineering – I; 1979) is a psychological investigation of the state of fear and insecurity created and conditioned by the lack of freedom. It is a narrative in the tradition of Kafka, about a nameless man who is afflicted by persecution mania. He travels somewhere to escape someone who is allegedly in his pursuit. The story can be read as the surrealistic dream of a prisoner who has lost his appreciation of freedom. In a more general sense, it can also be interpreted as reflecting the Soviet citizenry, who have surrendered all their rational being to the dictates of the totalitarian state.

The novel *Avtoportret s dogom* (1982), which is still regarded as Ivanchenko's best work, is different. It is a realistic first-person narrative, in confessional style, by the hero, Robert, a provincial painter-decorator over thirty. What appears to be, in the beginning, a family saga turns into an artistic exploration of self and an investigation of creativity in general. On the last page of the novel, the narrator admits that his attempt at self-portrayal is futile because one cannot observe oneself objectively. At the centre of the plot is the relationship of Robert with his wife, Alisa, a journalist. He is deeply in love with her; she is capricious, fickle, and unpredictable, which understandably makes him jealous and suspicious.

The plot structure is original. First, the reader is introduced to the friends of the family. Then, separate chapters are devoted to the psychological analysis of Alisa; Robert; Alisa's daughter, Katia; and their dog, Dezi. Subsequently, the subject shifts to Robert's business trip to Moscow, and his alleged affairs with several different women. As it turns out, the stories about Robert's infidelity are a product of his imagination and the result of his morbid jealousy. He imagines himself in the role of his wife's unknown lover, and the women he allegedly encounters in Moscow personify different aspects of Alisa's character and different stages in the relationship.

Love, according to Ivanchenko, is a positive force which stimulates artistic creativity. But the unfulfilled love of a desperate man can incite his sickly imagination and lead to the creation of a morbid vision of reality. Unlike 'Tekhnika bezopasnosti – I,' *Avtoportret s dogom* is conventionally realistic. The shallow and depraved Soviet middle-class *byt* environment of the Brezhnev era provides the background for penetrating character analysis. Straightforward narration, rich in subtle psychological detail, alternates with internal monologue and philosophical digressions. Failing in his attempt to come to terms with reality, the autobiographical hero makes up for in his imagination what he is unable to achieve in real life. On the surface, life appears to be simple, but the irony of this perception is unmistakable. The complexity of human nature, and the inability of people to communicate clearly and openly, lead to confusion, distress, and the destruction of the family unit. In fact, the marriage of Robert and Alisa is also the result of confusion and chance. They meet at an exhibition of semi-professional painters, which Alisa happens accidentally to attend, where Robert's painting *Avtoportret s molodym dogom* (Self-Portrait with a Young Great Dane) is displayed. In the end, Robert creates a perfect picture of the dog, but his attempt at self-realization through self-portrayal is futile.

Monogramma is different again, in terms of style, manner of narration, and images. The narrative has a realistic frame but contains metaphysical substance. One part of the novel deals with the history of a disenfranchised family; the other part discusses the system of Buddhist categories, meditations, and customs. The fragmentary structure of the novel, intercut with many digressions, reminds one of collage. The narrative and philosophical components of the novel are closely related, and the metaphysical part is supposed to illustrate, interpret, and substantiate the action of the heroine, Lida Chornovol. However, this novel is artistically inferior to *Avtoportret s dogom*. Its structure is diffused, character evolution is tentative, and much of the narrative is taken up by notes from abstracts intended for the education of beginning Russian Buddhists.

Like M. Kharitonov, V. P'etsukh, and A. Korolev, Ivanchenko makes use in his novels of a number of post-modernist devices. None the less, his art is rooted in the realistic tradition, and he is interested in the exploration of a variety of philosophical, sociological, and psychological issues.

VIKTOR PELEVIN

Viktor Pelevin is a young writer, just over thirty. In December 1993, his first collection of prose, *Sinii fonar'* (Blue Lamp), published in Moscow in

1991, was awarded the Booker Prize for the best work of short fiction. Pelevin's best known work is 'Omon Ra' (Omon Ra), published in the 1992 volume of *Znamia*.[99] Pelevin's prose is a combination of fantasy and reality. His heroes exist simultaneously in two different domains, the real world and the elusive realm of imagination. His mysterious universe is often inhabited by ghostly doubles who are real and illusory at the same time. On the surface, they may represent the exotic life of enigmatic creatures; however, in fact they reflect the human predicament of Soviet and Russian people.

'Omon Ra' is an example of socialist realism in reverse, and a peculiar version of the anti-utopia. It is a fantastic tale in a realistic setting. The first-person narrator, with the odd but highly symbolic name 'Omon,' has dreamt since childhood about a voyage to the moon. He enrols in an air force school where the lower extremities of the cadets are amputated and where the cadets are trained to become 'real people.' The reference is to Boris Polevoi's novel *Povest' o nastoiashchem cheloveke* (The Tale of a Real Man; 1947) which describes the heroic combat exploits of a Soviet pilot who has lost his limbs during the Second World War. Omon and his colleagues are trained for an essentially suicidal mission to the moon. They are supposed to reach the moon and send samples of moon soil back to earth, without ever being able to return home. None the less, the conclusion of the narrative offers some hope. The hero manages to escape the snares of brainwashing and deceit, and perhaps to begin a new life, free of the burdens of his past. Pelevin satirizes the Soviet space program, which is more concerned with the image of the Soviet state and its communist ideology than with scientific discovery. The story illustrates the shallowness of Soviet ideals, and the predicament of young people who are unable to escape the web of psychological manipulation.

Pelevin's new novel, *Zhizn' nasekomykh* (The Life of Insects; 1993),[100] is another example of his skill in reconstructing reality, intertwining the factual with the fantastic and turning the actual into the absurd. The characters in the novel are insects with human traits and the character features of real Soviet people. The novel is replete with philosophical deliberations and political dialogue. It addresses issues of education, sex, the arts, and the generation gap. In this work, Pelevin criticizes the Soviet system of government, ridicules socialist art, and hints at the futility of human endeavour. He is critical of the conservatives in post-Gorbachev Russia, yet rejects the notion that salvation may come from the West. The issues discussed in the narrative are serious, and the ideas expressed have merit, yet the style, language, and form of the novel are hardly conducive to the exploration of these problems at length.

Pelevin is certainly a promising writer and displays considerable creative imagination. His fantastic stories are inspired by real life and events rooted in human experience, but the artificiality of his plot construction, and the disparity between form and content, diminish the effect of his intended message. One wonders whether Pelevin will in the future diversify his artistic interests. His limited language skills and his reliance on melodramatic devices, such as surprise and shock, restrict the quality of his art.

PETR KOZHEVNIKOV

Vestnik novoi literatury (The Herald of New Literature) is one of the two journals awarded, in 1992, the special Booker Prize for the contribution to and development of contemporary Russian literature, intended to assist small Russian-language publications. (The other winner was *Solo*.) *Vestnik novoi literatury*, which first appeared in 1990, is published in St Petersburg, and most of its contributors are members of the former Leningrad literary underground. They include V. Krivulin, Iu. Mamleev, V. Erofeev, and F. Erskin (the pseudonym of M. Berg). According to its editor, Mikhail Berg, these authors lost their illusions about reality some fifteen to twenty years ago,[101] and, as Andrei Bitov suggests, 'the freedom they have acquired in the underground disintegrates now in the light of the day.'[102] It appears that writing for publication presupposes a certain degree of compliance, which restricts the freedom of the former underground writer. Contributors to *Vestnik* are known for their innovation and experimentation. However, some write conventional prose, while others produce post-modernist texts.

One of the contributors to *Vestnik novoi literatury* is the St Petersburg writer Petr Kozhevnikov (b. 1953). He began writing in the 1970s, and his first published work appeared in the notorious *Metropol'* (1979). His first official publication in the USSR appeared in the almanac *Krug* (Circle) in 1985. It was followed by a collection of prose, entitled *Ostrov* (Island; 1991), and a novella and stories published in *Iunost'*.[103] The thematic range of Kozhevnikov's prose is broad, but, as is true of the works of many other former underground writers, the structure is complex, the language unorthodox, and much of the characterization outside the mainstream of Soviet life.

The story 'Khudozhnik' (The Painter),[104] written in 1980 and published in 1990, has a loosely constructed plot. In it, unrelated events, details, and associations are indiscriminately mixed together. Lesha, a painter, wants to work but can find no inspiration. In the meantime, a friend arrives, and he and Lesha go out to look for drink and become involved in sexual activity with a public-washroom attendant. The story hints at prostitution, homosexuality, and the abuse of youngsters by mature women. It appears that, just as there is no consistency in the story, there is no set order in life: things are the way they happen to be and not the way they are ostensibly supposed to be. Life is far from perfect, and art is Lesha's escape from it. However, the creative process is arduous and inspiration does not come easily.

Kozhevnikov's novella 'Lichnaia neostorozhnost'' (Personal Carelessness; 1990), written in 1989, is thematically similar to former official narratives about the exploits of Soviet workers, but its style, structure, and objectives are different. It is a tale about a construction project, somewhere in a remote district, where many workers are former criminals and some are still in conflict with the law. This impressionistic account of human relationships in unusual circumstances comprises short chapters set in different locations. The language is an amalgam of underworld slang, officialese, and academic speech. In Soviet labour prose, the front-rank worker is usually the protagonist, and his main objective is the fulfilment of production quotas. In Kozhevnikov's novella, each worker seeks justice for himself and tries to satisfy his personal needs.

Kozhevnikov places his characters in difficult circumstances, because he believes that life is harsh. Yet, despite the sarcastic, often pessimistic, tone of his prose, he feels compassion for his heroes, who often find themselves in hopeless situations. Kozhevnikov's prose combines conventional Soviet themes with modern narrative techniques. It illustrates the uneasy process of fusion between former underground literature and current literary works.

NIKOLAI IAKIMCHUK

Petropol' (Petropol') is another St Petersburg almanac. It publishes prose and poetry of authors belonging to different generations, most of them members of the former Soviet literary underground. The contributors to *Petropol'* are united by the common denominator of non-conformity. Among them are post-modernists, such as V. Erofeev and E. Popov, as well as writers whose works combine elements of the post-modern with traditional realistic prose, such as A. Bitov and N. Iakimchuk.

The story 'Kartinki s vystavki' (Pictures from an Exhibition; 1990)[105] by N. Iakimchuk, the editor of *Petropol'*, has a well-defined plot, recognizable characters, and a conventional theme. San Sanych is a bureaucrat, soon to be demoted. Rita is his secretary and part-time lover. She decides to cast him off and seek the acquaintance of a successful writer. San Sanych follows Rita to her new lover's apartment, and the three meet in the ante-room.

The subject of the story is not new, but Iakimchuk's approach is original. Sentences and paragraphs are short, and the language is terse. There is no psychological analysis, but facts speak for themselves. Scenes, with little comment, follow one another swiftly, creating a cinematographic effect. Short passages concerning San Sanych and the writer, with Rita appearing in both instances, alternate. In the final scene, the heroes are compared to 'pictures from an exhibition.' Exhibition pictures are compared here to scenes from real life which express the irony of fate, as well as the author's message. Life resembles a whirlwind in which reality is in the process of constant dislocation, with people trying to adjust to the ever changing conditions of existence.

Among other writers who combine realistic portrayal with experimental narrative techniques it is worth mentioning Aleksandr Borodynia and Aleksei Slapovskii. In his novel *Spichki* (A Box of Matches; 1993),[106] Borodynia fuses a realistic setting with fantastic events. He introduces an array of images and scenes which mirror the corruption and moral decay of Soviet society. The distinction between fact and fiction in the narrative is fluid. In different chapters the author presents different versions of the same events. The novel is stylistically innovative, but portrayal is often incongruous, complex, and not easy to follow.

Slapovskii is a prolific writer able to produce in a variety of genres and styles. The hero of his novel *Pervoe vtoroe prishestvie* (The First Second Coming; 1993)[107] is a contemporary Messiah who believes in his calling. In 'Pyl'naia zima' (One Dusty Winter Day; 1993),[108] the narrator relates a story about an odd accident he concocts in his mind while waiting for a bus. Slapovskii's versatility is often rewarding, but it can also obscure his creative individuality.

The writers discussed here range in age from early thirties to close to sixty. Few of them published anything of substance prior to perestroika. Some, including Kuraev and Tolstaia, are currently in the process of stylistic and thematic experimentation. The writers in this group have different thematic interests, but all combine in their works realistic narration with modernist artistic devices. Kharitonov, P'etsukh, and Korolev rely heavily on secondary literary and historical sources. Pelevin blends the realistic with elements of fantasy and the absurd, and Kabakov's anti-utopias are evidence of their author's astonishing foresight. Writers such as Borodynia, Slapovskii, and Iakimchuk are still experimenting with subject, structure, and language. It is possible to conclude that, despite the reliance on a variety of post-modernist narrative techniques, most of the writers discussed above remain close to the realm of Russian conventional realism. The language of these writers is, in most cases, simple and straightforward, and their ideas are accessible.

C. Russian Post-modernism

Post-modernism is a term currently used and abused by Russian writers, critics, and literary scholars, who apply it to much of the new literature appearing in Russia in the late 1980s and early 1990s. The Russians did not invent this term. It was used first in 1934 by Federico de Onis in an anthology of Spanish poetry, published in Madrid, and later, in 1942, by Dudley Fitts in his *Anthology of Contemporary Latin-American Poetry*.[109] As a concept concerning dominant cultural characteristics, the notion of post-modernism has been in circulation since the end of the Second World War. Its meaning, however, remains vague, and its definitions and interpretations are often contradictory, owing to the fact that 'postmodernism suffers from a certain *semantic* instability: that is, no clear consensus about its meaning exists among scholars ... some critics mean by postmodernism what others call avant-gardism or even neo-avant-gardism, while still others would call the same phenomenon simply modernism.'[110] It is clear that 'modernism and postmodernism are not separated by an Iron Curtain or Chinese Wall,'[111] and they interact in a most intricate and perplexing manner. The argument of scholars studying post-modernist literature are diverse and contentious, and change rapidly. Hence, the study of each writer, or even work, requires new elaborations and qualifications. The situation is further complicated by the fact that politics and ideology often determine a given approach to literary theory – in Russia and the former Soviet Union as well as in the West.

It is accepted by most scholars that post-modernism is a response to modernism, which was, in turn, a reaction against nineteenth-century

cultural and aesthetic values. According to Ihab Hassan, 'postmodernism may be a response, direct or oblique, to the Unimaginable which
Modernism glimpsed only in its most prophetic moments ... it seems
bootless to compare Modern with Postmodern artists, range "masters"
against "epigones." The latter are closer to "zero in the bone," silence
and exhaustion, and the best of them brilliantly display the resources of
the void.'[112] And, yet, Hassan refuses to provide an unequivocal explanation of post-modernism. He asserts: 'I have not defined Modernism. I
can define Postmodernism less.'[113]
   More specifically, it is suggested that

the fundamental philosophical assumptions of modernism, its tendency toward
historical discontinuity, alienation, social individualism, solipsism, and existen-
tialism continue to permeate contemporary writing, perhaps in a heightened
sense. But the tendencies of the modernist to construct intricate forms, to interweave symbols elaborately, to create works of art that, however much they
oppose some established present order, create within themselves an ordered universe, have given way since the 1960s to a denial of order, to the presentation of
highly fragmented universes in the created world of art, and to critical theories
that are forms of phenomenology. Myth has given way to experiencing aesthetic
surfaces. Traditional forms, such as the novel, have given way to denials of those
forms, such as the anti-novel. The typical protagonist has become not a hero but
an anti-hero. Writers ... carry modernist assumptions about the world into the
very realm of art itself.[114]

Further, 'postmodern theory, criticism, and art today are all engaged in
contesting the modernist (humanist) premises of art's apolitical auton-
omy and of theory and criticism as value free activities.'[115] In their critical or ironic rereading of the past, post-modernists are contesting such
concepts as aesthetic originality and textual closure.[116] They also
endeavour 'to close the gap between past and present of the reader, and
... rewrite the past in a new context.'[117]
   In practical terms, in post-modernist art, irony is usually radical, com-
edy is absurd, and humour is black. There is a fusion of forms, and a
confusion of realms – a combination of fact and fiction, with emphasis
on improvisation, play, and abstraction. This literature is anti-élitist and
anti-authoritarian. The world described is not hierarchical but fragmented, and in a state of anarchy. Form is not conjunctive but disjunc-
tive and open, and metaphor is displaced by metonymy. Post-
modernism does not aspire towards accuracy of knowledge. It denies

the very ideas of reality and truth, and it elevates relativism into an end in itself. It is necessary to add, however, that, without perceiving the distinctive social, economic, philosophic, or political features of post-modernism, it is impossible to appreciate the true essence of post-modernist art. As Linda Hutcheon suggests, 'postmodernism is fundamentally contradictory, resolutely historical, and inescapably political.'[118] Postmodernism is more than an expression of literary theory. It is a worldview, a state of mind, and a reflection of the bewildering upheavals of our age.

In Soviet and Russian terms, 'post-modernism,' as it is currently applied, can be viewed as a misnomer. Modernism in Russia is a thing of the distant past. It goes back to the beginning of the century. Today, Russian post-modernism is not a reaction to modernism but rather a reflex of repugnance towards former Soviet social, ideological, and aesthetic values, and a reaction against socialist realism. It is a combination of what can be called post-socialist realism with an admixture of different elements of Western post-modernist art. In the late 1980s, most works previously forbidden by Soviet censors, or created in the Soviet cultural underground, were included in the realm of post-modernist art. This literature lifted former taboos and opened its pages to the discussion of issues such as sexual deviance, homosexuality, lesbianism, and drug abuse.

Russian writers apply post-modernist devices selectively and often emphasize some that are only marginally connected with post-modernist art in the West. The prose of most contemporary post-modernist Russian writers, whether those who have recently come out from the underground or those who had previously been published in official Soviet journals, is eclectic. They borrow freely from different sources, schools, and trends. Some combine post-modernist devices with those of realistic or modernist art. Others create on the verges of avant-gardism. But many are still steeped in their Soviet upbringing and education, and are unable to free themselves from the shackles of their past. Their literature, regardless of subject-matter and style, often sounds like socialist realism in reverse. They attack different targets, images, and ideas, but they exhibit the same lack of tolerance for the views and values of others and display an authoritarianism which is characteristic of socialist realism but alien to Western post-modernism.

Russian critics and scholars devote much time and effort to the discussion and elaboration of post-modernism as a theoretical notion. They argue about the relative merits of post-modernism, and its distinctions from avant-gardism. There are certainly many parallels between the two, but the current Russian avant-garde is interested primarily in the language which describes reality rather than in reality itself. For them, language becomes a new reality. Today those who consider themselves avant-garde artists ignore the Russian classical avant-garde heritage and include in avant-garde art everything that breaches the old system of Soviet taboos.[119] Furthermore, avant-garde literature advocates freedom and individualism. It expresses irony, cynicism, and nihilism. But its 'nothingness is not always a black hole where everything vanishes. It can also be a Divine Nothingness.'[120]

Some scholars suggest that 'Soviet postmodern is optimistic ... and that it is a phenomenon of a much broader scale' than Western post-modernism.[121] Others assert that it is not new to Soviet literature, and that works by writers such as A. Kim, V. Aksenov, and, in particular, the mature V. Kataev are close in style and spirit to post-modernism. Mark Lipovetskii asserts that Kataev's 'mauvisme' has many parallels with current post-modernist writings. He refers to Kataev's diffused prose, held together by the hero who is the author's alter ego, and to his dependence on the literary text.[122] Elaborating on the current state of Russian literature, Viacheslav Kuritsyn, a young critic from Ekaterinburg and one of the leading Russian theoreticians of post-modernism, suggests that 'post-modernism is an organic combination of all possible styles, trends, tendencies, and directions – in one word, all values of the former culture – within the framework of a single style. It is an exercise with a second actuality, the reality of culture ... Post-modernism functions not with "life" proper, but with a life impregnated by the seeds of culture.'[123] Writers, such as V. Erofeev, E. Popov, V. P'etsukh, V. Sorokin, and A. Vernikov, among others, are regarded by Kuritsyn as post-modernist authors. Kuritsyn is aware, however, that post-modernism has many enemies in Russia today. He claims that these are the people who 'defend hierarchical value systems, continue to believe in certain ideals, and are inclined towards religiosity ... These people are absolutely right. The non-hierarchical image of the world, suggested by post-modernism, is deadly to "traditional," "historical" (Christian, communist, etc.) thinking.'[124] Furthermore, 'post-modernism is the preoccupation of highly educated people ... who can easily deal with serious issues, and converse freely in the languages of different cultures.'[125]

Indeed, Russian conservative critics reject post-modernist literature entirely because it allegedly fosters the development of poor art and it is alien to the ethical spirit of the Russian people. Thus, Renata Gal'tseva

comes out with a vehement attack on post-modernism and its proponents. In a lecture delivered at a conference titled 'Literature and Religion,' she asserted that the world is currently in the process of 'the last
and decisive battle for the human soul. The name of the ideology,
instilled in the people with the purpose of replacing Marxism-Leninism,
is mystical hedonism ... Post-modernism invents horrors, but it is not
terrified by daily reality. All the macabre events described are not a play
of imagination, but the result of mental strains aimed at inventing something new from the realm of the satanic absurd ... The post-modernist
character is a moving source of atheistic anthropology of the epoch of
the end of the world. The cultural avant-garde teaches us to reject everything taught by Christian faith, by Russian literature, and by the principles of classical European humanism.'[126]

The sharp criticism of post-modernism is not limited, however, to
those who represent the conservative nationalist wing of Russian intellectual thought. Even some liberal critics have difficulty accepting it at
face value. They still adhere to traditional cultural values and fear that
post-modernism may fill the vacuum created by the demise of socialist
realism. Thus, one critic chides post-modernists because they allegedly
have no need to create anything new. All they do is plagiarize from the
works of others: 'a true post-modernist is *bound* to copy ... to eat the
crumbs from the table of culture ... The issue of talent makes no sense in
the framework of post-modernism. More important is to master the
appropriate set of recipes.'[127] According to another view, 'Russian post-
modernism, influenced by the specifics of the Russian literary tradition,
is a peculiar cultural *iurodstvo*,'[128] which can be loosely translated as
'playing God's fool.' Even Aleksandr Mikhailov, the editor of *Solo*, who
admires the internal freedom of expression exhibited by many post-
modernist authors, decries the fact that the meaning and essence of Russian post-modernism are vastly different from that accepted in the West.
He asserts that Russian post-modernism 'mystifies reality and turns it
into absurd. It is full of repulsive characters ... naturalism, and depravity.
Its language is monstrous. It claims to be intellectual while in fact it is
full of hidden and open quotations.'[129]

Karen Stepanian makes an attempt to place post-modernism within a
contemporary social context. He suggests that, to some, post-modernism
is a scarecrow which can be identified with all that is evil in contemporary Russian literature. To others, it is the only universal philosophy and
artistic method.[130] Stepanian believes that post-modernism, as a *Weltan-
schauung*, as well as a creative method, takes its roots in, and reflects in

turn, the social and philosophical phenomena coming to pass in Russian society today. These include 'the loss of faith in the higher meaning of existence, and in the super-personal aim of human life ... Reality is irrational and unknowable, and, therefore, its existence and meaning have just as much value as the illusions, fantasies, or ideas of each individual. And, finally, there can be no absolute truth, or any hierarchy of truths. Everyone exists in his own peculiar world, and everyone's personal truth ... is as real and important as the truth of everybody else.'[131] It is apparent, therefore, that the appearance of post-modernism in Russian social thought, as well as in literature, is a post-Marxist phenomenon. It is connected with the demise of official Soviet dogmatic ideology, and it aims to fill the theoretical vacuum in current Russian literary studies.

Much of the acrimonious discussion about the relative merits of post-modernism has been generated by two distinct events: the appearance in 1990 of the new periodical *Solo* (Solo), and the conference 'Post-modernism and Us,' organized in March 1991 at the Literary Institute in Moscow. The conference was attended by many prominent post-modernists, including V. Erofeev, V. Narbikova, T. Shcherbina, A. Bitov, and I. Zhdanov. Some opponents of this new literary trend in Russian culture also attended. In an article published in *Izvestiia*,[132] V. Malukhin, until recently the associate chief editor of *Oktiabr'*, discusses the proceedings of this conference and denounces post-modernism for its abolition of all aesthetic values and its indiscriminate appropriation of all intellectual wealth. He claims that 'the philosophy of post-modernism creates an intermediate world-view which is both an expression of and compensation for, the current general crisis of consciousness.' Malukhin's argument leads to the conclusion that, since current post-modernists have little talent, they resort to creative trickery and plagiarism. It did not take long before a response to Malukhin's attack appeared in the press. The Leningrad poet Viktor Krivulin came out in *Nezavisimaia gazeta* with a refutation of all Malukhin had to say. Krivulin suggested that Malukhin's hostility towards post-modernism was not motivated by aesthetic considerations but rather, was an expression of fear that this new literature would infiltrate the so-called thick journals, 'contaminating' what had been formerly known as the 'big literature.'[133]

It is obvious that the tone and substance of the literary debate is still in the language and spirit of official Soviet literary criticism of the period of stagnation. It is worth noting, however, that some young critics refuse to become involved in these highly politicized literary discussions. Instead, they resort to the study of Western literary theory and endeavour to place Russian post-modernism within the generally accepted theoretical context.[134] Others view Russian post-modernism as a temporary and transitional phenomenon, predicting its rapid decline.

It is clear that there is no unanimity in the assessment of the relative merits of post-modernism and its place on the current Russian literary scene. It is evident that there are many parallels between the Russian and Western versions of this phenomenon, yet it is necessary to stress that Russian post-modernism is in many respects different from its Western counterpart. Caryl Emerson points out that there are 'aspects of Western post-modernism that have been conspicuously absent, or present only in greatly weakened form, in the ex-Soviet context ... There is, first and most understandably, no *neo-Marxism* in any form ... In general ex-Soviet intellectuals are not sympathetic toward the justice-and-equality argument that fuels the best multiculturalist work in the West ... Finally ... there has been in Russia little sympathy for *feminism* of the sort we know here.'[135]

Russian post-modernism mirrors the violent and perplexing shifts in the political and social realities of Russia in the last decade. It is a rejection of the Soviet past without any expression of readiness, or willingness, to accept anything tangible in the future. It is a reaction to Soviet-style dogmatic philosophy and to the vacuous state of Soviet aesthetic theory. It signifies the deep crisis of consciousness, paralysing the actions of man and his social institutions. No wonder that, in such circumstances, young writers emerging from the underground, for the first time being able to make use of their newly acquired freedom, move from one extreme to another. The literature they produce may not be to the liking of everybody, but, because they owe nothing to the old regime and have seldom yielded to the pressures of censorship, they are able to create in a style to which former Soviet official writers have no access. They are perhaps not as skilful as their older colleagues and often lack a wide audience, but many are talented and may develop into good writers. Regardless of its artistic quality, the prose of Russian post-modernist writers is a true expression of a new pluralism. And that, in itself, is an important achievement.

VIKTOR EROFEEV

Viktor Erofeev (b. 1947) is one of the most interesting and controversial figures of the contemporary Russian literary scene. The son of a senior Soviet diplomat, he is a graduate of the Moscow State University and the

Institute of World Literature in Moscow. His first published work appeared in 1968, and he was admitted to the Writers' Union in 1978. He became well known in Russian literary circles in the late 1970s, in connection with his contribution to the almanac *Metropol'* (1979), banned by Soviet censors. This prompted his immediate expulsion from the Writers' Union, to which he was not readmitted until 1988. Erofeev, who is considered by many to be a proponent and practitioner of post-modernist art, is a prose-fiction writer as well as a literary scholar and critic. His novels and stories illustrate, in a way, what he preaches in his journalistic writings. Erofeev's article 'Pominki po sovetskoi literature' (A Funeral Feast for Soviet Literature),[136] provides a penetrating and provocative, but not completely objective, critique of Soviet literary history. Erofeev divides post-Stalin Soviet literature into three streams – official, liberal, and 'village prose' – and he claims that all Soviet writers have submitted, in varying degrees, to official pressure. He mocks socialist realism by asserting that 'it is the cultural emanation of totalitarianism. It is the rage of a literature locked up in spatial confines. It expresses the sado-masochistic complex of an atheistic writer who sells his soul to the devil, in the existence of which he does not believe.' Erofeev suggests that, in post-utopian society, it is time to return to real literature. The artist should concern himself with the creation of art, while the truth should remain the domain of *Pravda*. He calls for a dialogue, and perhaps a convergence, of all cultural and literary trends and styles which draw their inspiration from the experience of Russian and Western philosophers, until recently forbidden in the USSR.

Erofeev's article generated a lively reaction, but many disagreed with his unequivocal repudiation of everything created in the Soviet past. Indeed, while Erofeev scorns socialist realism, he applies in his criticism means and methods similar to those employed by official Soviet critics. He even questions the role of literature in a democratic society. He asserts that 'literature and democracy are incompatible. Literature is undemocratic by nature; it is unbelievably hierarchical.'[137] The substance of Erofeev's argument certainly has merit, but its tone, which does not leave any room for compromise, is reminiscent of Soviet official parlance. After all, Erofeev is himself a product of the Soviet system in which tolerance for the views of others has never been held in high esteem.

In 1989, Erofeev published a collection of stories entitled *Telo Anny, ili konets russkogo avangarda* (Anna's Body, or the End of the Russian Avant-Garde). It includes seven stories, written between 1985 and 1988, most of them narrated in the first person. Some stories or scenes are set in contemporary reality and others in pre-revolutionary Russia, but spatial and temporal confines are always vague, and chronology is lacking. In the stories, reality and fantasy are intertwined; ghosts and apparitions appear in episodes together with real people. The transition from reality to the imagined and fantastic is always abrupt, as is the transition from the discussion of elevated and spiritual subjects to the portrayal of the vulgar and profane. Erofeev's stories are intended for the sophisticated reader. They have many narrative dimensions; the terrible and sinister can coexist with the comic, while the tragic can turn into word play. Many stories express their message through their form. The intention is to surprise and shock the reader out of the stupor caused by years of adaptation, acquiescence, and passive acceptance of conventional didactic prose. In the titular story, Erofeev makes a symbolic attempt to bury, along with Soviet literature, the current Russian avant-garde. A woman, abandoned by her husband, an avant-garde writer, suddenly discovers that he is sleeping next to her in bed. Instead of waking him and showering him with love and affection, she devours him, and thus brings to an end the history of the Russian avant-garde.

Another story, 'Pis'mo k materi' (A Letter to Mother), begins with a letter by the author-narrator to his mother. He reports his determination to write a book. The story ends with an account of a New Year's Eve which the narrator spends in bed with a stranger, an old married woman. In between, there are observations about contemporary reality, the transition to democracy, as well as the struggle between the Whites and Reds in post-revolutionary Russia. Most important, the language shifts unexpectedly from traditional literary Russian to Soviet jargon and clichés. The shift creates a shocking aesthetic effect, the intention of which is to mock Soviet officialese.

It is not easy to summarize Erofeev's stories. Their meaning, if there is any, is most often under the surface, and different readers may perceive and interpret them in different ways. 'Popugaichik' (The Parakeet), written in epistolary form, is one tale which has the semblance of a definite plot. The language and tone of the letter are characteristic of nineteenth-century Russian prose, but the story is in fact an allegory of the Soviet system of justice. An official, who is an interrogator and executioner as well, replies to a letter of inquiry from a father who is concerned about the fate of his son. The boy has been incarcerated and accused of exhuming the body of a dead parakeet, and trying to make it fly again. When tortured, the boy admits that, by making the dead bird fly he indeed intended to prove the superiority of foreign parakeets over local birds, thus hurting the image and pride of his own people. There is no mention in the story of Russian or Soviet institutions, but the allusions are clear. The methods of interrogation, torture, and punishment are strikingly similar to those applied by the KGB. In the end, the interrogator torments and drives the boy to suicide. He forces him to jump from a belfry, watching attentively to see if he will try to fly, as the parakeet has allegedly done. The interrogator is a cynical tyrant, deriving sexual pleasure from torturing others. He has driven the boy to death and tortures the compassionate father. He gives vent to his sado-masochistic impulses and callously abuses the weak and helpless. The subject-matter of the story is human tragedy, while its tone is mocking and farcical.

Both 'Pis'mo k materi' and 'Popugaichik' are epistolary monologues, the first by an alleged liberal intellectual and the second by an executioner. Both characters are presented as types of the Russian historical absurd. The language in both stories comprises an array of rhetorical devices in which coarse and vulgar slang is indiscriminately blended with political clichés, accounts of torture, and elevated phraseology.

Erofeev's novel *Russkaia krasavitsa* (Russian Beauty; 1990), written in 1980–2, appeared simultaneously in Moscow and in Paris. Despite much advance publicity, its appearance pleased few and outraged many others. The novel is multidimensional, and it can be read in different ways – as a sentimental love story, a parable, an existential myth, or a social commentary. On the realistic surface, the plot of the novel seems uncomplicated – but only on the surface. The heroine, Irina Tarakanova, a poor but beautiful girl from the provinces, comes to Moscow in search of happiness and carries on an affair with the much older and married Vladimir Sergeevich, or, as she calls him, 'Leonardik,' who is an important personality in the arts. He claims to be in love with her but refuses marriage because it would ruin his professional reputation. He dies, in a state of sexual ecstasy, in bed with Irina, and, although she is thought to be barren, she becomes impregnated during this last encounter. Irina's affair with Leonardik continues even after his death. He appears in her sleep, makes love to her, and offers to marry her. Thus, dream offsets reality by creating in Irina's mind a new, imaginary life.

Irina's affair with Leonardik is the central episode in the novel, but there is also an array of subplots in which Irina's lovers, former husbands, women friends, foreign diplomats, cultural personalities, and simply shady characters appear and disappear in a haphazard manner. Few are remembered because they appear only fleetingly. Even Irina, the

Russian beauty, is never described in detail, and the reader may wonder what the external features of her beauty are. One thing is clear: it is not a spiritual beauty, but rather is a destructive beauty that reflects blind passion.

The novel is narrated in the first person by Irina, and most events are presented in the form of disjointed ruminations, passing through her morbid and sensitive mind. All we know is how she perceives reality, and how her subconscious reflects her life experiences. Irina's sickly imagination leads her to excesses: at one point she compares herself to Joan of Arc and assumes the role of the saviour of Russia; at another, she contemplates man's relation with God and her own attitude towards religion.

Russkaia krasavitsa experiments with plot and style and emphasizes different aspects and details of Soviet life that were previously taboo to the Soviet reader. A wide variety of sexual scenes, including allusions to homosexuality, lesbianism, bisexuality, exhibitionism, and *ménage à trois*, are included. According to Erofeev, 'erotica, in particular when connected with the subconscious, ... reveals the essence of man much better than his political and philosophical views do. Therefore ... a deeper and more valuable understanding of Soviet society can be obtained by investigating the fate of the heroine of *Russkaia krasavitsa* than by scrutinizing the works of Lenin, Stalin, the writer Rybakov, or the critic Lakshin.'[138] Unfortunately, sex in the novel is devoid of love and intimacy; rather, it is perverted, mechanical, and unemotional. While it caters to the whims of a reading public little exposed to erotica in Soviet literature, it also mirrors the decay and corruption of the Soviet intelligentsia.

The critical reception of *Russkaia krasavitsa* was as divided and contradictory as the novel itself. Some regarded it as 'an immoral story about dissolute Moscow courtesans, making use of the decaying system for personal enrichment.'[139] Others claimed that, in comparison with the corrupt Soviet system, Irina 'is ethically pure as a child.'[140] P. Basinskii suggested that the objective of Erofeev's prose was to 'expose the "animal" nature of people in order to separate it from the strictly "human."'[141] Another critic asserted that the novel 'espouses no cause beyond literary and sexual freedom.'[142] An original, albeit controversial, analysis of *Russkaia krasavitsa* was provided by the critic Oleg Dark and published in the journal *Strelets*. He discussed the novel within the context of the irreconcilable antinomy between the male and female principles, and the opposition between Christianity and paganism. He explored also the parallels between the views of Erofeev and those of V.

Rozanov, and suggested that the prose of Erofeev draws its inspiration from old cultural values. But, in the process of making ample use of these traditional sources in his art, Erofeev turned them upside down and transposed them in a shocking manner into burlesque, blasphemy, and travesty.[143]

Erofeev is a sophisticated and skilled craftsman, yet the language of the novel shows little respect for its readers. It is full of slang, obscenities, and expressions unacceptable in literary Russian. It is a mixture of different styles in which the 'low' and the 'high' intermingle freely. It includes naturalistic portrayal, grotesque, and hyperbole. It demystifies the sacred and exposes the dark side of human nature. It lays bare the triviality of daily existence and the decadence of Soviet society. It is possible to agree with Georges Philiph, who suggested that 'the author has set out to expose the fundamental spiritual and mental process symptomatic of the sick consciousness of the modern world,'[144] in particular as it relates to Soviet society of the Brezhnev era.

Erofeev's prose is not for the ordinary reader. It is controversial, it can be obscure, it often sacrifices characterization for external effect, and its temporal and spatial dimensions are indistinct. It can be even viewed as an expression of the author's personal rebellion against society, the state, and the established order of things. In his critical writings, Erofeev rejects the notion of the arts as a medium for different ideas. In his assessment of the current situation in Russia, he asserts that unexpected liberty can prove surprisingly frustrating. He claims that 'we are in [a state of] confusion now ... There are no taboo themes now ... When someone is unfree, he fights for freedom, and he loses all his energy fighting. But he is not free once the prison is open. He has nothing to say.'[145] And yet Erofeev cannot avoid broaching rebellious ideas in his prose. Even his style is an expression of his views. Erofeev and his prose mirror the difficult process of transition in Russia today. One cannot run away from oneself. Past experiences hide in the subconscious and affect the writer's creative imagination, and even his most rational acts.

EVGENII POPOV

Evgenii Popov (b. 1946) is one of the writers connected with the *Metropol'* affair. He was expelled from, and readmitted to, the Writers' Union, together with V. Erofeev. Many of his recent publications, appearing in the periodical press, were written in the literary underground prior to glasnost. His fiction is not conventionally realistic; rather, it is inventive, expressive, and humorous, but also paradoxical, absurd, and full of bitter irony. His long narrative *Prekrasnost' zhizni* (The Splendour of Life; 1990) has a ludicrous subtitle: 'Chapters from a "Novel (or Affair) with a Newspaper" which will never be started and finished.' The narrative, organized in chronological order, covers twenty-five years of Soviet experience. It includes excerpts from newspaper articles, speeches, headlines, and resolutions of different Soviet state and public institutions. Each chapter is devoted to one year and is composed of three distinct parts. It begins with an observation, comment, or short story in which the author-narrator is the main character, usually set in the year indicated in the title; excerpts and quotations from the daily or periodical press follow; and it concludes with another short story written some time in the early 1980s.

In the first chapter of *Prekrasnost' zhizni*, set in 1961, the reader is informed of the great accomplishments of Soviet science. The nation is proud of the first man in space, the Soviet major Iurii Gagarin. Today everyone appreciates Gagarin's feat, but most people also know that his life was wasted. He was killed during a training mission while he was intoxicated. Another great achievement is noted: the corn-planting campaign in the Soviet Union is a great success. Considering the perennial pathetic state of Soviet agriculture, raving of the achievements of Soviet farmers sound ludicrous today. In the last chapter of the narrative, set in 1985, we are informed about the death of K. Chernenko, and there is a hint that a new era is about to begin. The book is open-ended: it could be continued at any time. The sheer accumulation of historical facts and the array of diverse fictional characters, mostly failures, alcoholics, have-beens, and insipid personalities, turn the narrative into a peculiar encyclopedia of Soviet life, which illustrates convincingly the oppressive nature of Brezhnev's rule.

The stories which open each chapter accord the author-narrator a platform for self-expression and provide the reader with a lyrical portrait of the writer. They combine a variety of styles, narrative techniques, and devices, but the author-narrator's personality is always at the centre, helping unify the plot. According to Popov, life is beautiful, and one has to make the best of it while one is still alive. Ideologies and theoretical conceptions about life are not important, but practical experiences are. Popov is selective in his choice of quotations. Many relate to the life of Soviet cultural institutions and the literary establishment. In some cases, he juxtaposes contrasting excerpts in order to shock the reader. In other instances, he reminds us, for example, that the very writers and bureaucrats who today worship and idolize A. Solzhenitsyn were among those who previously condemned and repudiated him, and demanded his blood.

Popov's stories, whether incorporated into a larger narrative structure or published separately, are similar in style, tone, and spirit. There is nothing stable in them. Tragedy and farce, happiness and despair, are easily transformed one into the other. In 'Tetia Musia i diadia Leva' (Aunt Musia and Uncle Leva; 1988),[146] the first-person narrator stands in a queue, observes the world, and meditates about the past. He reminisces about his relatives, friends, and life in general. He rambles freely in time and space, providing sketchy and impressionistic observations about people, events, or values. This disorderly outpouring reflects the unmanageable essence and unpredictability of life itself. People act and move in time and space, but only some experiences are remembered; all the rest vanishes from sight, just as people do.

'Rasskazy' (Stories; 1989),[147] stories set in provincial Russia, provide sketches from Soviet life, pointing at such phenomena as homosexuality, alcoholism, and permissiveness. Events rather than people are at the centre of these stories, which are full of sarcasm and sad irony. A variety of stylistic devices intermingle in each story. First – and third-person narration are interspersed with dialogue, excerpts from the press, and narration in poetic form. Some characters reappear in different stories, but confusion and lack of order – virtual chaos – is the unifying thread.

The stories 'Udaki' (Udaki; 1992)[148] are similar. They dwell on the remote and the unusual. Popov blends the paradoxical and the sentimental in his writing, and is able to combine the sad and the comic in an unobtrusive manner. Dejection and gloom in his stories can depress the reader but can also evoke laughter. After all, Popov believes that life is beautiful, and that should be enough to make people happy.

VLADIMIR SOROKIN

A slim collection of prose, 'providing a cross-section of unofficial literature of the 1980s,' entitled *Vidimost' nas* (The Appearance of Us), was published in Moscow in 1991.[149]It includes two stories by Vladimir Sorokin (b. 1955), as well as works by A. Gavrilov, Z. Gareev, Nina Sadur, Valeriia Narbikova, and others. A year later a small volume containing seventeen stories and simply titled *Vladimir Sorokin* (Vladimir Sorokin; 1992) was published in Moscow. V. Sorokin is a graphic artist by profession, and literature appears to be his second love. Having established residence in West Germany, he currently moves freely between Russia and the West. Sorokin is regarded today as one of the most talented writers to come out from the Soviet literary underground. However, his prose is peculiar and highly eccentric. Sorokin regards himself as a post-modernist, although many view his art as an expression of conceptualism. The philosophical doctrine of conceptualism asserts that universals do exist but only as mental concepts. The mind can form an image that corresponds to a particular concept and may later be properly affirmed by reality. As opposed to post-modernism which is an expression of relativism, conceptualism in literature is play with language signs which have no meaning. Some have suggested that 'Moscow conceptualism is in fact post-literature ... post-modernism, instead, does not advocate the complete dissolution of literature, but it shatters its foundations from within.'[150] According to Sorokin, in conceptualist art 'the relation to the object is more important than the essence of the object itself. Conceptualism means a remote relationship to a work of art, and to culture in general.'[151] Sorokin claims that a conceptualist writer is usually recognized by his idiosyncratic style. Sorokin, however, is a master of multiple styles, moving freely from nineteenth-century Russian literary language to the language of 'village prose,' the Soviet construction novel, *byt* literature, or *Pravda*. His stories can always be recognized by recurring narrative patterns, and his realistic narratives are interlaced with the grotesque, the absurd, and the surrealistic. In most of his stories, he alternates the real with the unreal, the absurd, and the nonsensical.

The beginnings of Sorokin's stories are usually set in Soviet reality, and they are parodies of well-known themes of socialist realism. After the introduction of the realistic characters and the exposition of the plot, an abrupt and unexpected change in style and narrative tone follows. In some instances, it leads to the portrayal of scenes that are totally absurd and make little sense. In other cases, they involve perverse sexual exploits, senseless murder, or horrid cannibalistic scenes. The transition from one narrative mode to another is so sudden that the reader is stunned and may take a while to recover from the initial shock. The chaos in Part two undermines the stability and ideological dogma contained in Part one. Furthermore, since the conclusion of a story seldom makes real sense, it destroys the reader's initial perception of the text, and creates a new, very different impression. And that is precisely Sorokin's objective. By intertwining the language and subject-matter of official Soviet literature with outrageous scenes, obscene language, and despicable abusive expressions, Sorokin brings the former down to the level of the latter and illustrates that the gibberish which concludes most of his stories is 'just as senseless and philistine as the ravings of socialist realism.'[152] This new perception of the narrative revolts and disgusts the reader, who is led to view the 'high' style of Soviet socialist art as camouflage that obscures its fraudulent essence.

The narrative pattern mentioned above recurs in story after story. After a while, the reader is no longer shocked and expects in the next story, after the realistic introduction, a frantic, often senseless, conclusion. The story 'Delovoe predlozhenie' (A Business Proposition; 1992)[153] begins with an orderly and logical discussion that takes place at the editorial office of a students' newspaper. The subject of the discussion is serious, and so are its participants. But, as soon as the meeting is over, two young men stay behind and become involved in sexual interplay. One of them produces a gift box containing a severed portion of a male's face. It is obvious that the two are lovers, yet one of them is also involved in an incestuous relationship with his own mother.

In another story, 'Sorevnovanie' (Competition; 1992),[154] two woodcutters, Lokhov and Budziuk, discuss the issue of production quotas and socialist competition. Budziuk suggests that competition is important, and that they should challenge another brigade. Lokhov, on the other hand, is against it because he believes that winning the pennant is meaningless. The exchange of opinions is brief, and Budziuk is soon back at work, cutting trees. That is when Lokhov approaches him, cuts of his head with his saw, and runs off to the nearby river, muttering on his way contemptuously: 'now we will compete, now we will compete.' Boys who are fishing at the river sense something ominous, and one of them embarks upon a long tirade, which is a mixture of Soviet clichés and absurd horrific detail and ends with the words 'pus and lard.'

'Otkrytie sezona' (The Opening of the Season; 1991)[155] describes a hunting trip to the Russian countryside. The young Sergei returns to his native village and, together with the old huntsman Kuz'ma Egorych, ventures into the forest. The language of the first few pages is reminiscent of I. Turgenev's *Hunter's Sketches*, and the general atmosphere in the countryside is related in the spirit of Russian 'village prose'. But then, all of a sudden, everything changes. Sergei aims and shoots, and the dark running shadow collapses. They approach what turns out to be a dead human body, then cut it into pieces and prepare to cook and consume its liver. Thus, what begins as a description of an idyllic episode in rustic life ends with the portrayal of an incongruous cannibalistic scene.

The pattern in which the realistic, business-like, and often sentimental alternates with the gruesome and absurd repeats itself time and again. In 'Sergei Andreevich' (Sergei Andreevich; 1992),[156] a graduating-class outing into the forest ends with the best student eating the excrement of his favoured teacher. In 'Proezdom' (Passing Through; 1992),[157] a business meeting of the district party committee ends with a scene in which a visiting party official from the regional centre relieves himself on the desk of a local bureaucrat. In 'Zasedanie zavkoma' (A Meeting of the Trade Union Committee; 1991),[158] a meeting at which the unseemly behaviour of a factory worker is discussed ends with the torture and violent murder of a cleaning woman. 'Kiset' (Tobacco-Pouch; 1991)[159] begins with a sentimental story of a war veteran, searching for a woman who presented him during the war with a tobacco-pouch. When he finally manages to locate her, the account of their meeting turns into senseless mad raving.

Sorokin's published prose currently receives mixed reviews in Russia. However most Russian editors refuse to accept his stories for publication.[160] Representatives of the conservative nationalist wing express contempt for such literature and vehemently oppose it. But even liberal critics have difficulty in accepting the sexual perversion, horrifying detail, and mad delirium described in his prose. Some compare Sorokin's stories with those of members of the Oberiu group of the late 1920s.[161] But the literature of the absurd, by such writers as Daniil Kharms and Aleksandr Vvedenskii, the leading members of this group, appears to be tame in comparison with Sorokin's prose. It eschews the use of foul language, and avoids the cynical and nihilistic message contained in Sorokin's stories, and often provides a sense of optimism. Sorokin sets himself apart, not only from the writers of the absurd of the 1920s, but from society in general. He separates literature and morality and asserts that he has no social interests and is absolutely apolitical. It makes no difference to him whatsoever who rules the country and whether representatives of democracy, perestroika, or totalitarianism are in charge. According to Sorokin, 'Evtushenko [and] Aitmatov have social interests; therefore, literature for them is, at least partially, a cause for political activity ... Hence, they write in a language understood by the masses. They write for the people, while [Sorokin] writes for himself.'[162] Conceptualism, he claims, allows him to approach literature in a detached manner and spares him having to take into consideration the needs or interests of the reading public.[163] All he is concerned with is the text. He does not separate language into 'high' and 'low' styles but

accepts all words and expressions as parts of one language, and one culture. He claims that, by introducing swear words and foul language into
literary use, one deprives these expressions of their aggressiveness and
turns them into an ordinary means of communication.[164]

Sorokin is, of course, free to create as he sees fit, and to interpret his
work in accordance with his own philosophical and social beliefs, but a
literary text usually acquires an existence independent of its author's initial intentions. Hence, his reliance on subject-matter from Soviet daily life
and his interest in, and preoccupation with, the manipulation of 'socialist
realism as an autonomous aesthetic trend'[165] make his prose socially rel-
evant and open to different interpretations. Thus, for example, 'Zasedanie
zavkoma' may assert that, in the Soviet Union, those who are charged
with the responsibility of chastising and upbraiding others are themselves criminals and murderers. In 'Proezdom' the scene in which a high-
ranking official relieves himself on a document he has just signed may
indicate this official's low regard not only for the particular document but
for the whole system, which produces mountains of useless paper. Similarly, the scene in 'Sergei Andreevich,' in which a student eats the excrement of the teacher he worships may allude to the pitfalls of
indoctrination and the shortcomings of the Soviet system of education,
which provides the young with much useless and unnecessary information but fails to prepare them for independent activity in mature life.

Sorokin's prose is a phenomenon peculiar to the changing realities of
Soviet and Russian life in the last decade. It reflects this life in many different ways, and expresses rebellion against the established order of
things. It offers a cynical view of reality with little hope for the future.
Sorokin subverts meaning, illustrating, at the same time, that, in the final
analysis, nonsense may also have meaning. In the concluding parts of
his stories, Sorokin employs the same devices he uses as a graphic artist.
He often includes in his stories contrasting graphic images, collage, and
a disorderly accumulation of seemingly unimportant detail, which create an atmosphere of chaos, absurdity and futility, and a realization, that,
as Sorokin suggests, '"social life" ... cannot change human nature.'[166]

VALERIIA NARBIKOVA

Valeriia Narbikova (b. 1958) is one of the young writers whose appearance on the Russian literary scene generated controversy and discord
among readers and professional critics alike. Some regard her as a talented prose writer; others view her as a modern hack. Narbikova pro-

duced her first pieces of prose in 1980, while still a student at the Moscow Literary Institute.[167] But before the advent of glasnost, she had no chance of publishing anything. Her first published novella, 'Ravnovesie sveta dnevnykh i nochnykh zvezd' (The Equilibrium of the Day and Night Stars), appeared in 1988.[168] 'Okolo ekolo ...' (Around and About ... ; 1990),[169] 'Probeg – pro beg' (On the Run; 1990),[170] and several other stories followed.

A. Bitov, Narbikova's teacher at the Literary Institute, has been exceedingly generous to his former student. In the introduction to her first novella, he wrote that she is extremely talented, and her style is unique: 'The spatial and temporal relationships in the perception and experiences of her heroes, i.e., the poetics of Narbikova, are new and convincing to me. Anyone endowed with traditional literary taste can appreciate the beauty and the stridently lyrical strength of ... her prose ... It is more difficult to comprehend her plots, her architectonics, and general meaning. But even that is possible.'[171] It is apparent that Bitov is captivated by Narbikova's style, paying less attention to structure, plot, and meaning in her works. Indeed, it is difficult to provide a summary of any of Narbikova's stories. All that emerges is a blurred picture of reality, interspersed with a generous admixture of fantasy. Indistinct characters, many with uncommon names that are difficult to pronounce, converse, move, copulate, and talk about love. In between are scattered comments, remarks, and aphorisms relating to the works of classical literary giants or to certain current political and social events.

In 'Ravnovesie sveta dnevnykh i nochnykh zvezd,' the heroine, Sana,[172] is married to Avvakum, but allegedly in love with Otmatfeian,[173] who is also married. Otmatfeian has a friend with a weird name, Chiashchiazhyshyn. Sana bears Otmatfeian's child conceived by way of a telephone conversation. In another story, 'Vidimost nas' (The Appearance of Us; 1991),[174] written apparently before glasnost, Sana, Otmatfeian, and Chiashchiazhyshyn appear again. The first two are lonely lovers, somehow associated with the creative world. The latter, an acquaintance of theirs, is a sculptor who admits the two into his studio, where they apparently consummate their love. Chiashchiazhyshyn produces monuments so that the image of creative people, whose works are forbidden, should not disappear.

The plot of 'Okolo ekolo ...' is easier to follow, but it is also a combination of fantasy, the grotesque, and the bizarre. Petia, a young female student, lives with her older sister, Ezdandukta, and is in love with Boris. All three intend to spend New Year's eve together. In the meantime,

Petia visits a male student friend, Kostroma, and returns home late. She learns then that Boris has made love to Ezdandukta, and that they intend to marry. As an act of vengeance, Petia makes love to another friend, but that does not quench her passion for Boris. In one of his scientific experiments, Kostroma manages to bring to life a little monster, who drives his creator to destruction.

Seemingly unrelated, scenes, images, and dialogue are indiscriminately mixed together in Narbikova's stories. With the help of such devices as collage, repetition, and tautology, she endeavours to break down the accepted logical meaning of words and phrases. Narbikova's language is the vernacular of contemporary Moscow youth, and her stories are apparently directed at the same audience. This prose often resembles a sequence of internal monologues in which the stream-of-consciousness technique prevails. The distinction between the voice of the author-narrator and that of the protagonists is tentative and ill defined. The reader is under no illusion that most of the thoughts, reflections, or doubts expressed by the characters belong to the author-narrator rather than to the protagonists. There is no exposition of plot or character identification in the stories. We learn little about the heroes. They have no faces, and it is even difficult to remember their names. Yet, this is apparently the intention of the author: it symbolizes the ethereal essence of our existence, in which nothing is stable and everything is futile.

Love is one of the recurring themes in Narbikova's stories. But the love portrayed is lifeless and unemotional; it is not the romantic, passionate, or spiritual love that usually entails selflessness and the care for others. There is much talk about sex, but there is no explicit description of it. In fact, sex is treated as a casual occurrence, intended to satisfy one's animal urges only. Hence, Petia is surprised and horrified that, at the mature age of thirty-five, her sister, Ezdandukta, is still a virgin. She is outraged that her sister wants to love Boris as a human being rather than as an object of sex. Petia views her sister as a relic of another age.

It is possible to assume that Narbikova, a married woman and the mother of a young daughter, is articulating the views of her own generation. In reply to the question 'How does eroticism combine with morals?' Narbikova has the following to say: 'Morals are indispensable, but they must be natural, not forced or dictated. The individual should arrive at a moral code of his or her own free will.'[175] It is clear, then, that Narbikova's fictional world, in which chaos reigns, resembles closely her notion of a real world in which everyone is free to establish his or her own boundaries between good and evil. This view apparently reflects the opinions of many young people, and it also mirrors the situation in the Soviet Union in the late 1980s and early 1990s, when social instability became a way of life. The rejection of the Marxist myth and the repudiation of Soviet class morality have left an ethical vacuum which cannot be filled instantaneously by faith. Judging by one of her stories, in which Narbikova exhibits an obvious lack of respect for religion in general, and for the Christian creed in particular, it is hard to believe that she relies on faith when seeking solutions for existing problems.[176]

Many critics berate Narbikova for the shallowness and the lack of moral values in her prose. The well-known writer Georgii Vladimov suggests that, despite the fact that Narbikova is skilful in her own way, 'she does not fit into the mainstream of Russian literature, which has always concerned itself acutely with ethical issues.'[177] M. Lipovetskii asserts that Narbikova attempts 'to cover up her primitive emptiness with a deceptive appearance of significance.'[178] It is clear that Narbikova sacrifices ethics for style and forsakes meaning for external effect. But, in doing so, she exhibits great ingenuity in experimenting and playing with words. K. Stepanian suggests that 'the *word* has lost its inherent connection with meaning and, by implication, with the truth. The words with which young poets and writers operate today are virtually meaningless in the minds of their young contemporaries. Furthermore, these words have become symbols of falsehood ... hence the attempt to restore the spiritual strength of the word by discovering new and unexpected combinations and associations, and the restoration of almost forgotten meaning.'[179]

Narbikova's prose mirrors her times. She began her creative path in the literary underground but was fortunate enough to come out soon into the open. Her stories do not make for easy reading, and her prose is certainly not for the mass readership, rooted in old Russian and Soviet literary traditions. Instead, she reaches out to an audience which is literate, sophisticated, and tired of old Soviet plots and clichés; it is an audience with which she shares a common language and can identify with ease. Only time will tell whether her early success will endure; however even negative critical recognition is a mark of achievement for a young writer in Russia today.

NINA SADUR

Born in 1950 in the city of Novosibirsk, and at present residing in Moscow, Nina Sadur has come into literature with her own set of characters, until recently ignored in Russian and Soviet prose. The daughter of a professional poet and a 1983 graduate of the Moscow Literary Institute, she regards the playwright R.S. Rozov and the writer E. Kharitonov as her literary teachers.[180] Sadur writes stories, novellas, and plays in which she places the feeble-minded and mentally unstable at the centre. Most of her images are suggestive of phantoms who may appear from nowhere and disappear into thin air.

The title of her story 'Chto-to otkroetsia' (Something Will Appear; 1991)[181] is appropriate to its subject-matter. It is a story about appearances, and the reader is never sure whether the characters are real or a figment of the main hero's imagination. Petrov, who has previously suffered several unspecified painless fits, returns after many years from Moscow to his native city. He intends to visit his parents' graves; however he never reaches the cemetery and, instead, walks the streets in a morbid state of mind, conversing with different people who are inventions of his sick imagination. In fact, he is talking to his own double. From the deep recesses of his subconscious, it is brought out of hiding by his visit to long-forgotten places. The dialogue with oneself is reminiscent of an internal monologue of a mentally unstable man.

The main character of the story 'Iug' (The South; 1991),[182] Olia, is a young woman on a visit to the resort of Sochi. Like Petrov, she knows that she is not well but cannot identify her illness. Recently she has become depressed and forgetful, losing weight and experiencing extreme anxiety. Married before, but now single, she antagonizes and is afraid of people, yet makes sexual advances to a fifteen-year-old boy. Little by little, Olia disintegrates mentally and emotionally. She loses her faculty of speech and the ability to communicate with others, and she ends up starving and without a place to live. Day and night she spends at the seashore in the cold. Finally, she is saved by two old, God-seeking women who are on their way to one of the holy places in the Caucasus, which they unfortunately never manage to reach.

The story is narrated on several different levels. The omniscient narrator places the story in a certain perspective. Parts of the story are narrated by Olia when she is still rational and can relate to the world around her. As well, there is a third-person account of Olia's sickly and totally irrational state of mind. Most characters in the story, with the exception of the two old women, are perceived through Olia's eyes. The images of these characters appear in a cinematographic sequence. As Olia's mental illness becomes more pronounced, these characters become increasingly indistinct and blurred, and reflect the disintegration of Olia's mental faculties.

Sadur explores in her stories the subconscious and the surrealistic. She follows her protagonists on their path to mental disintegration, examining their transition from semi-normal cognition of real life to the morbid and irrational perception of the world around them. She uncovers the way ordinary human passions are experienced by those who are mentally unstable, and she seeks, in the end, solace for some of her heroines in religion. Sadur's prose is intense, subtle, metonymical, and highly individualistic. Her stories address the darker side of human nature, a subject that received little attention in official Soviet literature prior to glasnost.

ALEKSANDR LAVRIN

Aleksandr Lavrin does not fit easily within the currently accepted designations in Russian literature, as is aparent from his recent collection of prose, *Liudi, zveri i angely* (People, Animals, and Angels; 1992). His story 'Babochka' (Butterfly),[183] a parody of the art and personality of Vladimir Nabokov, is dedicated to Viktor Erofeev, the current guru of Russian post-modernist art. 'Vechernii zvon' (The Evening Chime)[184] is one long paragraph in which many different characters appear, telling seemingly unrelated tales, all shrouded in metaphoric language and interlaced with fantastic detail.

Lavrin's novella 'Iama' (The Pit),[185] is different. It contains components of 'village prose,' a detective novel, and psychological realism, combined with elements of fantasy, magic realism, dreams, and hallucinations. The hero, Lekha Zhikharev, is a habitual loafer who likes to philosophize about life. He lives in the village Karacharovo with his wife, Dar'ia, who works to support him. Life has no meaning for him, and he is depressed most of the time. His former teacher tells him that the 'most horrible thing is the slavery of freedom.' It is an aimless existence, to which Lekha has been exposed most of his mature life. On the advice of some travelling etymologists, Dar'ia tries to keep him busy digging a new cellar in the house. To his surprise, Lekha discovers an inexhaustible source of blood, at the bottom of the pit, which gives new meaning to Lekha's life. In his attempt to make the blood useful to the people, Lekha visits friends, physicians, and bureaucrats to present his case. Unfortunately his efforts land him a place in the local madhouse. He does manage to escape, but can find no solution to his problem. That is when he retreats into the realm of imagination, dreams, and hallucinations.

Having been turned away by all the officials he has approached, Lekha goes for advice to an old woman who is a quack doctor. She tells him that the blood from his pit is of no use to people because it is the blood of the dead. The earth is soaked with the blood of those who have been tortured, murdered, and made to suffer, and now gives back this blood to the people because it can retain it no longer. Lekha's quest to help his fellow humans is futile because the blood is the product of human cruelty. In the end, Lekha realizes that human nature cannot be changed, and that people will never be able to make the final necessary step that would separate them from the animals.

In his own simple peasant way, Lekha rebels against the animal essence of human nature, as well as against the values of the Soviet state. His apathy and passivity are the consequence of this rebellion. The term 'iama' – the pit – appears time and again. It refers to the real pit, dug in the cellar, but it is a symbol of the mental pit and spiritual vacuum in society. It refers further to history as a pit in which everything can get lost, and it symbolizes the universal pit in which all mankind loses its path. The world is compared to a pit, at the bottom of which are people blinded by ignorance and egomania and unable to find their way out. In a parallel to A. Chekhov's 'Ward 6,' normal people are locked up in a madhouse because they disturb the maniacs who run state and social institutions.

Lavrin is certainly a talented writer, and 'Iama' is an absorbing, subtle, and imaginative story. Despite some shortcomings in characterization and structure, it can serve as proof that it is possible to experiment with language and style without destroying the structural foundation of the plot, and providing, at the same time, meaningful insights into social and human problems. Lavrin's prose shows that the distinction between traditional realism and post-modernism in current Russian literature is not as clearly defined as one would expect, and that, in that respect, Russian literature differs greatly from its Western counterpart.

ALEKSANDR VERNIKOV

Aleksandr Vernikov is closely connected with the new literature of perestroika. His story 'Pustynia Tartari' (The Tartari Desert; 1991) was published in Sverdlovsk in the collection of prose *Sramnaia proza* (Shameful Prose; 1991), dedicated to 'Ural Literature of the New Wave.'[186] The story features a first-person nameless narrator who uses simple, direct, and declarative language. The narrator is infatuated with a nameless young woman. Before she leaves town on a business trip, she asks him to see a rarely shown film so that, upon her return, he can tell her everything about it. The narrator goes to see the movie, but he is drunk and falls asleep. Then, he goes to meet the woman at the airport but is embarrassed to face her. At the airport, he learns that the plane has crashed and she will never return. Heart-broken, he feels that there is something fateful in her disappearance, and he decides to see the movie at any cost. The film, entitled *Pustynia Tartari*, is about a fortress in a remote desert. The people in the garrison believe that one day the desert will bloom, and they wait years for this miracle to happen. At the same time, they prepare to face an imaginary enemy that is allegedly supposed to attack them. This enemy never appears, just as the desert never blossoms, yet they continue to hope and expect the improbable.

The symbolism of the film expresses the reality that only the unchangeable and the constant can exercise a firm hold on the human psyche. There is nothing in the world that is more consistent with the endless and insatiable human quest for the supernatural than the image of the desert. The author-narrator is pleased that the authors of the foreign scenario share the views of some Soviet people; they understand that lofty notions of duty, honour, and bravery are just the means used by those in power to create the 'great fog' which blinds the people.

'Pustynia Tartari' is realistic in form but post-modernist in substance. It has an original plot, with a story within a story, but except for the narrator, who is also a character, the story does not have a single identifiable protagonist. The time sequence in the story is confusing, and the location obscure. Most individuals mentioned are atypical. The only woman in the story is frigid, and apparently asexual; she is a great conversationalist, but discussion with her is compared to sexual stimulation. As well, there are strong insinuations of homosexuality; the members of the garrison are all male, and spend years in the desert without a woman. In the story, the reader is exposed not to reality per se, but to reality as it is perceived by the narrator. Authorial self-reflexiveness determines the reader's comprehension. The conclusion of the story suggests that man's eternal quest is determined by the intricacies of the human mind, but the conditions of the real, or imaginary, desert influence and shape the workings of the human psyche – hence, the allusion that everything is indeterminable and left to chance.

THE AUTHORS OF *SOLO*

Solo is one of the new periodicals devoted chiefly to the publication of experimental literature. It publishes works produced by representatives of the former literary underground as well as by little-known writers of the younger generation. The first issue of *Solo* appeared in 1990. By the end of 1991 eight issues had been published. In 1992, lack of money forced, *Solo* to suspend publication. The award to *Solo* of the special Booker Prize for small Russian-language publications for contributing to the development of contemporary Russian literature made possible the periodical's reappearance in print. In the spring of 1993 nos. 9 and 10 were published. The bimonthly journal is slender, yet it has already become an important outlet for the creative output of many post-modernist and avant-garde writers. Aleksandr Mikhailov is its editor, and A. Bitov and E. Popov joined its editorial board after the appearance of its first number.

In an editorial in 1991's third issue of the journal, A. Mikhailov explained that the title *Solo* has been selected in order to make it abundantly clear that its authors are absolutely independent and free individuals, and that neither the journal nor its authors belong to any political or literary group. Moreover, most contributors to *Solo* are not professional writers, and support themselves by being gainfully employed in a variety of different trades and professions. According to Mikhailov, this literature is not for everyone; it is for 'gourmands; for those who get a "high" from the order of words in the text, and from the author's "play" with these words.'[187] In an introduction to the fourth issue of *Solo*, A. Bitov clarified its essence and stated its objectives. He asserted that it publishes literature by a generation of abandoned and forgotten writers, authors who have just come out from the underground. They live 'in the same country, in the same room and family, but on different planets, and in different historical times.'[188]

The authors of *Solo* have come out into the open, identifying the problems of a mute generation silenced in the period of stagnation. They are all distinct. Each writes in a different manner, but 'style expresses for them, first of all, the human being. In the final analysis it is all about one thing – namely about the evaporation and disappearance of man. About stagnation – the primary and only experience. At first sight, they appear to be removed from social issues and politics ... in their own way, however, they are socially conscious ... The disappearance and dematerialization of the hero is not only the theme but also the plot common to most authors. Life loses meaning to each of them in a different way, but the result – the loss of this meaning – is the same for all of them.'[189] According to Bitov, literature is the starting-point for the authors of *Solo*; they are readers who are also researchers and investigators. Their literature may be playful, it may accept and reject certain values and truths at the same time, but it is serious literature and not a game.

The first number of *Solo* opened with the prose of Anatolii Gavrilov, a mailman in the provincial city of Vladimir. He was over forty but made his literary debut in 1989. Since then, he has published two collections of prose,[190] but his best-known work is the short story 'Istoriia maiora Simin'kova' (The Story of Major Simin'kov; 1990).[191] It is a first-person narrative describing the reality of Soviet army life in the mid-1960s and written in the language, tone, and spirit of early nineteenth-century literature. The young officer Simin'kov arrives at a rocket detachment, located in a remote Russian provincial town. His academic credentials are excellent; he is well mannered and impeccably dressed; he does not drink or use foul language; but he is disliked by his immediate superior who is jealous of able young officers. None the less, Simin'kov is noticed at the top; his good work is appreciated and he advances rapidly. But then his downfall begins. He accidentally slips at a parade in front of the inspecting general. He is embarrassed, and his confidence is shaken, and this occurrence leads to his ruin. Soon afterwards, he misplaces a secret document and becomes frantic, searching all over for it, but fruitlessly. The loss of a secret document is viewed in the Soviet Army as a disgrace and a crime, often compared to treason. In this case, however, the irony of fate seems to favour Simin'kov. He gets off lightly and is not even demoted. The document in question turns out to be instructions, regarding potato peeling for the soldiers' kitchen. But Simin'kov is heart-broken and the collapse of his spirit is complete. He soon resigns from the army and takes an insignificant job in Moscow.

The first-person narrative by a fellow officer moves smoothly. Portrayal is terse, and there is no redundant detail. Psychological analysis is absent, but the picture drawn provides a convincing image of psychological shock. Simin'kov is a perfectionist, but he is also vain. He has a strong sense of duty and great expectations from life, but the fall in front of his superiors undermines his confidence, hurts his self-esteem, and brings him down from soaring heights to ordinary human dimensions. In the beginning of the story, Gavrilov builds up the image of his hero in order to make his fall more appalling. The intention is to show that chance rules human destiny, that we are all fallible, and that the invincibility of some is only an illusion.

Parody is a device widely used by Russian post-modernists, and Gavrilov's language is reminiscent of that in A. Pushkin's *Povesti Belkina* (The Tales of Belkin; 1831). The general atmosphere of army life described here has parallels with that of Pushkin's 'Vystrel' (The Shot). But the polished and stylized phrases Gavrilov uses are also a contrastive device that expresses the great paradox of Soviet daily existence and the extreme senselessness of certain Soviet army regulations. One wonders why information that has no relevance to state security is classified in the first place. Gavrilov's other stories are short vignettes of people, encounters, or events. Some rely on phantasmagoric invention, others on surrealistic detail, but all are blended with realistic portrayal.

Igor' Klekh, a resident of the city of L'viv in Ukraine, is another contributor to *Solo*. Like many other post-modernists, he views contemporary life through the prism of Russian and universal culture and tradition. Most of his short stories and sketches, which take root in the past, are a combination of reality, fantasy, and the absurd. Other stories, dealing with provocative contemporary issues, are a mixture of fiction and journalism. His stories pose a number of monumental questions but offer no answers to them. In the story 'Inostranets' (The Foreigner; 1991)[192] a foreigner who has for many years lived in Russia becomes ill and is admitted to hospital. There he realizes that an invisible wall separates him from all other patients. He sees them but does not perceive them; he cannot comprehend their mentality. He joins other patients in playing cards and domino, games that have their roots in antiquity, Christianity, astrology, and spiritualism. Today these games have conquered Russia and have become 'a secret national religion – a synthetic faith.'[193] The foreigner cannot overcome the chasm dividing him from the rest and is driven to suicide.

Another story, 'Intsident s klassikom' (An Occurrence with a Classicist; 1991),[194] relates an incongruous occurrence with a poet from Kiev. He comes to Mirgorod with the purpose of being able to better understand the creative spirit of N. Gogol. He wants to inhale the same air that has nurtured the latter's genius. Unfortunately, the hapless poet loses his keys in the railway station's lavatory and spends most of the day searching for a magnet to help retrieve the keys from the cesspool. Back in Kiev, it takes a while before he can rid himself of the Mirgorod stench. The bizarre story about the poet is a farce, but it has also serious meaning: it hints that real talent is at the root of artistic creation, and that feeding on the fruits of the labour of others seldom provides for original ideas. Whether intentionally or unintentionally, the story is a paradox. It mocks the very essence of post-modernist art, which intends to debunk the actual notion of genius yet takes generously from the cultural heritage of its illustrious predecessors.

Another publication by Klekh, under the general title 'Monolog' (Monologue; 1991),[195] includes a number of short sketches, mostly about writers and literature. In one of them, he explores the parallels between the circumstances preceding the murder of John Lennon and those of assassination attempt on President Ronald Reagan, and he asks a pointed question: why are future murderers avid readers of J.D. Salinger's *The Catcher in the Rye*? In another sketch he offers his own critique of M. Bulgakov's *Master i Margarita* (The Master and Margarita; 1966–7), asserting that it is 'a deeply philistine book ... with a number of poor stereotypes.'[196] Yet another sketch discusses the parallels in the lives and death of Edgar Allan Poe and F. Dostoevsky. Klekh's language is distinct, and his metaphors are precise. His stories are plotless and full of paradoxes, and they read as a continuous saga, with no beginning or end.

In 1993, Klekh published the novella "Khutor vo vselennoi" (Farmstead in the Universe) in *Novyi mir*.[197] The narrative is set in the Carpathian mountains. Episodes and impressions from the life of those who live in the hills are augmented by keen observations about the nature of people and the general human condition. The mountaineers are isolated and secluded, but they are simple, warm, and straightforward. Klekh contrasts the people in the hills with those in the city. Physically, they are close to each other but mentally and emotionally they are worlds apart. None the less, Klekh suggests that there is uniformity among all people. The farmstead in the hills is part of the global village which embraces all humanity. All are lost in the convoluted labyrinth of human existence in which it is difficult to find one's way.

The fourth issue of *Solo* for 1991 contains three stories by Zufar Gareev.[198] They are different in tone, language, and subject-matter. 'Stereoskopicheskie slaviane' (Stereoscopic Slavs; 1991) has no definite plot or time sequence. The ghost-like characters, who are Russians and apparently reside in Moscow, move freely back and forth between reality and the world of fantasy. They are involved in activities which are never explained and make little sense. And yet this confusing narrative contains clear allusions to the repulsive state of Soviet institutions and the corruption of the Soviet bureaucracy, as well as to the dangers and likelihood of an ecological disaster. The story 'Podrazhanie letu' (The Imitation of Summer; 1991) is the complete opposite of 'Stereoskopicheskie slaviane.' It is told in crisp language by a female narrator who wants to become acquainted with a student travelling in the same train compartment. She finally manages to attract his attention, and they even exchange telephone numbers. Unfortunately, when she calls him, she learns that she has the wrong number. It is not clear whether the mistake was accidental or intentional, but the girl is extremely disappointed. She loses faith in life and wants to escape reality. Gareev seems to point out here that chance can determine human destiny but can also breed illusions, and that it is devastating to learn that people cannot be trusted and that one has mistaken an illusion for reality.

The story 'Multiproza' (Multiprose; 1991) is different again. It is about the life of vagrants roaming the large expanses of the Russian land. Scattered all over the country, they travel, sometimes work, steal, and drink, yet retain a close and intimate relationship with one another. The story is a mixture of the comic and the tragic. The characters can be recognized only by the language they speak. The first half is narrated in a slang peculiar to vagabonds and outlaws. The second half, describing the death of one of them, is in the language of the heroic epos. On the surface, it may appear that the vagrants lead a carefree existence, but the intention of the author is to show that their lives are at once difficult and wasteful.

Evgenii Laputin's 'Litsa ptits' (The Faces of Birds; 1991)[199] is another example of current Russian post-modernist prose. At the root of the plot is a conventional conflict: the young Andrei despairs when he discovers that Kublitskii, a family friend and his chess partner, is also his mother's lover. When Kublitskii moves in with them, Andrei is devastated; he contemplates suicide and tries to run away. When he returns home, he realizes, that Kublitskii is no longer there. On the surface the story is simple: a jealous and possessive son begrudges his mother's short-lived joy; he is too young to understand that, to enjoy real happiness, she needs both her son and a lover, friend, and husband, preferably in one and the same person. The story is presented in a fragmented and disjointed manner. First- and third-person narrators alternate continuously. There is constant transition from reality to fantasy, and from one narrative mode to another. There is almost no dialogue in the story. Most associations are remote and indistinct, and it is difficult at times to discern what is real and what is in Andrei's mind. The temporal dimensions in the story are vague. The main protagonists are Russians, but the story is set somewhere in France. Long digressions relating events from centuries of French history are intertwined with the portrayal of human relationships and the morbid state of Andrei's mind. Interlaced through all are discussions of homosexuality, infidelity, and other frailties of human nature. This creates an atmosphere of instability and chaos. Life appears to flow, in its unpredictable and disorderly way, like a river without a beginning or an end.

It is interesting to note that some of Laputin's stories have been published by conservative journals specializing primarily in traditional realistic prose. Thus, for example, his 'Pamiatnik obmanshchiku' (A Monument to a Deceiver; 1990)[200] appeared in *Moskovskii vestnik* (Moscow Herald), a journal published by the Moscow conservative Writers' Union and edited by Vladimir Gusev. It is a story about the experiences of a forty-year-old widow in search of an eligible man. She has many lovers and suitors, all of them friendly, considerate, and married. They all pretend and lie to get sex from her, and then they disappear into the darkness of the night. Continuously exposed to liars and cheaters, the heroine loses faith in humanity. When she finally meets an inconspicuous individual who appreciates her and appears to be single, she mistreats him and suspects that he is like all her other suitors – married and a liar. She drives him to distraction, and he disappears, never to return. But then loneliness devastates her, and she disintegrates, both mentally and emotionally. Laputin does not analyse the psychological motivation of the heroine's actions, nor does he tell us anything about her past. All we learn is that life experience leaves an indelible mark on the human psyche. People always aim at the inaccessible and illusory but seldom appreciate what they have before it is too late. The two stories by Laputin, published in different journals, corroborate the assumption that, even today, when there is no official censorship in Russia, some writers continue to produce prose that conforms with the expectations of editors rather than honestly reflecting their innate creative impulses.

Most contributors to *Solo* are individualists. They do not struggle with their past, nor do they offer a vision for the future. They simply ignore both. Instead, they are busy creating literary texts that reflect the new spirit of intellectual freedom in a society still in a state of chaos. This situation explains the stress and tension, and abrupt changes in location and point of view, in Gareev's stories: they simply mirror the general atmosphere of confusion and social discord in the country. In Klekh's stories, the image of the hero is vague, and the situations described are indistinct. Klekh draws heavily on the cultural heritage of the past; but, instead of paying detailed attention to conventional characterization, he concentrates on the perceptions, contemplations, and insights of his protagonists and places himself at the centre of all his narratives.

The writers discussed here, as well as other contributors to *Solo*, such as D. Dobrodeev, A. Kavadeev, R. Marsovich, and V. Zuev,[201], have created for themselves a niche in *Solo*. Until very recently, no established journal would even consider publishing their works. Today, these authors publish books and continue to appear in newly established journals and almanacs. Some old established periodicals, including *Novyi mir*, *Znamia*, and *Druzhba narodov*, have also opened their pages to the prose of this formerly mute generation.

Most proponents of Russian post-modernism are different from each other. Their prose is fluid, often ambiguous, and difficult to classify. Like their Western counterparts, they debunk old notions, reject rational language, and present a fragmented reality. They manipulate form, emphasize the play of words and sounds, and alternate a variety of narrators. They ignore the importance of conventional characterization and rely heavily on the extraordinary and the fantastic. Russian post-modernists avoid direct didacticism, but in many instances the very nature of their subject-matter may have important social significance. In most cases social meaning is not on the surface and can be discerned only through careful investigative reading.

6

Conclusion

December 1991 marks the date of the dissolution of the Soviet Union and the creation of the Commonwealth of Independent States, composed of former Soviet republics. It denotes the beginning of transition from communist dictatorship to democracy, and from a planned economy to a free market. In December 1993, Russia adopted a new constitution, which marks the formal end of communist-Soviet rule in the country. Adjustment to life after communism is proving to be a traumatic experience. The process of change is painful. It is identified with ideological squabbles; economic and political instability; the disintegration of former social, cultural and state institutions; and the re-evaluation of old Soviet values.

The abolition of single-party rule in the former Soviet Union has led to a rift within the writers' community, and the former Writers' Union has split into a number of warring associations with different political and ideological agendas. Liberal writers such as Nagibin, Pristavkin, and Evtushenko cherish their new freedom of expression. They support democratic reforms, the transition to a market economy, and most policies of the Yeltsin government. Other writers, some formerly identified with 'village prose,' such as Belov and Rasputin, as well as Bondarev and Prokhanov, oppose democratic reform, and support the conservative-nationalist opposition to Yeltsin's policies. This opposition is an alliance of convenience among extreme Russian nationalists; adherents of conservative Orthodoxy; and the most reactionary elements of the former *nomenklatura*, the armed forces, and the KGB. Prior to the August 1991 coup, each writers' clan presented a unified front and acted in a cohesive manner. By the end of 1992, rifts within these camps began to appear, generated by political disagreement and the struggle for power and money.

The abolition of censorship in 1990 changed the face of the literary press. Most literary weeklies and monthlies have become independent and have cut their ties with their former sponsoring writers' organizations. By 1990, the circulation of most literary journals had grown into the millions. However, this success, connected with the publication of formerly forbidden works by dissident, exiled, and foreign authors, was short-lived. The circulation of journals soon dropped drastically, and by 1994 it was smaller than at the beginning of perestroika. The interests of the reading public have changed as well, and inflation has made literary journals inaccessible to most middle-class readers.

The book-publishing business has also changed its mode of operation. Having become independent and self-supportive, publishers today refuse to publish money-losing scholarly and academic books, printing instead foreign detective novels and erotic literature. The situation is somewhat alleviated by the appearance of many new small private publishing outlets which cater to the needs of different artistic interest groups. Similarly, new almanacs and periodicals, appearing daily and disappearing as fast, provide platforms for new and aspiring authors.

The situation on the Russian literary scene has changed drastically in the last six years. In 1988, the party and the state still exercised control over literary production. By 1992, writers acquired total freedom of expression and publication, and the political and ideological distinction between Russian émigré writers and those residing in their native land has, for all practical purposes, disappeared.

The demise of socialist realism has been gradual and painful. Most liberal writers and scholars always regarded it as an artificial creation that hampered the development of creative talent. Yet, even as late as 1991, some old academics and conservative writers continued to stress its importance as a method of artistic creation. Today, socialist realism is a relic of the past and a part of Soviet literary history.

No writer born, raised, and educated in the Soviet Union could avoid the influence of Soviet upbringing and the Soviet way of life. The degree of this influence is often affected by age, as well as by the adherence to certain ideological, social, or religious values. Today, writers of the older generation make use of, and some abuse, the new possibilities of freedom of expression, but artistically they remain true to themselves. It is too late for them to change. Many middle-aged authors suffer from a crisis of identity. Some, such as Makanin and Kim, continue to work within their former artistic perimeters, at the same time, extending, their thematic and philosophical range. They often indulge in metaphysical contemplation and set their narratives in an anti-utopian environment. Some authors, like Evtushenko and Kurchatkin, try to capitalize on the topicality of perestroika and the anti-Gorbachev coup, and turn it, albeit not quite successfully, into the subject of their fiction.

The new authors of perestroika are a diverse group. Some are young and the product of the times. Others are mature writers who have just recently emerged from the literary underground. The prose of these writers can be divided into three broad streams: one group consists of writers who create in the traditions of Russian conventional realism; the second group is composed of writers who combine in their works realistic and modernist narrative techniques; and the third group consists of representatives of what is called today Russian post-modernism.

The prose of many authors is challenging and experimental. Realistic writers stress thematic innovation and dramatic intensity. Russian post-modernism mirrors the violent and perplexing shifts in the political and social realities of Russia in the last decade. Russian post-modernist writers reject old values, rely heavily on secondary sources, and turn language into word play. It is difficult to generalize about the quality of recent Russian prose as it is controversial and uneven. Some works are infused with serious ideas but are artistically deficient; others are artistically sophisticated but lack depth. The situation is further complicated by the fact that, as in the cases of Pristavkin, P'etsukh, Kuraev, and Tolstaia, an author may produce an excellent work of art and follow it with a work of little artistic merit.

The Russian literary scene is today dynamic and vibrant but also chaotic and unpredictable. There is more artistic innovation and experimentation in Russian prose today than at any other time since the early 1920s. However, the new experimental prose is addressed solely to a small and sophisticated audience. It is not easy to follow, and its message, if any, is buried deep beneath the surface. The Russian mass readership, nurtured for many years on solid realistic fare, has little interest in such literature. It appears that Russian post-modernism has reached its apogee and is at a crossroads. Some of its proponents have started to cater to the lower tastes of the reading public by turning to kitsch. It is purely a matter of surmise that the future of Russian prose lies in a new realism – sincere, profound, inspired by serious ideas, and free of the constraints of censorship and external interference.

In the past, literature was at once a vehicle of ideology and an important cultural, intellectual, and political factor of everyday Soviet life. The writer was a philosopher, sociologist, politician, and missionary. Today, literature continues to reflect the social and political situation in the country, but the role and prestige of the writer have diminished, and literature is turning gradually into a form of art.

In general terms, the Russian creative intelligentsia is now undergoing a painful process of self-examination and a reassessment of its place in society. The destabilization of social and cultural institutions, economic anarchy, and the increasing poverty of the masses affect even the recent works of liberal writers such as Bitov and Iskander. They do not clamour for the past but are dejected by the present. They turn to religious imagery as to a sign of hope, but their search for God is feeble and only symbolic; it is not yet a spiritual quest or a statement of faith.

Russia today is still in a state of chaos. Whatever the result of the current political infighting and its effect on the economic and cultural transformation, it is unlikely that the old regime could ever return to power. The old Soviet myth has been destroyed, and it is doubtful whether the Russian people could ever be chained and muzzled again. None the less, there is still potential in Russia for the appearance of a new dictator who could curtail some of the liberties enjoyed by the Russian people today.

The Russian prose of the period 1988–94 is the literature of transition. Its future will be influenced, to a degree, by the outcome of the current changes in Russian society. But the Russian people are a reading nation, and the appearance in the last few years of a number of young and promising authors bodes well for the future of Russian literature.

Notes

CHAPTER 1 Politics, Literature, and Society

1 *Pravda*, 1 March 1991, 2.
2 *Literaturnaia gazeta*, 8 July 1992, 4.
3 Ibid., 18 September 1990, 3–6.
4 V.I. Belov, 'My znaem, chto delat'/' *Russkii vestnik*, 23/56, (17–24 June 1992), 2.
5 *Literaturnaia Rossiia*, 2 March 1990, 3.
6 *Literaturnaia gazeta*, 7 March 1990, 2.
7 *Sovetskaia Rossiia*, 23 July 1991, 1.
8 *Literaturnaia gazeta*, 24 January 1990, 2.
9 'My gotovy k vlasti,' *Den'*, 28 June– July 1992, 2.
10 Aleksandr Romashov, 'Russkii vektor,' *Den'*, 21–7 June 1992, 4.
11 Aleksandr Romashov, 'Pritiazhenie edinnogo mira,' *Den'*, 21–7 June 1992, 4.
12 Mikhail Antonov, 'Davaite vnesem iasnost'/' *Russkii vestnik* 23/56 (17–24 June 1992), 4.
13 Aleksandr Dugin, 'Islam i patriotizm,' *Den'*, 28 June–4 July 1992, 4.
14 Ibid.
15 See, for example, Andrei Novikov, 'Giperboloid inzhenera Kurginiana,' *Literaturnaia gazeta*, 15 December 1993, 11.
16 *Moskovskie novosti*, 7 June 1992, 22.
17 For a detailed discussion of the history of the Writers' Union see: John and Carol Garrard, *Inside the Soviet Writers' Union* (New York 1990).
18 *Aprel'*, 1989, no. 1, 9–15.
19 *The New York Times*, 11 May 1989, c22.
20 *Literaturnaia gazeta*, 22 November 1989, 7.
21 Ibid., 5 July 1989, 1, and 22 August 1990, 1.
22 Ibid., 6 June 1990, 7.

23 Ibid., 10 January 1990, 7.

24 Ibid., 5 December 1990, 2.

25 *Literaturnaia Rossiia*, 14 December 1990, 2.

26 *Literaturnaia gazeta*, 3 and 10 July 1991.

27 Ibid., 28 August 1991, 9.

28 Ibid., 18 September 1991, 2.

29 Ibid., 4 December 1991, 2.

30 Ibid., 24 April 1992, 3.

31 Ibid., 15 July 1992, 3.

32 *Literaturnaia Rossiia*, 12 June 1992, 4.

33 *Literaturnaia gazeta*, 25 November 1992, 3. See also Sergei Lukashin, 'Statisty i "reformator",' and Valerii Rogov, 'Povorot v sud'be,' *Den'*, 14–20 March 1993, 6.

34 *Literaturnaia gazeta*, 14 June 1989, 3.

35 Ibid., 20 December 1989, 7.

36 Ibid., 11 January 1989, 1–4.

37 Ibid., 4.

38 *Pravda*, 14 July 1990, 2.

39 Ibid., 3 October 1990, 2.

40 Ibid., 20 September 1990, 1–2.

41 Ibid., 3 October 1990, 1.

42 Ibid., 2.

43 Ibid. For a discussion of the terms *narodnost'* and *partiinost'* see N.N. Shneidman, 'The Russian Classical Literary Heritage and the Basic Concepts of Soviet Literary Education,' *Slavic Review* 31/3 (September 1972), 626–38.

44 *Pravda*, 3 October 1990, 3.

45 Ibid., 30 September 1990, 2.

46 *Literaturnaia gazeta*, 22 September 1993, 3.

47 See 'Proekt. Zakon SSSR o pechati i drugikh sredstvakh massovoi informatsii,' ibid., 13 December 1989, 7.

48 Ibid., 13 February 1991, 3.

49 Ibid., 28 August 1991, 3.

50 *Iskuplenie* (Atonement), *Iunost'*, 1990, nos. 11 and 12; *Koiko-mesto* (Some Place), *Znamia*, 1990, nos. 1 and 2; *Psalom* (The Book of Psalms), *Oktiabr'*, 1991, nos. 10–12, and 1992, nos. 1 and 2.

51 *Ukreplennye goroda* (The Fortified Cities), originally published in 1980, in Jerusalem.

52 *Zhizn' Aleksandra Zil'bera* (The Life of Aleksandr Zil'ber), *Druzhba narodov*, 1990, nos. 6 and 7.

53 *Literaturnye novosti*, 1992, no. 4, 10.
54 Vl. Novikov, 'Promezhutochnyi finish,' *Znamia*, 1992, no. 9, 225.
55 *The Toronto Star*, 23 January 1993, D5.
56 *Literaturnaia gazeta*, 26 February 1992, 7.
57 *Den'*, July 1991, no. 13, 5.
58 *Literaturnaia gazeta*, 10 January 1990, 11.
59 Elena Tokareva, 'Dvulikii Ianus knizhnogo razvala,' ibid., 9 June 1993, 7.
60 Ibid., 11 December 1992, 6.
61 *Nezavisimaia gazeta*, 1 October 1992, 7.
62 *The Toronto Star*, 23 January 1993, D5.
63 *Literaturnaia gazeta*, 31 October 1990, 3.
64 Ibid., 15 July 1992, 3.
65 Ibid., 20 May 1992, 3.
66 Ibid., 25 November 1992, 10.
67 Ibid., 3.
68 Stepan Bokoch, 'K voprosu o russkoi kul'ture,' *Domostroi*, 2 July 1991, 13.
69 *Pravda*, 13 October 1990, 3.
70 *Domostroi*, 2 July 1991, 13.
71 *Sovetskaia Rossiia*, 30 May 1992, 2.
72 *Moskovskie novosti*, 1992, no. 11, 19. Quoted in *Literaturnaia gazeta*, 20 May 1992, 3.

CHAPTER 2 The Russian Literary Scene

1 *Literaturnaia gazeta*, 8 June 1994, 3.
2 *Novyi mir*, 1992, no. 10, 60–106; no. 11, 188–226; and no. 12, 168–248.
3 *Novyi mir*, 1989, no. 4, 5–48, no. 5, 42–115, and no. 6, 111–45.
4 See the narrative 'Baikal,' *Nash sovremennik*, 1989, no. 7, 12–44. It summarizes Rasputin's efforts to save Lake Baikal from pollution and to protect it from the intrusion of technological progress.
5 Valentin Rasputin, 'Blizhnii svet iz daleka,' *Molodaia gvardiia*, 1992, no. 9, 11.
6 Pavel Basinskii, 'Memento Mori,' *Literaturnaia gazeta*, 28 October 1992, 4.
7 *Novyi mir*, 1989, no. 6, 149–237, and no. 7, 85–133.
8 For a detailed discussion of Russian post-modernism see chapter 5, Part C.
9 Viacheslav Kuritsyn, 'Do i vo vremia Bukera,' *Literaturnaia gazeta*, 29 December 1993, 4.
10 Aleksandr Solzhenitsyn, 'The Relentless Cult of Novelty and How It Wrecked the Century,' *The New York Times Book Review*, 7 February 1993, 17.
11 Ibid., 3

12 Caryl Emerson, 'The Shape of Russian Cultural Criticism in the Postcommunist Period,' *Canadian Slavonic Papers*, 34/4 (December 1992), 369.

13 See for example Vadim Dubichev, Aleksandr Vernikov, Viacheslav Kuritsyn, *Sramnaia proza* (Sverdlovsk 1991).

14 See, for example, T. Mamonova, ed., *Women in Russia* (Boston 1984).

15 See Sigrid McLaughlin, 'Contemporary Soviet Women Writers,' *Canadian Woman Studies*, 10/4 (1989), 77–80.

16 For a discussion of current women's literature see Helena Goscilo, '*Domostroika* or *Perestroika*? The Construction of Womanhood in Soviet Culture under Glasnost,' in Thomas Lahusen and Gene Kuperman, eds., *Late Soviet Culture: From Perestroika to Novostroika* (Durham, NC, 1993), 233–55.

17 Viacheslav Semiletov, 'Peizazh posle bitvy,' *Literaturnaia gazeta*, 10 March 1993, 4.

18 For an analysis of the socialist realism canon see Katerina Clark, *The Soviet Novel: History as Ritual*, 2d ed. (Chicago 1985). For a discussion of socialist realism in the 1980s see N.N. Shneidman, *Soviet Literature in the 1980s: Decade of Transition* (Toronto 1989), 22–32.

19 Vl Gusev, 'Otkazyvat'sia li nam ot sotsialisticheskogo realizma?' *Literaturnaia gazeta*, 25 May 1988, 3.

20 See, for example, E. Sergeev, 'Neskol'ko zastarelykh voprosov,' *Novyi mir*, 1988, no. 8, 142–46; Mikhail Golubkov, 'Konkretika metoda,' *Literaturnaia gazeta*, 24 August 1988, 3; Vadim Kovskii, 'Kul't metoda: prichiny i sledstviia,' *Literaturnaia gazeta*, 7 September 1988, 3.

21 *Literaturnaia gazeta*, 22 March 1989, 3

22 For a discussion of *partiinost'* and narodnost' see N.N. Shneidman, 'The Russian Classical Literary Heritage and the Basic Concepts of Soviet Literary Education,' *Slavic Review* 31/3 (September 1972), 626–38.

23 *Literaturnaia gazeta*, 20 December 1989, 2.

24 Ibid., 29 May 1991, 9.

25 Aleksandr Vial'tsev, 'Literatura i moral',' *Znamia*, 1993, no. 6, 193.

26 Ibid., 195.

27 Pavel Basinskii, 'Ad"iutanty ikh prevoskhoditel'stv,' *Literaturnaia gazeta*, 15 December 1993, 4.

28 See, for example, *Repetitsia*, *Neva*, 1992, no. 1, 6–91, and no. 2, 98–188, and *Do i vo vremia*, *Novyi mir*, 1993, no. 3, 6–76, and no. 4, 11–77.

29 Excerpts have been published in *Novyi mir*, 1992, no. 9, 78–120, and no. 11, 228–81.

30 I. Rodnianskaia, 'Shall We Live Without a Great Author?' *Russian Studies in Literature* 28/4 (Fall 1992), 59. Quoted from *Literaturnaia gazeta*, 29 May 1991, 11.

CHAPTER 3 The Old Guard

1 'Chto pishu? Chto chitaiu?' *Literaturnaia gazeta*, 9 January 1991, 9.
2 *Literaturnaia gazeta*, 22 May 1991, 9.
3 For a discussion of V. Astaf'ev's early prose see N.N. Shneidman, 'Viktor Astaf'ev: The Soviet Bard of Siberia,' *Russian Language Journal*, 33/114 (1979), 99–107, and N.N. Shneidman, *Soviet Literature in the 1980s: Decade of Transition* (Toronto 1989), 108–13.
4 *Nash sovremennik*, 1988, no. 8, 3–30.
5 *Novyi mir*, 1989, no. 9, 3–27.
6 *Nash sovremennik*, 1988, no. 8, 29.
7 For a discussion of Ch. Aitmatov's early works see N.N. Shneidman, 'Soviet Literature at the Crossroads: The Controversial Prose of Chingiz Aitmatov,' *Russian Literature Triquarterly*, 1979, no. 16, 244–63 and 340–41, and Shneidman, *Soviet Literature in the 1980s*, 194–208.
8 *Novyi mir*, 1980, no. 11, 3–185. The original title of the novel, submitted to *Novyi mir* was *Obruch* (The Hoop). It referred to the ring of rockets around the earth to prevent mankind from learning the truth about the universe, as well as to the caps, made from the udders of a camel, which turned prisoners into devoted slaves – mankurts, oblivious of their past. When the work was published in book form, the title, *I dol'she veka dlitsia den'*, was changed by the Molodaia gvardiia publishing house to *Burannyi polustanok* (Burannyi Siding). In the forthcoming edition, to be published soon, Aitmatov intends to reinstate the original title. See *Literaturnaia gazeta*, 27 June 1990, 4.
9 *Moscow News*, 29 July–5 August 1990, 14.
10 *Literaturnaia gazeta*, 27 June 1990, 4.
11 *Znamia*, 1990, no. 8, 7–57.
12 *Literaturnaia gazeta*, 27 June 1990, 4.
13 'Vstrecha s Chaadaem,' Ibid., 19 January 1994, 7.
14 *Literaturnaia gazeta*, 25 July 1990, 7.
15 Ibid., 21 December 1988, 6.
16 *Soviet Literature*, 1989, no. 5, 3–14.
17 *Literaturnaia gazeta*, 21 December 1988, 6.
18 Ibid., 29 June 1994, 3.
19 Ibid., 1 January 1992, 7.
20 Ibid., 9 September 1992, 7.
21 Ibid..
22 Chinghiz Aitmatov, 'Pis'mo molodomu pisateliu,' Ibid., 13 January 1993, 4.
23 Ibid., 19 January 1994, 7, and 29 June 1994, 3.
24 For a discussion of Bondarev's early prose see N.N. Shneidman, *Soviet Litera-*

ture in the 1970s: Artistic Diversity and Ideological Conformity (Toronto 1979), 54–60, and Shneidman, *Soviet Literature in the 1980s*, 124–32.

25 *Nash sovremennik*, 1991, no. 1, 28–119, and no. 2, 62–155.

26 *Literaturnaia gazeta*, 18 December 1985, 4.

27 Irina Strelkova, 'Iskusheniia i prozreniia,' *Literaturnaia Rossiia*, 5 April 1991, 19.

28 *Nash sovremennik*, 1991, no. 1, 79.

29 5 April 1991, 10 and 19.

30 1991, no. 4, 247–77.

31 Oleg Davydov, 'Iskushenie Iuriia Bondareva,' *Nezavisimaia gazeta*, 4 July 1991, 7.

32 Iurii Bondarev 'Zapiski po povodu ...,' *Molodaia gvardiia*, 1992, no. 10, 3–34.

33 For a discussion of V. Bykov's early prose see: N.N. Shneidman, *Soviet Literature in the 1970's*, 47–54, and Shneidman, Soviet Literature in the 1980's: 132–8.

34 *Novyi mir*, 1990, no. 1, 97–140.

35 Ibid., 121.

36 V. Oskotskii, 'Za chto?' *Znamia*, 1990, no. 4, 225.

37 *Novyi mir*, 1964, no. 2, 3–80.

38 *Znamia*, 1993, no. 11, 7–76.

39 'Lenin na "Amre",' (Lenin at the 'Amra'), *Znamia*, 1992, no. 2, 2–33; 'Rapira' (The Foil); 'Krasota normy, ili Mal'chik zhdet cheloveka' (The Beauty of the Norm, or the Boy Waiting for a Man) and 'Kremovyi kitel" (The Cream-Coloured Tunic), *Znamia*, 1992, no. 6, 100–47; 'Kutezh starikov nad morem' (The Drinking-Bout of Old Men at the Seashore), *Znamia*, 1992, no. 11, 3–17.

40 *Znamia*, 1992, no. 2, 6.

41 Ibid., 1993, no. 8, 3–36.

42 *Druzhba narodov*, 1988, no. 9, 5–110, and no. 10, 7–115.

43 Ibid., 1990, no. 9, 6–123, and no. 10, 6–132.

44 *Nash sovremennik*, Book one, 1993, no. 2, 5–49, and no. 3, 19–70.

45 *Novyi mir*, 1989, no. 3, 6–95; 1991, no. 3, 4–44, and no. 4, 91–134; and *Nash sovremennik*, 1994, no. 1, 11–51, and no. 2, 7–51.

46 *Moskva*, 1987, no. 9, 3–92, and no. 10, 5–143; 1990, no. 7, 16–146, no. 8, 33–131, and no. 9, 116–45.

47 *Znamia*, 1987, no. 3, 3–75, and no. 4, 25–79.

48 *Iunost'*, 1989, no. 11, 46–57, and no. 12, 7–46.

49 *Znamia*, 1991, no. 3, 9–64, and no. 4, 51–91.

50 For a discussion of E. Evtushenko's prose of the 1980s see Shneidman, *Soviet Literature in the 1980s*, 159–66.

51 *Znamia*, 1993, no. 3.

52 Ibid., no. 12, 3–39.

53 A. Anan'ev, *Skrizhali i kolokola*, Book one, *Oktiabr'*, 1989, no. 1, 3–126, and no.

2, 76–135, and *Liki bessmertnoi vlasti. Tsar' Ioann Groznyi*, Book one, *Oktiabr*, 1992, no. 3, 3–74, no. 4, 24–103, no. 5, 69–135, and no. 6, 24–115, and *Prizvanie Riurikovichei ili tysiacheletniaia zagadka Rossii, Oktiabr'*, 1993, no. 9, 3–77, and no. 10, 24–98.

54 *Oktiabr'*, 1993, no. 9, 3–77, and no. 10, 24–98.

55 *Novyi mir*, 1993, no. 12, 3–106.

56 *Znamia*, 1993, no. 9, 4–55, and 10, 77–125.

CHAPTER 4 The Intermediate Generation

1 *Novyi mir*, 1991, no. 5, 92–133.

2 Ibid., 83–92.

3 *Znamia*, 1991, no. 4, 3–47.

4 Ibid., 1993, no. 1, 9–53.

5 *Novyi mir*, 1993, no. 7, 124–47.

6 Ibid., 1989, no. 4, 5–48; no. 5, 42–115, and no. 6, 111–45. For a discussion of the novel see Natasha Kolchevska, 'Fathers, Sons, and Trees: Myth and Reality in Anatolij Kim's *Otec-les*,' 36 no. 3 (1992), 339–52.

7 *Novyi mir*, 1989, no. 5, 90; emphasis in original.

8 'Mozhno li zhit' buntom,' *Literaturnaia gazeta*, 4 October 1989, 4.

9 Marina Dutko, '... ne prinimaiu vashego "prigovora" A. Kimu,' *Literaturnaia gazeta*, 10 January 1990, 4.

10 'Muzhestvo govorit' pravdu,' *Moskva*, 1990, no. 9, 201.

11 'Proiti cherez otchaianie,' *Iunost'*, 1990, no. 1, 88.

12 *Novyi mir*, 1992, no. 3, 6–57.

13 'Bei babu molotom,' *Literaturnaia gazeta*, 7 October 1992, 4.

14 *Znamia*, 1990, no. 1, 8–63.

15 '"... i vse vezde stanet inache" ili Absoliutnoe Metro,' *Literaturnoe obozrenie*, 1990, no. 11, 58–9.

16 *Iskusstvo kino*, 1989, no. 6, 150–75. For a discussion of Kabakov's narrative see chapter 5, part two.

17 *Znamia*, 1993, no. 5, 7–72, and no, 6, 38–106.

18 'Tri rasskaza,' *Avrora*, 1987, no. 2, and 'Tri rasskaza,' *Neva*, 1987, no. 7.

19 *Novyi mir*, 1988, no. 1, 116–30.

20 Ibid., 116.

21 Ibid., 130.

22 Ibid., 1989, no. 9, 88–96.

23 *Literaturnaia gazeta*, 27 December 1989, 2.

24 See, for example, Evgenii Ovanesian, 'Raspada venok,' *Literaturnaia Rossiia*, 6 November 1991, 21–3.

25 *Novyi mir*, 1990, no. 8, 7–18.

26 Ibid., 7.

27 *Aprel'*, 1990, no. 2, 107–15.

28 *Novyi mir*, 1992, no. 2, 65–110.

29 Ibid., 1993, no. 3, 105–13, published under the general title 'V sadakh drugikh vozmozhnostei,' 105–26.

30 *Sintaksis* (Paris), 1990, no. 3, 44–9.

31 *Novyi mir*, 1993, no. 8, 130–59.

32 E. Nevzgliadova, 'Siuzhet dlia nebol'shogo rasskaza,' *Novyi mir*, 1988, no. 4, 259.

33 Natal'ia Ivanova, 'Neopalimyi golubok,' *Znamia*, 1991, no. 8, 19.

34 *Novyi mir*, 1993, no. 10, 6–102.

35 'The Park of Our Culture. Andrei Bitov Considers How to Assert One's Freedom in the Awakening World,' *Moscow News*, 25 November–2 December 1990, 14.

36 Ibid.

37 *Novyi mir*, 1991, no. 9, 129–51.

38 Sigrid McLaughlin, 'An Interview with Viktoria Tokareva,' *Canadian Woman Studies*, 10/4 (Winter 1989), 76.

39 *Novyi mir*, 1991, no. 9, 130.

40 In 1992, V. Krupin has been replaced in the position of editor of *Moskva* by the writer Leonid Borodin.

41 *Nash sovremennik*, 1991, no. 12, 3–43.

42 Ibid., 10.

43 Vladimir Krupin, 'Knigi vse tolshche, smysla vse men'she,' *Literaturnaia gazeta*, 14 October 1992, 3.

44 For a discussion of A. Prokhanov's early prose see N.N. Shneidman, *Soviet Literature in the 1980s: Decade of Transition* (Toronto 1989), 142–54.

45 *Oktiabr'*, 1988, no. 8, 3–117, and no. 9, 21–142.

46 Aleksandr Prokhanov, *Shest'sot let posle bitvy* (Moscow 1990), 245.

47 *Nash sovremennik*, 1991, no. 10, 5–60, no. 11, 91–141, and no. 12, 46–107.

48 Ibid., 1993, no. 7, 7–46, no. 8, 15–61, and no. 9, 10–50.

49 Eduard Volodin, 'Russkii epos. Pesn' pervaia,' 11 February 1992, 4.

50 *Diadia Vania*, 1991, no. 1, 65–220.

51 Iurii Arakcheev, 'Da pomozhet nam Bog,' *Zavtra*, July 1994, no. 28 (33), 8.

CHAPTER 5 New Writers of Perestroika

1 *Novyi mir*, 1989, no. 4, 59–89.

2 One of the first works to describe military service in negative terms is Iurii Poliakov's 'Sto dnei do prikaza,' *Iunost'*, 1987, no. 11, 47–68.

3 Vasil' Bykov, 'Obosnovannaia trevoga,' *Znamia*, 1989, no. 8, 221.

4 Aleksandr Pozdniakov, 'Poslednii parad nastupaet,' *Nash sovremennik*, 1990, no. 5, 135–43.

5 *Novyi mir*, 1991, no. 11, 87–116.

6 Elena Iakovich, interview with Sergei Kaledin, *Literaturnaia gazeta*, 20 March 1991, 9.

7 *Novyi mir*, 1989, no. 6, 149–237, and no. 7, 85–133.

8 Zh. Vasil'eva, 'Padshikh liudei net ...,' interview with Leonid Gabyshev, *Literaturnaia gazeta*, 6 March 1991, 11.

9 *Znamia*, 1989, no. 3, 93–103, and 103–19.

10 *Novyi mir*, 1989, no. 8, 156–64.

11 *Znamia*, 1989, no. 10, 83–128.

12 *Literaturnaia gazeta*, 29 August 1990, 6.

13 *Znamia*, 1992, no. 6, 6–86, and no. 7, 99–171.

14 *Druzhba narodov*, 1990, no. 7, 5–87.

15 *Literaturnaia gazeta*, 10 February 1993, 2, and 6 October 1993, 13.

16 *Aprel'*, 1989, no. 1, 256–97.

17 *Soglasie*, 1991, no. 2, 8–72.

18 Aleksandr Terekhov, 'My vpitaem vsiu pyl' ...,' *Literaturnaia gazeta*, 13 June 1990, 4.

19 *Znamia*, 1991, no. 5, 3–82.

20 *Literaturnaia gazeta*, 13 June 1990, 4.

21 1990, no. 7, 10–45.

22 See, for example, Ol'ga Kuchkina, 'Poema o kvadratnykh metrakh,' *Literaturnoe obozrenie*, 1991, no. 3, 51–2.

23 *Khronograf. Ezhegodnik 90* (Moscow 1991), 374–88.

24 *Novyi mir*, 1991, no. 3, 47–81.

25 Ibid., 1993, no. 3, 82–95.

26 Vladimir Kharitonov, 'Vozvrashchenie labirinta,' *Ekstsentr-labirint* (Leningrad-Sverdlovsk), 1991, no. 2, 11.

27 *Ekstsentr-labirint* 1991, no. 2, 88–158, and no. 3, 84–139. Two other novels by A. Matveev, *V poiskakh blizhnego* (1988) and *Chastnoe litso* (1991), were published in the literary journal *Ural*.

28 *Predlagaemye obstoiatel'stva* (Moscow 1988), 150–259.

29 'O proze Iriny Polianskoi,' Ibid., 264.

30 *Predlagaemye obstoiatel'stva*, 16–29.

31 Ibid., 7–16.

32 'Chistaia zona,' in S.V. Vasilenko, comp., *Novye Amazonki* (Moscow 1991), 32–51. Originally published in *Znamia*, 1990, no. 1, 64–73.

33 *Konets veka*, 1991, no. 1, 114–54.

34 *Novyi mir*, 1992, no. 7, 61–88.

35 *Oktiabr'*, 1993, no. 9, 81–111.

36 *Iunost*, 1993, no. 4, 10–39.

37 Moscow: Knizhnyi sad 1993.

38 *Znamia*, 1993, no. 6, 9–26.

39 *Novyi mir*, 1993, no. 9, 58–70.

40 *Druzhba narodov*, 1992, no. 1, 38–117, and no. 2, 94–178.

41 The novella 'Prokhor Men'shutin' (Prokhor Men'shutin), written in 1971 and published in *Den' v fevrale* in 1988, opens this cycle, and *Linii sud'by* concludes it. The same heroes appear in all three, and the action takes place in the same location.

   It is interesting to note, that after the award of the Booker Prize to Kharitonov, *Druzhba narodov*, in which *Linii sud'by* initially appeared, refused to publish 'Provintsional'naia filosofiia.' According to its editor, Viacheslav P'etsukh, it 'can hardly be regarded as a new novel. These are preparatory notes and sketches to the prose, published last year in our journal under the title of *Linii sud'by, ili sunduchok Milashevicha*. Since the final version of the novel is already in print, what is the use of publishing its rough copy?' (See *Literaturnaia gazeta*, 17 March 1993, 3.) 'Provintsional'naia filosofiia' was eventually published in *Novyi mir*, 1993, no. 3, 7–86.

42 *Literaturnaia gazeta*, 16 December 1992, 7.

43 Karen Stepanian, 'Realizm kak zakliuchitel'naia stadiia postmodernizma,' *Znamia*, 1992, no. 5, 236.

44 Konstantin Kedrov, 'Vybor Bukera: mezhdu modernizmom i realizmom,' *Izvestiia*, 9 December 1992, 6.

45 *Znamia*, 1992, no. 3/4, 184–8.

46 *Novyi mir*, 1989, no. 1, 54–124.

47 V. P'etsukh, *Novaia moskovskaia filosofiia* (Moscow 1989), 286.

48 Ibid., 265.

49 Ibid., 258.

50 *Novyi mir*, 1990, no. 4, 5–20.

51 Benedikt Sarnov, *Smotrite, kto prishel* (Moscow 1992), 478.

52 *Oktiabr'*, 1991, no. 2, 3–19.

53 Ibid., 16.

54 Interview with V. P'etsukh, conducted by S. Taroshchina. See *Literaturnaia gazeta*, 17 May 1989, 7.

55 *Ibid.*

56 *Znamia*, 1992, no. 2, 67–107.

57 *Druzhba narodov*, 1992, no. 2, 179–87.

58 *Ia i prochee* (Moscow 1990), 121–4.

59 Ibid., 187–216.

60 V. P'etsukh, 'Duraki i sumashedshie,' *Literaturnaia gazeta*, 24 April 1992, 3.

61 *Neva*, 1990, no. 7, 6–61.

62 *Znamia*, 1992, no. 7, 7–66.

63 Ibid., 59.

64 Ibid., 14.

65 Ibid.

66 Ibid., 19.

67 The lack of identifiable remains gave rise to rumours that Hitler had escaped the advancing Soviet Army. According to newspaper reports, Soviet agents obtained fragments of Hitler's skull to prove to Stalin that his fears that Hitler had survived the war were groundless. It has been recently reported in *Izvestiia* that, according to secret files from the Soviet Commissariat of the Interior, secret-police investigators were sent to Berlin in May 1946, and recovered skull fragments at Hitler's headquarters, the Reich Chancellery. See *The Miami Herald*, 20 February 1993, 20A.

68 *Znamia*, 1992, no. 7, 62.

69 Ibid., 49.

70 Ibid., 63.

71 Tat'iana Rasskazova, 'Pushkin strelialsia by s Gogolem,' Interview with A. Korolev, *Literaturnaia gazeta*, 19 May 1993, 5.

72 'Vsled za "neistovym Vissarionom,"' Ibid.

73 *Znamia*, 1992, no. 7, 62.

74 For a discussion of anti-utopia in Soviet literature and society, see Natal'ia Ivanova, 'Proshchanie s utopiei,' in *Gibel' bogov* (Moscow 1991), 8–16.

75 *Iskusstvo kino*, 1989, no. 6, 150–75.

76 Konstantin Shcherbakov, introduction to *Nevozvrashchenets*, *Iskusstvo kino*, 1989, no. 6, 150.

77 Moscow: Tekst, 1991.

78 *Znamia*, 1990, no. 4, 43–76.

79 Aleksandr Kabakov, 'Tikhaia, schastlivaia smert',' *Literaturnaia gazeta*, 18 September 1990, 7.

80 For a detailed discussion of M. Kuraev's early works, see Colin F. Dowsett, 'Rewriting History and Reviving Modernism: Mikhail Kuraev's "Kapitan Dikshtein" and "Nochnoi dozor," ' *Canadian Slavonic Papers*, 33/2 (June 1991), 113–22.

81 *Novyi mir*, 1988, no. 12, 80–114.

82 Ibid., 1990, n. 3, 9–30.

83 *Znamia*, 1991, no. 3, 9–58.

84 'Daesh' krutuiu energetiku!' *Literaturnaia gazeta*, 24 April 1991, 10.

85 *Novyi mir*, 1992, no. 8, 6–40.

86 *Znamia*, 1992, no. 11, 24–37.

87 *Novyi mir*, 1992, no. 8, 40.

88 Ibid., 1993, no. 5, 3–68, and no. 6, 67–131.

89 Translated by Antonina W. Bouis (New York 1989).

90 *Novyi mir*, 1988, no. 7, 8–26.

91 Ibid., 26.

92 Karen Stepanian, 'Tri shaga k istine,' *Neva*, 1989, no. 1, 187.

93 See, for example, *Stolitsa*, 1991, no. 33, also *AATSEEL Newsletter* 344 (February 1992), 28–9.

94 *Znamia*, 1991, no. 11, 45–70. Originally published in *Sintaksis* (Paris), 1990, no. 27.

95 'A za prazdnik – spasibo,' *Literaturnaia gazeta*, 11 November 1992, 4.

96 *Sintaksis* (Paris), 1991, no. 31, 100–9.

97 Originally published in the journal *Ural* (Sverdlovsk).

98 *Ural*, 1992, nos. 2–4.

99 *Znamia*, 1992, no. 5, 11–63.

100 Ibid., 1993, no. 4, 6–65.

101 *Literaturnaia gazeta*, 20 January 1993, 4.

102 *Vestnik novoi literatury,* 1990, no. 2, 284.

103 'Uchenik,' 1989, no. 4, 5–23, and 'Lichnaia neostorozhnost','' 1990, no. 5, 10–23, and no. 6, 50–61.

104 *Vestnik novoi literatury,* 1990, no. 2, 82–103.

105 *Petropol'*, 1990, no. 2, 175–85.

106 *Novyi mir*, 1993, no. 6, 3–62.

107 *Volga* (Saratov), 1993, nos. 8 and 9.

108 *Znamia*, 1993, no. 10, 29–50.

109 Ihab Hassan, *The Postmodern Turn: Essays in Postmodern Theory and Culture* (Columbus, OH, 1987), 85.

110 Ibid., 87.

111 Ibid., 88.

112 Ihab Hassan, *Paracriticism. Seven Speculations of the Times* (Urbana, IL. 1975), 53.

113 Ibid., 54.

114 Hugh Holman and William Harmon, *A Handbook to Literature*, 6th ed. (New York 1992), 370.

115 Linda Hutcheon, *A Poetics of Postmodernism: History, Theory, Fiction* (New York 1988), 230.

116 Ibid., 23.

117 Ibid., 118.

118 Ibid., 4.

119 Sergei Biriukov, 'Sigma avangarda,' *Literaturnaia gazeta*, 17 February 1993, 4.
120 Sergei Stratanovskii, 'Igra s besom,' *Literaturnaia gazeta*, 18 March 1992, 4.
121 Mikhail Epstein, 'After the Future: On the New Consciousness in Literature,' in T. Lahusen and G. Kuperman, *Late Soviet Culture: From Perestroika to Novostroika* (Durham, NC, 1993), 286–7. Originally published in *Znamia*, 1991, no. 1, 217–30.
122 'Zakon krutizny,' *Voprosy literatury,* 1991, no. 11–12, 7.
123 'Na poroge energeticheskoi kul'tury,' *Literaturnaia gazeta*, 31 October 1990, 5.
124 'O nashikh raznoglasiiakh po povodu postmodernizma,' *Literaturnaia gazeta*, 14 October 1992, 4.
125 Viacheslav Kuritsyn, 'Postmodernizm: novaia pervobytnaia kul'tura,' *Novyi mir*, 1992, no. 2, 232.
126 'Sem' zleishikh dukhov,' *Literaturnaia gazeta*, 15 January 1992, 4.
127 Boris Kuz'minskii, 'Post vo vremia chumy,' *Literaturnaia gazeta*, 10 April 1991, 11.
128 Mark Lipovetskii, 'Apofeoz chastits, ili dialogi s khaosom,' *Znamia*, 1992, no. 8, 217.
129 Aleksandr Mikhailov, 'Priznanie v liubvi, ili vospominanie ob odnom simpoziume,' *Literaturnaia gazeta*, 22 January 1992, 4.
130 'Realizm kak zakliuchitel'naia stadiia postmodernizma,' *Znamia*, 1992, no. 9, 232.
131 Ibid.,233.
132 V. Malukhin, 'Post bez modernizma,' *Izvestiia*, 8 May 1991.
133 'Nasha literatura ne rezinovaia,' 4 June 1991, 7.
134 See for example V. Kuritsyn, 'O nashikh raznoglasiiakh po povodu postmodernizma,' *Literaturnaia gazeta*, 14 October 1992, 4.
135 Caryl Emerson, 'The Shape of Russian Cultural Criticism in the Postcommunist Period,' *Canadian Slavonic Papers* 34/4 (December 1992), 367–8.
136 *Literaturnaia gazeta*, 4 July 1990, 8.
137 *Moscow News*, 8–15 July 1990, 14.
138 Interview with Viktor Erofeev, *Gumanitarnyi fond*, 1992, no. 12 (115), 2.
139 Quoted from an article by Ann McElvoy in *The Times, Literaturnaia gazeta*, 30 September 1992, 3.
140 Natal'ia Ivanova, 'Zhizn' prekrasna,' *Iunost'*, 1991, no. 1, 62.
141 'Grustnoe vozvrashchenie Chatskogo,' *Literaturnaia gazeta*, 6 May 1991, 4.
142 Dan Cryer, 'Erostroika,' *Fanfare. Newsday's Weekly Report on Entertainment and Living* (Nassau, NY), 9 May 1993, 35.
143 Oleg Dark, 'Chernoe pis'mo,' *Strelets*, 1992, no. 1 (68), 187.
144 'The Labyrinth of a Sick Man,' *Moscow News*, 6–13 January 1991, 14.
145 Dan Cryer, 35.

146 *Iunost'*, 1988, no. 9, 74–9.

147 *Novyi mir*, 1989, no. 10, 8–23.

148 *Druzhba narodov*, 1992, no. 1, 3–27.

149 Compiled by Oleg Dark.

150 *Vestnik novoi literatury*, 1990, no. 2, 280. Quoted from an article by Vasilii Betaki in *Russkaia mysl'* (Paris), 10 November 1989.

151 *Vladimir Sorokin* (Moscow 1992), 120.

152 Dmitrii Lekukh, 'Metamorfozy melkogo besa,' *Literaturnaia gazeta*, 20 May 1992, 4.

153 *Vladimir Sorokin*, 11–16.

154 Ibid., 16–20.

155 *Vidimost' nas*, 37–43.

156 *Vladimir Sorokin*, 58–9.

157 Ibid., 70–6.

158 *Strelets*, 1991, no. 3 (67), 122–35.

159 *Vidimost' nas*, 28–36.

160 A printing house in the city of Kharkov recently returned a manuscript by Sorokin, complaining that 'the text offended the workers and administration.' See Petr Vail', and Aleksandr Genis, 'Vesti iz onkologicheskoi kliniki,' interview with Vladimir Sorokin, *Sintaksis* (Paris), 1992, no. 32, 139.

161 Oberiu stands for 'Ob"edinenie real'nogo iskusstva' or Association for Real Art. This group was active in Leningrad between 1927 and 1930. Its leading members, D. Kharms and A. Vvedenskii, were arrested in the beginning of the Second World War, and perished in the Gulag.

162 *Vladimir Sorokin*, 125.

163 Ibid., 121.

164 Interview with Vladimir Sorokin, *Gumanitarnyi fond*, 1992, 12 (115), 3.

165 *Vladimir Sorokin*, 122.

166 Ibid., 123.

167 *Moscow News*, 1 April 1990, 14.

168 *Iunost*, 1988, no. 8, 15–29.

169 Ibid., 1990, no. 3, 10–35.

170 *Znamia*, 1990, no. 5, 61–87.

171 *Iunost'*, 1988, no. 8, 15.

172 In Latin for 'healthy.'

173 An illusion to the Russian swear word 'mat.'

174 *Vidimost' nas* (Moscow 1991), 118–34.

175 *Moscow News*, 1 April 1990, 14.

176 See Narbikova's story 'Plan pervogo litsa. I vtorogo,' which appeared in the collection of prose *Vstrechnyi khod* (Moscow 1989).

177 G. Vladimov, 'Ia by khotel seichas byt' riadom s sootechestvennikami,' *Literaturnaia gazeta*, 6 June 1990, 5.

178 'Svobody chernaia rabota,' *Voprosy literatury*, 1989, no. 9, 17.

179 'Tri shaga k istine,' *Neva*, 1989, no. 1, 186.

180 S.V. Vasilenko, comp., *Novye amazonki* (Moscow 1991), 244.

181 *Vidimost' nas* (Moscow 1991), 44–55.

182 *Na izlote veka. Povesti i rasskazy molodykh pisatelei* (Moscow 1991), 89–136. It was also published in *Znamia*, 1992, no. 10, 9–40.

183 A. Lavrin, *Liudi, zveri i angely* (Moscow 1992), 168–84.

184 Ibid., 184–201.

185 Ibid., 3–140.

186 *Sramnaia proza*, compiled by Vadim Dubichev, Aleksandr Vernikov, and Viacheslav Kuritsyn.

187 *Solo*, 1991, no. 3, 4.

188 A. Bitov, 'Ot "solista" shestidesiatykh,' *Solo*, 1991, no. 4, 5.

189 Ibid., 5–6.

190 *V preddverii novoi zhizni* (Moscow 1990) and *Starukha i durachok* (Vladimir 1992).

191 *Solo*, 1990, no. 1, 5–14.

192 Ibid, 1991, no. 2, 5–12.

193 Ibid., 11.

194 Ibid., 12–14.

195 Ibid, 1991, no. 5, 86–95.

196 Ibid., 88.

197 *Novyi mir*, 1993, no. 9, 34–49.

198 *Solo*, 1991, no. 4, 41–73.

199 Ibid., 1991, no. 3, 25–44.

200 1990, no. 2, 238–69.

201 For a collection of stories by V. Zuev, see *Pravila igry. Alkhimiia liubvi. Goroskop* (Moscow 1991).

Selected Bibliography

This bibliography is far from exhaustive but is intended to provide the reader with the necessary background for a better understanding of Soviet and Russian literature and to act as a guide for the future investigation of contemporary Russian prose.

The list of suggested background reading contains several Russian and Western histories of literature, as well as important monographs and articles dealing with different aspects of contemporary Russian literary theory and practice. The list of contemporary Russian prose includes works representing different thematic and artistic trends by authors residing both in Russia and in the West, and published in Russia between 1988 and 1994. The list of Russian prose in English translation includes works originally published before 1988 but recently translated into English. The list of new periodicals and almanacs includes journals that began publication between 1989 and 1993.

BACKGROUND READING

Apukhtina, V.A. *Sovremennaia sovetskaia proza*. Moscow, 1984.

Arkhangel'skii, Aleksandr. *U paradnogo pod"ezda: Literatura i kul'turnye situatsii perioda glasnosti, 1987–1990*. Moscow, 1991.

Belaia, Galina A. *Literatura v zerkale kritiki*. Moscow, 1986.

Bocharov, Anatolii. *Literatura i vremia*. Moscow, 1988.

Brown, Deming B. *Soviet Russian Literature since Stalin*. New York, 1978.

– *The Last Years of Soviet Russian Literature. Prose Fiction 1975–1991*. New York, 1993.

Brown, Edward J. *Russian Literature since the Revolution*, revised and enlarged edition. Cambridge, MA, 1982.

Chances, Ellen. *Andrei Bitov. The Ecology of Inspiration*. New York, 1993.

Clark, Katerina. *The Soviet Novel: History as Ritual*. 2nd ed. Chicago, 1985.

Clowes, Edith W. *Russian Experimental Fiction. Resisting Ideology after Utopia*. Princeton, 1993.

Dement'ev, A.G., ed. *Istoriia russkoi sovetskoi literatury v 4-kh tomakh. 1917–1965*. Moscow, 1967–71.

Dunham, Vera. *In Stalin's Time: Middleclass Values in Soviet Fiction*. Cambridge, 1976.

Ermolaev, Herman. *Soviet Literary Theories 1917–1934: The Genesis of Socialist Realism*. Berkeley, 1963.

Friedberg, Maurice. *Russian Culture in the 1980s*. Washington, DC, 1985.

Garrard, John, and Carol Garrard. *Inside the Soviet Writers' Union*. New York, 1990.

Gibian, G. *Interval of Freedom: Soviet Literature during the Thaw, 1954–1957*. Minneapolis, 1960.

Graham, Sheelagh D., ed. *New Directions in Soviet Literature*. New York, 1992.

Hayward, Max, and Leopold Labedz. *Literature and Revolution in Soviet Russia, 1917–1962*. London, 1963.

Hosking, Geoffrey. *Beyond Socialist Realism: Soviet Fiction since Ivan Denisovich*. London, 1980.

Kuz'menko, Iu. *Soviet Literature Yesterday, Today and Tomorrow*. Moscow, 1983.

Lahusen, Thomas, and Gene Kuperman, eds. *Late Soviet Culture. From Perestroika to Novostroika*. Durham, NC, 1993.

Lowe, David. *Russian Writing since 1953: A Critical Survey*. New York, 1987.

Maguire, Robert A. *Red Virgin Soil: Soviet Literature in the 1920s*. Princeton, 1968.

Markov, D. *Problemy teorii sotsialisticheskogo realizma*. Moscow, 1975.

– 'O nekotorykh voprosakh teorii sotsialisticheskogo realizma.' *Voprosy literatury*, 1988, no. 3, 3–22.

Mathewson, Rufus W. *The Positive Hero in Russian Literature*. 2d ed. Stanford, 1975.

Metchenko, A.I., and S.M. Petrov, eds. *Istoriia russkoi sovetskoi literatury 40–80e gody*. Moscow, 1983.

Ovcharenko, Aleksandr. *Bol'shaia literatura*, 3 vols. Moscow, 1985.

Parthé, Kathleen F. *Russian Village Prose: The Radiant Past*. Princeton, 1992.

Robin, Regine. *Socialist Realism: An Impossible Aesthetic*. Translated from the French by Catherine Porter. Stanford, 1992.

Shneidman, N.N. *Soviet Literature in the 1970s: Artistic Diversity and Ideological Conformity*. Toronto, 1979.

– *Soviet Literature in the 1980s: Decade of Transition*. Toronto, 1989.

Slonim, Marc. *Soviet Russian Literature: Writers and Problems, 1917–1977*, 2d ed. New York, 1977.

Struve, Gleb. *Russian Literature under Lenin and Stalin, 1917–1953*. Norman, OK 1971.

Svirski, Gregori. *A History of Post-War Soviet Writing: The Literature of Moral Opposition*. Ann Arbor, MI, 1981.

Vail', Petr, and Aleksandr Genis. *Sovremennaia russkaia proza*. Ann Arbor, MI, 1982.

RUSSIAN PROSE FICTION, 1988–1994

Aksenov, Vasilii. *V poiskakh grustnogo Bebi* [In Search of a Sad Baby]. 1991.

Alekseev, Ivan. *Muzhchina na odnu noch'* [A Man for One Night; collection of prose]. 1993.

Aleksievich, Svetlana. *Tsinkovye mal'chiki* [Boys in Metal Coffins]. 1990.

Aleshkovskii, Petr. 'Chaika' [Seagull]. 1992.

– 'Zhizneopisanie Khorka' [Polecat's Biography]. 1993.

Anan'ev, Anatolii. *Skrizhali i kolokola* [Tablets and Bells]. 1989.

– *Liki bessmertnoi vlasti. Tsar' Ioann Groznyi* [The Images of Immortal Power. Tsar Ivan the Terrible]. 1992.

– *Prizvanie Riurikovichei, ili tysiacheletniaia zagadka Rossii* [The Mission of the Ruriks, or the One-Thousand-Year Puzzle of Russia]. 1993.

Arakcheev, Iurii. *Istoriia odnogo razocharovaniia* [The History of One Disappointment]. 1991.

Astaf'ev, Viktor. 'Liudochka' [Liudochka]. 1989.

– *Prokliaty i ubity* [The Cursed and the Slain Book One]. 1992–4.

Bakin, Dmitrii. 'Logoftalm' [Logoftalm]. 1991.

Belov, Vasilii. *God velikogo pereloma. Khronika deviati mesiatsev* [A Year of Great Change. A Chronicle of Nine Months]. 1989–94.

Berg, Mikhail. *Tri romana* [Three Novels]. 1991.

Bitov, Andrei. *Chelovek v peizazhe. Povesti i rasskazy* [Man in the Landscape; collection of prose]. 1988.

– *Uletaiushchii Monakhov: roman punktir* [The Disappearing Monakhov: A Dotted-Line Novel]. 1990.

– 'Ozhidanie obez'ian' [Waiting for the Apes]. 1993.

Bondarev, Iurii. *Iskushenie* [Temptation]. 1991.

Borodin, Leonid. 'Zhenshchina v more' [A Woman in the Sea]. 1990.

– *Tret'ia pravda* [The Third Truth]. 1990.

Borodynia, Aleksandr. *Spichki* [A Box of Matches]. 1993.

Buida, Iurii. 'Don Domino' [The Domino-Player]. 1993.

Butov, Mikhail. *Izvaianie pana* [The Carved Image of a Gentleman; collection of prose]. 1994.

Bykov, Vasil'. 'Oblava' [The Cordon]. 1990.
- 'Stuzha' [Cold Spell]. 1993.
Davydov, Iurii. 'Zorovavel'' [Mr Zorovavel']. 1993.
- 'Zagovor sionistov' [A Zionist Conspiracy]. 1993.
Dolliniak, Igor'. 'Mir tretii' [Another World]. 1993.
Dombrovskii, Iurii. *Fakul'tet nenuzhnykh veshchei* [Faculty of Useless Things].
    1988.
- 'Afganskie rasskazy' [Afghan Stories]. 1989.
- 'Blagopoluchnoe vozvrashchenie' [Safe Return]. 1989.
Ermakov, Oleg. 'Kreshchenie' [Baptism]. 1989.
- 'Zheltaia gora' [The Yellow Mountain]. 1989
- 'Kolokol'nia' [Belfry]. 1990.
- *Znak zveria* [Sign of the Beast]. 1992.
Erofeev, Viktor. *Telo Anny, ili konets russkogo avangarda* [Anna's Body, or the End
    of the Russian Avant-Garde; collection of prose]. 1989.
- *Russkaia krasavitsa* [Russian Beauty]. 1990.
- *Izbrannoe, ili karmannyi apokalipsis* [Selected Prose, or the Pocket Apocalypse].
    1993.
Evtushenko, Evgenii. *Ne umirai prezhde smerti* [Don't Die Before Your Death].
    1993.
Gabyshev, Leonind. *Odlian, ili vozdukh svobody* [Odlian, or the Air of Freedom].
    1989.
Galkovskii, Dmitrii. *Beskonechnyi tupik* [The Endless Impasse]. 1992.
Gareev, Zufar. 'Stereoskopicheskie slaviane' [Stereoscopic Slavs]. 1991.
- 'Multiproza' [Multiprose]. 1991.
Gavrilov, Anatolii. 'Istoriia maiora Simin'kova' [The Story of Major Simin'kov].
    1990.
- *Starukha i durachok* [The Old Woman and the Fool; collection of prose].
    1992.
Golovin, Genadii. *Den' rozhdeniia pokoinika* [The Birthday of a Dead Man; collec-
    tion of prose]. 1991.
- 'Pokoi i volia' [At Peace and Liberty]. 1993.
Gorenshtein, Fridrikh. *Iskuplenie* [Atonement]. 1990.
- *Koiko-mesto* [Some Place]. 1990.
- *Psalom* [The Book of Psalms]. 1991.
Granin, Daniil. *Begstvo v Rosiiu* [Escape to Russia]. 1994.
Grossman, Vasilii. 'Vse techet' [Forever Flowing]. 1989.
Iakimchuk, Nikolai. 'Kartinki s vystavki' [Pictures from an Exhibition]. 1990.
Iskander, Fazil'. *Chelovek i ego okrestnosti* [Man and His Surroundings]. 1992.
-'Pshada' [Pshada]. 1993.

Ivanchenko, Aleksandr. *Avtoportret s dogom* [Self-Portrait with a Great Dane; collection of prose]. 1990.
- *Monogramma* [Monogram]. 1992.
Kabakov, Aleksandr. *Nevozvrashchenets* [No Return]. 1989.
- 'Bul'varnyi roman' [A Cheap Novel]. 1990.
- *Sochinitel'* [The Scribbler]. 1991.
Kaledin, Sergei. 'Stroibat' [Construction Battalion]. 1989.
- 'Pop i rabotnik' [The Priest and the Worker]. 1991.
Karabchievskii, Iurii. *Zhizn' Aleksandra Zil'bera* [The Life of Aleksandr Zil'ber]. 1990.
- *Toska po domu* [Longing for Home; collection of prose]. 1991.
Khandus', Oles'. *Polkovnik vsegda naidetsia* [The Colonel Will Always Be Found]. 1992.
Kharitonov, Mark. *Den' v fevrale* [A Day in February; prose Collection]. 1988.
- *Linii sud'by, ili sunduchok Milashevicha* [Lines of Fate, or Milashevich's Little Trunk]. 1992.
Kim, Anatolii. *Otets-les* [Father-Forest]. 1989.
- *Poselok kentavrov* [Hamlet of Centaurs]. 1992.
Kireev, Ruslan. 'Pesni Ovidiia' [The Songs of Ovid]. 1992.
Klekh, Igor'. 'Inostranets' [The Foreigner]. 1991.
- 'Intsident s klassikom' [An Occurrence with a Classicist]. 1991.
- Monolog' [Monologue]. 1991.
- 'Khutor vo vselennoi' [Farmstead in the Universe]. 1993.
Kormer, Vladimir. *Nasledie* [Heritage]. 1990.
Korolev, Anatolii. *Ozhog linzy* [The Burn of a Lens]. 1988.
- 'Genii mestnosti' [The Genius of the Place]. 1990.
- 'Golova Gogolia' [Gogol's Head]. 1992.
- *Eron* [Eron]. 1994.
Kozhevnikov, Petr. *Ostrov* [Island; collection of prose]. 1991.
Krupin, Vladimir. 'Proshchai, Rossiia, vstretimsia v raiu' [Farewell, Russia, We Will Meet in Heaven]. 1991.
Kuraev, Mikhail. 'Malen'kaia domashniaia taina' [A Little Family Secret]. 1990.
- 'Nochnoi dozor' [Night Patrol]. 1988.
- 'Petia po doroge v Tsarstvo Nebesnoe' [Petia on His Way to Heaven]. 1991.
- 'Druzhby nezhnoe volnenie' [The Tender Excitement of Friendship]. 1992.
- 'Kuranty b'iut' [The Bells Ring]. 1992.
- *Zerkalo Montachki* [Montachka's Mirror]. 1993.
Kurchatkin, Anatolii. 'Zapiski ekstremista' [Notes of an Extremist]. 1990.
- *Strazhnitsa* [A Guardian for Gorby]. 1993.

Laputin, Evgenii. 'Pamiatnik obmanshchiku' [A Monument to a Deceiver]. 1990.
– 'Litsa ptits' [The Faces of Birds]. 1991.
Lavrin, Aleksandr. *Liudi, zveri i angely* [People, Animals, and Angels. Collection of Prose]. 1992.
Levitin Mikhail. 'Sploshnoe neprilichie' [Total Indecency]. 1993.
Lipkin, Semen. *Zapiski zhil'tsa* [Notes of a Lodger]. 1992.
Makanin, Vladimir. 'Laz' [Manhole]. 1991.
– 'Tam byla para ...' [There Was a Pair ...]. 1991.
– 'Dolog nash put'' [Long Is Our Way]. 1993.
– 'Stol pokrytyi suknom i s grafinom poseredine' [Cloth-Covered Table with Carafe in the Middle]. 1993.
– 'Kvazi' [Quasi]. 1993.
Matveev, Andrei. *Istoriia Lorimura ili obretenie very* [The Story of Lorimur, or the Discovery of Faith]. 1991.
Miloslavskii, Iurii. *Ukreplennye goroda* [The Fortified Cities]. 1990.
Mozhaev, Boris. *Izgoi* [The Outcast]. 1993.
Nabatnikova, Tat'iana. *Zagadai zhelanie* [Make a Wish; collection of prose]. 1990.
– *Dar Izory* [The Gift of Izora; collection of prose]. 1991.
Nagibin, Iurii. *Vstan' i idi. Povesti i rasskazy* [Arise and Walk; collection of prose]. 1989.
– *Prorok budet sozhzhon* [The Prophet Will Be Burnt]. 1990.
– *Rasskazy sinego liagushenka* [Tales of the Little Blue Frog]. 1991.
Narbikova, Valeriia. 'Ravnovesie sveta dnevnykh i nochnykh zvezd' [The Equilibrium of the Day and Night Stars]. 1988.
– 'Okolo Ekolo ...' [Around and About]. 1990.
– 'Probeg – pro beg' [On the Run]. 1990.
– *Izbrannoe, ili shepot shuma* [Selected Prose, or the Whisper of Noise]. 1994.
Novikova, Ol'ga. *Zhenskii roman* [A Woman's Novel]. 1993.
Okudzhava, Bulat. *Uprazdnennyi teatr* [The Closed down Theatre]. 1993.
– *Zaezzhii muzykant* [The Travelling Musician]. 1993.
Palei, Marina. 'Evgesha i Annushka' [Evgesha and Annushka]. 1990.
– 'Kabiriia s Obvodnogo kanala' [Cabiria from By-Pass Canal Street]. 1991.
– *Otdelenie propavshikh* [The Ward of Those Ruined; collection of prose]. 1993.
– 'Reis' [The Trip]. 1993.
Pelevin, Viktor. *Sinii fonar'* [Blue Lamp; collection of prose]. 1991.
– 'Omon Ra' [Omon Ra]. 1992.
– *Zhizn' nasekomykh* [The Life of Insects]. 1993.
Petrushevskaia, Liumila. 'Novye Robinzony. (Khronika kontsa 20 veka') [The New Robinsons. (A Chronicle of the End of the Twentieth Century)]. 1989.
– 'Novyi Gulliver' [The New Gulliver]. 1990.

- 'Medeia' [Medeia]. 1990.
- 'Pesni vostochnykh slavian' [Songs of the Eastern Slavs]. 1990.
- 'Vremia noch'' [The Time: Night]. 1992.
- *Po doroge Boga Erosa* [In the Ways of God Eros; collection of prose]. 1993.

P'etsukh, Viacheslav. *Novaia moskovskaia filosofiia* [The New Moscow Philosophy; collection of prose]. 1989.
- 'Anamnez i epikriz' [Anamnesis and Epicrisis]. 1990.
- 'Aleksandr Krestitel'' [Aleksandr the Baptist]. 1991.
- *Zakoldovannaia strana* [Enchanted Country]. 1992.

Polianskaia, Irina. *Predlagaemye obstoiatel'stva* [Proposed Circumstances; collection of prose]. 1988.
- 'Chistaia zona' [Clear Zone]. 1990.

Popov, Evgenii. *Prekrasnost' zhizni* [The Splendour of Life]. 1990.

Pristavkin, Anatolii. 'Kukushata ili zhalobnaia pesn' dlia uspokoeniia serdtsa' [The Cuckoos, or a Sad Song for the Calming of One's Heart]. 1989.
- *Riazanka (Chelovek s predmest'ia)* [Riazanka (A Man from the Suburb)]. 1991.

Prokhanov, Aleksandr. *Shest'sot let posle bitvy* [Six Hundred Years after the Battle]. 1988.
- *Angel proletel* [An Angel Flew By]. 1991.
- *Poslednii soldat imperii* [The Last Soldier of the Empire]. 1993.

Proskurin, Petr. *Otrechenie* [Disavowal]. 1987 and 1990.

Radov, Egor. *Zmeesos* [Snake Eater]. 1992.

Rosliakov, Aleksandr. 'Such'i petli' [The Loops of a Bitch]. 1991.
- *Lovushka D'iavola* [The Devil's Snare]. 1993.

Rybakov, Anatolii. *Tridtsat' piatyi i drugie gody* [Nineteen-Thirty-Five and Other Years]. 1988.
- *Strakh* [Fear]. 1990.
- *Prakh i pepel* [The Dregs and Ashes]. 1994.

Sadur, Nina. 'Iug' [South]. 1991.

Sharov, Vladimir. *Repetitsia* [Rehearsal]. 1992.
- *Do i vo vremia* [Before and in the Time of]. 1993.

Shishkin, Mikhail, 'Urok kalligrafii' [A Lesson of Calligraphy]. 1993.
- 'Slepoi muzykant' [The Blind Musician]. 1994.

Shmelev, Nikolai. *Sil'vestr* [Sil'vestr; novel and stories]. 1992.

Slapovskii, Aleksei. *Pervoe vtoroe prishestvie* [The First Second Coming]. 1993.
- 'Pyl'naia zima' [One Dusty Winter Day]. 1993.

Sokolova, Ol'ga, comp. *Abstinentki* [Women Who Abstain; collection includes works by N. Gorlanova, O. Sokolova, N. Doroshko, E. Semashko, and others]. 1991.

Soloukhin, Vladimir. *Smekh za levym plechom. Kniga prozy* [Laughter Over the Left shoulder; collection of prose]. 1989.

Sorokin, Vladimir. 'Zasedanie zavkoma' [A Meeting of the Trade Union Committee]. 1991.

– *Vladimir Sorokin* [Vladimir Sorokin; collection of prose]. 1992.

– 'Serdtsa chetyrekh' [Four Stout Hearts]. 1993.

Svetov, Feliks. *Tiurma* [Jail]. 1992.

Terekhov, Aleksandr. 'Zema. Ironicheskii dnevnik' [Zema. Ironic Diary]. 1989.

– 'Memuary srochnoi sluzhby' [Memoirs of a Conscript]. 1991.

– 'Zimnii den' nachala novoi zhizni' [The Wintry Day of the Beginning of a New Life]. 1991.

– *Proshu prostit'* [I Beg Your Pardon; collection of prose]. 1993.

Tokareva, Viktoriia. 'Ia est'. Ty est'. On est' [I Am Here. You Are Here. He Is Here]. 1991.

– *Korrida* [Corrida; collection of prose]. 1994.

Tolstaia, Tat'iana. 'Somnambula v tumane' [Sleepwalker in a Fog]. 1988.

– 'Limpopo' [Limpopo]. 1990.

– 'Siuzhet' [Plot]. 1991.

Ulitskaia, Liudmila. 'Sonechka' [Sonechka]. 1992.

Varlamov, Aleksei. *Zdravstvui, kniaz'!* [Good Morning, Prince!; collection of prose]. 1993.

Vasilenko, S.V., comp. *Novye amazonki* [The New Amazons. includes works by N. Gorlanova, I. Polianskaia, T. Nabatnikova, V. Narbikova, M. Palei, S. Vasilenko, N. Sadur, and others]. 1991.

Vasil'ev, Boris. *Dom, kotoryi postroil ded* [The House Built by Grandfather]. 1991.

Vernikov, Aleksandr. 'Dozornyi na granitse' [Border Patrol]. 1991.

– 'Pustynia Tartari' [The Tartari Desert]. 1991.

Vladimov, Georgii. *General i ego vremia* [The General and His Time]. 1994.

Voinovich, Vladimir. *Delo No. 34840* [Case No. 34840]. 1993.

Zalygin, Sergei. *Ekologicheskii roman* [Ecological Novel]. 1993.

Zuev, Vladimir. *Pravila igry. Alkhimiia liubvi. Goroskop* [The Rules of the Game. Alchemistry of Love. Horoscope]. 1991.

– *Chernyi iashchik* [Black Box]. 1992.

Zviagin, Evgenii. *Kladoiskatel'* [Treasure Seeker; collection of prose]. 1991.

RUSSIAN WRITERS IN ENGLISH TRANSLATION

Aitmatov, Chingiz. *Mother Earth and Other Stories*. Translated by James Riordan. London, 1989.

– *Piebald Dog Running Along the Shore and Other Stories*. Moscow, 1989.

– *The Place of the Skull.* New York, 1989.

Alexievich, Svetlana. *Zinky Boys: Soviet Voices from a Forgotten War.* Translated by Julia and Robin Whitby. London, 1992.

Astafiev, Victor. *To Live Your Life and Other Stories.* Moscow, 1989.

– 'Lyudochka.' Translated by David Gillespie. *Soviet Literature,* 1990, no. 8, 3–39.

Baranskaya, Natalya. *A Week Like Any Other: Novellas and Stories.* Seattle, WA., 1990.

Belov, Vasilii. *The Best Is Yet to Come.* Moscow, 1989.

Bitov, Andrei. *A Captive of the Caucasus.* Translated by Susan Brownberger. New York, 1992.

Borodin, Leonid. *The Third Truth.* Translated by Catriona Kelly. London, 1989.

– *The Story of a Strange Time.* Translated by Frank Williams. London, 1990.

Bykov, Vasil'. *Sign of Misfortune.* Translated by Alan Myers. New York, 1990.

Chukhontsev, Oleg, ed. *Dissonant Voices: The New Russian Fiction.* London, 1991.

Erofeev, Victor. *Russian Beauty.* New York, 1993.

Goscilo, Helena, ed. *Balancing Acts. Contemporary Stories by Russian Women.* Bloomington, IN 1989.

– *Lives in Transit: A Collection of Recent Russian Women's Writings.* Ann Arbor, MI 1993.

Goscilo, Helena, and Byron Lindsey, eds. *Glasnost: An Anthology of Russian Literature Under Gorbachev.* Ann Arbor, MI 1990.

– *The Wild Beach: An Anthology of Contemporary Russian Stories.* Ann Arbor, MI 1992.

Granin, Daniil. *The Bison: A Novel about the Scientist Who Defied Stalin.* Translated by Antonina W. Bouis. New York, 1990.

Grekova, I. ed. *Soviet Women Writing: Fifteen Short Stories.* New York, 1990.

Iskander, Fazil. *Rabbits and Boa Constrictors.* Translated by Ronald E. Peterson. Ann Arbor, MI 1989.

Kabakov, Aleksandr. *No Return.* Translated by Thomas Whitney. New York, 1990.

Kaledin, Sergei. *The Humble Cemetery.* Translated by Catriona Kelly. London, 1990

Kalina, I., comp., Jacqueline Decter, ed. *Soviet Women Writing; Fifteen Short Stories.* New York, 1990.

Kim, Anatolii. *Father-Forest* (Excerpts from the novel). Translated by Alexander Postnikov and Charlotte Foster. *Soviet literature,* 1989, no. 7, 6–111.

Kupriyanova, Nina, ed. *Always a Woman: Stories by Soviet Women Writers.* Moscow, 1988.

Kuraev, Mikhail. *Night Patrol and Other Stories.* Translated by Margaret O. Thompson. Durham, NC, 1994.

McLaughlin, Sigrid, ed. and trans. *The Image of Women in Contemporary Soviet Fiction: Selected Short Stories from the USSR.* New York, 1989.

Nagibin, Yuri. *An Unwritten Story by Sommerset Maugham*. Moscow, 1989.
– *Arise and Walk*. Translated by Catriona Kelly. London, 1990.
Rasputin, Valentin. *Siberia on Fire. Stories and Essays*. Translated and Introduction by Gerald Mikkelson and Margaret Winchell. Dekalb, IL, 1989.
– *Farewell to Matyora*. Translated by Antonina W. Bouis. Evanston, IL, 1991.
– *Live and Remember*. Translated by Antonina W. Bouis. Evanston, IL, 1992.
Rybakov, Anatoli. *Fear*. Translated by Antonina W. Bouis. New York, 1992.
Soloukhin, Vladimir. *Scenes from Russian Life*. Translated by David Martin. London, 1989.
– *Laughter Over the Left Shoulder*. Translated by David Martin. London, 1991.
– *A Time to Gather Stones*. Translated by Valerie Z. Nollan. Evanston, IL, 1993.
Sorokin, V. *The Queue*. Translated by Sally Laird. New York, 1988.
– 'A Month in Dachau.' *Grand Street*. New York, no. 48, 232–53.
Tolstaya, Tatyana. *On the Golden Porch*. Translated by Antonina W. Bouis. New York, 1989.
– *Sleepwalker in a Fog*. Translated by Jamey Gambrell. London, 1992.
Trifonov, Yuri. *Exchange*. Translated and Introduction by Michael Frayn. London, 1990.
– *Disappearance*. Translated by David Lowe. Ann Arbor, MI, 1991.
– *The Exchange and Other Stories*. Eds. Ellendea Proffer and Ronald Meyer. Ann Arbor, MI, 1991.
Vasilyev, Boris. *Don't Shoot the White Swans and Other Stories*. Moscow, 1990.
Vukolov, Leonid, ed. *Modern Soviet Stories*. Moscow, 1989.
Yevtushenko, Yevgeny. *Don't Die before Your Death*. New York, 1993.
Zalygin, Sergei, comp., Jacqueline Decter, ed. *The New Soviet Fiction: Sixteen Short Stories*. New York, 1989.
– *The Commission*. Translated by D.G. Wilson. DeKalb, IL, 1993.

NEW PERIODICALS AND ALMANACS

Aprel' (April) (Moscow)
Bezhin lug (The Bezhin meadow) (Moscow)
Diadia Vania (Uncle Vania) (Moscow)
Drugie berega (Other Shores) (Moscow)
Ekstsentr-labirint (Eccentricity-Labyrinth) (Ekaterinburg)
Fenniks-XX (Fenniks-XX) (Moscow)
Indeks (Index) (Moscow)
Kliukva (Cranberries) (Moscow)
Kol'tso A (Ring A) (Moscow)
Kommentarii (Commentary) (Moscow)

Konets veka (The End of the Century) (Moscow)

Laterno-Magika (Laterno-Magic) (Moscow)

Leksikon (Lexicon) (Moscow)

Lepta (Mite) (Moscow)

Literaturnyi zhurnal (Literary Journal) (Moscow)

Litsei na chistykh prudakh (Lyceum on Clean Ponds) (Moscow)

Moskovskii vestnik (Moscow Herald) (Moscow)

Nezamechennaia zemlia (The Unnoticed Land) (Moscow-St. Petersburg)

Noi (Noah) (Moscow)

Novaia iunost' (New Youth) (Moscow)

Novoe literaturnoe obozrenie (New Literary Review) (Moscow)

Orfei (Orphrey) (Rostov-na-Donu)

Peterburgskie chteniia (Petersburg Readings) (St. Petersburg)

Petropol' (Petropol') (Petersburg)

Predvestie (Omen) (Feodosiia, Crimea)

Rubezh. Tikho-okeanskii almanakh (The Boundary. Pacific Almanac)

Rubikon (Rubicon) (Moscow)

Russkaia viza (Russian Visa) (Moscow)

Russkii raz"ezd (The Russian Track) (St Petersburg)

Russkoe bogatstvo (Russian Wealth) (Moscow)

Rus' (Russia) (Iaroslavl', Kostroma, Vladimir)

Sfinks (Sphinx) (Moscow)

Slavianin (The Slav) (Moscow)

Slovo (The Word) (Moscow)

Soglasie (Concord) (Moscow)

Solo (Solo) (Moscow)

Strannik (The Wanderer) (Moscow)

Stremia (Stirrup) (Moscow)

Svoi golos (One's Own Voice) (Irkutsk)

Teplyi stan (Warm Stature) (Moscow)

Utes (Rock) (Saratov)

Vest' (News) (Moscow)

Vestnik novoi literatury (The Herald of New Literature) (St Petersburg)

Vsemirnoe slovo (Universal Word) (St Petersburg)

Vstrechnyi khod (Counter Move) (Moscow)

Zerkala (Mirrors) (Moscow)

Zolotoi vek (The Golden Age) (Moscow)

Index